D1785103

Ethnic Literary Traditions in American Children's Literature

Ethnic Literary Traditions in American Children's Literature

Edited by Michelle Pagni Stewart
and Yvonne Atkinson

Elizabeth Gargano's essay was first published in Children's Literature Quarterly 31, no. 1 (2006): 27–39. The chapter appears here with permission of Johns Hopkins University Press.

First published in 2009 by
PALGRAVE MACMILLAN®
in the United States – a division of St. Martin's Press LLC,
175 Fifth Avenue, New York, NY 10010.

Where this book is distributed in the UK, Europe and the rest of the world, this is by Palgrave Macmillan, a division of Macmillan Publishers Limited, registered in England, company number 785998, of Houndmills, Basingstoke, Hampshire RG21 6XS.

Palgrave Macmillan is the global academic imprint of the above companies and has companies and representatives throughout the world.

Palgrave® and Macmillan® are registered trademarks in the United States, the United Kingdom, Europe and other countries.

ISBN: 978-0-230-61875-6

Library of Congress Cataloging-in-Publication Data is available from the Library of Congress.

A catalogue record of the book is available from the British Library.

Design by Macmillan Publishing Solutions

First edition: December 2009

10 9 8 7 6 5 4 3 2 1

Printed in the United States of America

For Wayne, Ryan, and Nathan
For Donald, Eric, Daniel, and Aaron

Contents

Acknowledgments

We would like to thank all of the contributors to this collection for their work, their patience with the process, and their dedication to the project. We received much encouragement from colleagues in children's literature who saw a need for a project such as this one, and we appreciate their support: Anne Phillips, Christine Doyle, Naomi Wood, and especially Katharine Capshaw Smith.

Many thanks to Michelle Martin for her editorial feedback. We also want to thank Rebecca Coleman and David Smith for assistance with the bibliography and indexing.

We appreciate the patience from our families who more than once heard, "Not now—I'm working on the book!" We wish to thank Michelle's brother, Michael, for a crash course in contract law, Yvonne's husband, "The Donald," for the photography and layout of the cover art, and Larry Barkley for being our sounding board and voice of reason.

We are also grateful for our colleagues at Mt. San Jacinto College, especially our office mates in the English Department.

For Yvonne: from the airport in Ontario to New Orleans to NYC to "Yvonne's room" down the hall, the journey of our friendship has been one adventure after another. Thank you for coming into our lives and adopting "the boys"—all three of them!

For Michelle: thank you for keeping this project alive, holding down the fort, and listening to me gripe about indexing.

CHAPTER 1

Do Dick and Jane Still Live Here? Reading Children's Literature as Ethnic Literature

Yvonne Atkinson and Michelle Pagni Stewart

To date, most book-length studies of ethnic children's literature analyze the texts as children's literature first and foremost with a secondary—if at all—consideration of the text's ethnic and cultural roots. We are aware of the complexities of defining the terms race, ethnicity, and even culture as well as how the definitions of these words are connected to history, hegemony, and colonial thinking. The term "race" has been closely associated with blood: at one time in America the "one-drop rule" was the law of the land—a single drop of "negro blood" marked a person as Black. While no longer the rule of thumb for the nation, nevertheless, blood is still connected with race. The terms "ethnicity" and "race" have become analogous because of the belief that somehow blood is the essence of ethnicity, while ethnicity and culture have been, over time, generally conflated to refer to the characteristics of a people who share a common and distinctive culture, religion, and/or language. For purposes of this introduction, the word "culture" refers to the shared knowledge and values of a society, and "ethnicity" refers to that which is derived from a culture, race, or religion, as well as linguistic traditions of a people. Admittedly, not all races or cultural groups are included in this book, but a dialogue needs to begin so that future conversations can embrace even more variety and inclusion.

This collection of essays looks at ethnic children's literature as ethnic literature first and as literature for children second. Children are cognitively able to understand ethnicity and its literary variations, something that some analyses overlook, as if children are not capable of being ethnically aware beyond the differences in color of skin, types of food, shape of eyes, or other more obviously "readable" signs of ethnic identity. We want readers of all ages to see beyond the sometimes-stereotypical signifiers to the cultural foundations that create meaning in the text. This book, then, can serve as the doorway for entry into understanding another culture, an entry into another way of viewing the world. When people read or teach ethnic children's literature without the enhanced knowledge of the literary and contextual traditions from which the book arises, they miss something—a richer and deeper meaning. Having cultural and ethnic insight will enhance the understanding of the literature and the literary experience.

Although books dealing with ethnic children's literature exist, many of them are edited or written by experts in the field of education, rather than the field of literature. This means that ethnic children's literature is viewed through a pedagogical lens rather than with a literary perspective, giving guidance on what to look for and what to avoid in ethnic literature (such as looking for books that depict a culture accurately while avoiding stereotypes, etc). While these books serve a need with respect to ethnic children's literature since so many of those who educate future teachers as well as those who currently teach may be unfamiliar with various ethnic cultures and what can be offensive, our book seeks to expand the range of possibilities for reading, understanding, and teaching children's literature so that the analysis shifts to an emphasis on *ethnic* literature rather than *children's* literature. Because many of those who teach children's literature or children's literature courses may not have been trained in ethnic literature, they may not have the tools to see what makes ethnic literature ethnic. In contrast, those writing in our collection have a view from within either because of their own ethnic background and/or because of their scholarship in the ethnic literature. While we do not wish to further the complicated notions of the insider/outsider binary, those who have been educated and/or are metacognitively aware of the culturally shared knowledge and values of a society and/or ethnic group can, through their knowledge, enlighten others to approach children's literature from a more cultural/ethnic perspective. With so many more ethnic children's books being published, there is even more of a need to give people who read and teach these books another tool to access what is culturally significant about these books.

While there are now presses devoted to publishing ethnic children's literature, they typically do not have access to the large and variable consumers or retail outlets, which then limits the accessibility and number of readers of these texts. Because bookstores have also become more driven by mass-marketed and commercial texts, which tend not to be ethnic in content, this also affects reader awareness of these diverse books. With restricted audiences, public knowledge of these books is limited from the outset, something that Rigoberto Gonzalez discusses in more depth in his interview (Chapter 14). Often, then, to become published by mainstream presses requires a compromise of ethnic content and style, those aspects that are highlighted in the analyses of this book.

As the country has become more aware of our cultural differences, we need to celebrate those differences and avoid "mainstreaming" or "ghettoizing" ethnic literature: we should not teach ethnic children's literature only during Black History Month or within multicultural units but all year long and within all genres and types of courses. America is not a homogenous society—we recognize the people, the groups, but we still ignore what makes those cultural groups who they are: the beliefs, values, traditions, ways of life, etc., those aspects that are promoted in the literary traditions of the cultures, traditions that are, unfortunately, often misunderstood because they are viewed from a Western literary perspective rather than from a literary perspective based in the specific cultural background from which the texts arise. Furthermore, we have yet to validate ethnic literary traditions as an identifiable, worthy, teacherly source. This book takes a step in that direction: rather than segregating our discussions of children's and ethnic literature, we need to understand those theoretical, critical ethnic perspectives that have empowered ethnic literature written for adults and apply them to children's literature, just as we have applied the theories of Mikhail Bakhtin, Jacques Derrida, Jacques Lacan, and others to children's literature. Now that children's literature is recognized as literature worthy of study so that scholars approach it with the same kind of theoretical and academic rigor devoted to literature as a whole, so we seek to have ethnic literature—including that written for a younger audience—treated with the same critical, scholarly attention it warrants.

Previously those writing ethnic children's literature were more inclined to follow a traditional Western European literary style since to be published as an ethnic writer was enough of a hurdle without the additional onus of trying to tell a story in a narrative style unfamiliar to those who had been schooled in Western European literary traditions. As more ethnic books are being published and recognized by winning major children's awards, ethnic authors are freer to use literary traditions from within their cultural basis. They are increasingly doing so without didactic explanations for those outside of their particular cultural background, without taking on the role of "native informant." Our book helps readers understand the cultural nuances of ethnic literature and how they may affect meaning within the story.

Because ethnic literature is often based on different forms of literacy such as oral traditions, unaware readers and teachers can miss part of the performative aspect of the narrative. In literary traditions of Western European origin, reading is often a passive event: the story is told to the reader through the words on the page. In most literary traditions that are based on orality, however, meaning is created by both the teller and the listener: active reading is necessary for understanding. When those oral traditions are the basis for written narratives, the reader and the written narrative have to work together to create meaning. This participatory reading can be viewed negatively if one is not aware. In fact, books written from ethnic traditions that do not follow the customs of Western European literary traditions can be penalized because they are "different." As Cynthia Leitich Smith explains in an interview, her books have been criticized for relying on the number four, rather than the number three, despite the fact that the former is more culturally significant to American Indians, as more fully discussed by Michelle Pagni Stewart in "Alive and Well and Reclaiming Their Cultural Voice: Third Generation Native American Children's Literature" (found in this collection [Chapter 5]). In similar fashion, Toni Morrison's novel *The Bluest Eye* was at first rejected by publishers because the narrative did not follow the style of Western European literature in that the story was not linear, there were too many narrators, and it was "too hard to read." Yet Morrison narratives have a foundation in her ethnic background: she is an African American. She was not writing for, or about, the dominant culture. Awareness of other literary traditions allows readers to understand that other cultures have and are able to name/own their own literary styles, themes, and ways of storytelling. Understanding other literary traditions therefore allows for the recognition that references are not always going to be European/American-based, that not all historical moments are going to be the history of the dominant culture or from the perspective of the victors, as Rocio G. Davis discusses in her essay "Examining History: Representing War in Asian American Autobiographies for Children" (Chapter 13); instead, readers will have to be able to make connections to other cultural texts, moments, and people.

Within each section, the essays include diverse perspectives: renowned children's authors discuss their own work, especially the extent to which they see themselves as "ethnic" authors; scholars give introductions to the literary traditions of various ethnicities, an overview of the kinds of ideas one might find in an introductory literature class focused on that particular ethnicity; and children's literature scholars provide analyses of specific children's texts, with a focus on the application of the literary traditions, contexts, and critical perspectives of the particular culture. The analytic essays are not meant to serve as "touchstones" of a book or two that must be taught, but are instead models of ways of looking at the literature from its ethnic base. Further, although this book deals with selected texts used for analysis, we are not creating a canon of children's ethnic literature; rather, we open up possibilities for the classroom and for young readers through an analysis of the variety of ethnic children's literature that is available. In fact, some of the authors in this book have used the same text in their discussions but always from a different perspective, demonstrating the richness of possibilities with which we can approach ethnic children's literature. The book also includes a bibliography that suggests other texts for a further study of the various ethnic literatures as well as further reading of selected texts of children's and adolescent ethnic literature.

P. Jane Hafen, Yvonne Atkinson, Traise Yamamoto, and Tanya González—as their chapter titles indicate–give in their essays an overview of American Indian, African American, Asian American, and Latina/o literature, an introduction to the literature itself, not necessarily children's literature from that ethnicity. The specifics on children's literature come from the authors' discussions in essay and interview form of the extent to which they see themselves as ethnic authors and the extent to which their cultural heritage informs the texts they write for children and adolescents. Children's authors Joseph Bruchac, Julius Lester, Cynthia Kadohata, and Rigoberto González enlighten readers with an understanding of their own cultures and how that informs the literature they write.

The other essays throughout the collection demonstrate ways that some scholars of children's literature are treating children's and adolescent literature as ethnic literature. In the section on American Indian literature, Elizabeth Gargano (Chapter 4) explores Ojibwe storytelling as depicted in Louise Erdrich's children's novels (*The Birchbark House* and *The Game of Silence*), demonstrating how an understanding of Ojibwe worldview and the sacred and secular importance of stories can allow readers to engage with those values and traditions for a more enlightened literary experience. Whereas Gargano deals exclusively with historical fiction, Michelle Pagni Stewart (Chapter 5) analyzes contemporary depictions of American Indians, creating a new paradigm for analysis of Native American texts as she defines the concepts of Second and Third Generation novels, demonstrating how Third Generation books deconstruct notions of Indian identity. In the section on African American literature, Katharine Capshaw Smith (Chapter 8) reminds us that Black culture is not a monolith as she examines the liminal quality of Caribbean American texts (specifically Haitian American) written for young people. Neal Lester (Chapter 9) provides an analysis of the picture books that might be considered more traditional African American children's literature, looking at the illustrations and texts through the optic of African American culture. In the section on Asian American literature, the authors also recognize that Asian American children's literature involves more than Japanese and Chinese texts, such as in Melinda de Jesús's (Chapter 12) piece that acknowledges the "invisible yet hypervisible" South Asian Americans while explaining the concepts of hybridity and "desicreation" in the young adult novel *Born Confused*. Rocio G. Davis (Chapter 13) examines narratives of war in Asian American autobiographies for children, interrogating the way these children's texts provide an alternate view of the representations of war depicted by the "winners," a view from the eyes of a child who experienced war. In the section on Latina/o literature, Phillip Serrato (Chapter 16) analyzes Luis Rodríguez's picture books that depict the harsh realities of life for young Chicano/as while questioning the purpose of the more optimistic endings. Tiffany Ana López (Chapter 17) offers an analysis of what she calls *critical witnessing* in which Latina/o authors often write from their autobiographical experiences to provide young readers with ways of dealing with trauma that can empower them and provide hope, much as Rigoberto González himself has done both through his picture books as well as through his work in impoverished schools as a visiting writer.

This book provides a bridge *over* boundaries created by cultural and ethnic differences so that readers can negotiate and cross over the barriers, both imagined and real, that limit and restrict the understanding of ethnic literature. While we have separated our book into ethnic groupings so that readers can perhaps see the connections within each culture, to create a gestalt for that group, the book as a whole also represents a beginning foundation for access into ethnic literature as a larger concept, one that recognizes there are ways to write and read that do not rely on Western traditions, styles, and beliefs. Further, there are numerous connections among the essays across cultures, not just within. For example, Davis and López make similar arguments about the way that life experiences become ways of rewriting the past and connecting generations. Many of the authors discuss children's literature in terms of orality and aurality, such as Bruchac, Atkinson, Gargano, and Neal Lester, to name a few. De Jesús and Stewart discuss the ways that contemporary ethnic literature deconstructs stereotypical depictions of cultural identity. Several of the introductions, such as Yamamoto's and González's make clear that one label does not "fit all," as do Capshaw Smith and de Jesús provide analyses that expand our understanding and definitions of race as monolith, just as Julius Lester explains that ethnicity does not define a totality of who someone is. Serrato, Hafen, and Kadohata all discuss the way notions of place impact representations of self.

The essays and interviews in this book contribute to understandings of difference from the perspective of those who have been named Other.

We hope that this book is the beginning of necessary conversations about children's literature as ethnic literature. While we do not want to leave behind that which makes children's literature such an important genre, we want to honor all aspects that contribute to the wonderful texts of ethnic children's literature. As the title of our introduction recognizes, children's literature for quite some time was founded on the white world of Dick and Jane, a world that excluded so many American children, children of cultures represented by the texts and authors found in the pages of this book. Perhaps Dick and Jane still live here, but so do children of Native American, Asian American, Latina o, and African American cultures, and their stories warrant a place on the shelf as well.

SECTION 1

American Indian Literature

CHAPTER 2

Listening to the Loon: On Finding the Ideas for My Books

Joseph Bruchac

A loon flies low over our heads on its way to the Moose River, just beyond the trees at the edge of the yard. It is so close that I can hear the whistling sound made by its swift wings cutting through the late summer air. We both look up as it passes. Then, as if the passage of that bird whose name he shares was a signal for him, my Abenaki friend and elder Medawelasis puts down his chisel. He places his right hand on the shape he's been bringing out on the face of the cedar log that rests between two rough sawhorses. A curlicue of smoke rises from the smudge fire we built to keep away the black flies.

"Kina," he says. "Look here, Sozap. How many plates do you see here on Turtle's back?"

I lean close to look carefully at the carved turtle. "Thirteen," I answer.

He nods his head. "Thirteen," he agrees. "Always thirteen. One for each of our old Abenaki nations. Thirteen nations before there were thirteen colonies. Thirteen. One for each of the moons in the circle of the seasons. Thirteen moons on Old Turtle's back."

Where do I get the ideas for my books that deal with Native American themes? That moment I have just described with one of my teachers, Maurice Dennis, whose Abenaki name of Medawelasis means "Little Loon," is a perfect example. Rather than basing my insights on the frozen facts found on paper or a computer screen, the poems and plays, novels and stories that I've written have often grown out of some unplanned event, some contact with real human beings living their cultures, that turned out to be the first step on a creative journey.

Before I go further, I should admit that I also engage in a great deal of scholarly research. That is especially true when my story deals with historical events. I have little patience at all with books that contain unintentional anachronisms or writers who change major events just to suit their purpose. I'm presently involved in writing a novel that takes place during the last two years of the American Civil War. I've read thousands of pages and searched out every relevant piece of source material that I can find. My years in the academic world, where I obtained a PhD in Comparative literature and taught at several colleges, stand me in good stead for that sort of pursuit.

However, even in that historical novel I'm presently writing, there are intimate connections to oral tradition. One of those connections came from my Abenaki grandfather's stories about his own father's experience in the Civil War, where he was wounded and left for dead on the battlefield. He would not have survived if it hadn't been for a thunderstorm that rolled in after the battle. "He was just strong enough to crawl over to one of them pools of rainwater and drink," my grandfather said. My main character is based on that great-grandfather—Louis Bowman, a Canadian Abenaki Indian who joined the Union Army in 1864 and took part as a member of the Army of the Potomac in the Virginia Campaign that included the siege of Petersburg.

Not only that, when I was a child, my grandmother and I made many visits during the summer to Warm Springs, Virginia, where we would stay with her brother Orvis Dunham. Orvis was a devoted amateur Civil War historian. One of great-uncle Orvis's favorite things to do with us during those summer visits was to take us out on those battlefields to share the stories he'd learned from men who had fought over that ground about the great events that took place there.

'The sound of those guns," great-uncle Orvis said to us on one of those battlefield walks, "were like thunder. That is what some of those old veterans said. When they became confused in the smoke of the battlefield they were told to just walk toward the thunder."

Thunder. Those stories would strike an even deeper chord for me when I would learn later from such elders as Medawelasis and another of my Abenaki teachers Stephen Laurent that the Abenaki name for Thunder is Bedagi and that he is often seen as a friend to the human beings. When Bedagi hurls down his arrows of lightning, he is trying to destroy monsters. The rain that he brings washes away the damage done by those monsters.

Had it not been for those stories from my grandfather and my great-uncle, or those words about Thunder from my Abenaki elders, I doubt I would ever have come to the writing of the novel nor would I have found the working title for the manuscript *March toward the Thunder*.

Listening and paying attention to my surroundings—those are at least as important to my writing as is reading. I do not believe it is possible for any one person to fully express the depth of American Indian cultures. I am not just talking about the Native American societies of the past—which all too many non-Indian writers for young people choose as their only focus, making it seem as if Indians only existed long ago. I am talking about here and now. Those who have had no real social contact with contemporary American Indians, those who've never spent any significant amount of time in any of our rich, diverse, often confusing, and sometimes contradictory communities, find this hard to understand. Or they think that Indians who go to Walmart, play basketball, and speak English are pitiful, "assimilated," and no longer "real" Native Americans and thus not worthy subjects for a children's book. But if you are a good listener and look at things with at least partially unjudgemental eyes, you may find as I have always found, a wealth of wonderful stories. Often, those contemporary stories are an antidote for the stereotyping and outright racism that are often found in books about American Indians.

Native Americans are very aware of the simplistic images that have been created about them and just as aware of who they actually are. On the one hand, they are saddened by the ways they have been portrayed as savages or as noble but pitiful losers. If you say you are a writer to modern Indians, do not be surprised if they look at you with some skepticism. On the other hand, Native Americans are hungry for books that show them as fully realized human beings.

Some of the books I've written have come about as a result of being asked directly by Native people who have come to know my work when I am going to write a book about some particular subject dear to them. Six years ago, while I was doing an author visit to the Onondaga Nation School, a teenager I later learned was the best lacrosse player in the region asked me "When are you going to write a book about someone like me?" I heard what he was saying. There is a surprising lack of portrayals in books written for young people of modern American Indian youths, successful kids who are able to compete in the modern world, but who still have to deal with the weight of those preconceptions and expectations that are still loaded onto Indian shoulders. The result was a novel of mine called *The Warriors* that focuses on an Onondaga lacrosse star who ends up as the only Native American in a Baltimore prep school where everyone more or less worships lacrosse—although their vision of that traditional Iroquois game is different from the protagonist's.

I've been reminded by any number of Native elders over the years that our Creator made every person with two ears and only one mouth.

That means we must listen twice as much as we talk. That's a hard thing for many Americans, who are always trying to get a word in edgewise, to do. Or breaking in, as so many interviewers do, when someone is only halfway through their first sentence. In majority culture, just because someone asks you a question doesn't mean they actually want to hear *your* answer.

My late friend, the Lakota writer and activist Vine Deloria Jr., exemplified our Native awareness of that chatty Kathy nature of Euro-American culture when he titled one of his books *We Talk, You Listen*. But if, when you are around our Native people, you listen, folks take note of that. Show enough patience to be comfortable with silence, and folks will decide that you really do want to hear what they have to say. Chatter away like a jaybird and you may find yourself confronted with the stereotypical taciturn, silent Indian.

I don't always succeed in being quiet enough. But I have done so often enough to be trusted as one who will actually justify someone taking their time to tell me a story. And so it was that day at the edge of the town of Old Forge in the heart of the Adirondack mountains near the Moose River when my friend Little Loon trusted me with that story about the Moons on Turtle's back. It led to a discussion of the ways the moons are named for the things happening at that time in the natural world, such as the Moon of Falling Leaves that comes every autumn.

And, years later, when Jonathan London (who was a well-published poet before he was a children's writer and has always been a good listener!) and I collaborated on a children's book about the cycle of Native moons, I was able to use the memory of that afternoon. It gave us the title of the book, *Thirteen Moons on Turtle's Back*. And also, as I worked with Thomas Locker, the wonderfully gifted artist who illustrated the book and has gone on to be a dear friend, it helped Thomas find the first image in the book—that of an Abenaki elder carving a cedar pole like the one Medawelasis was working on that day.

I need to add an additional word about the creation of that illustration. Thomas Locker is as much a stickler for accuracy as I am. As a result, whenever he illustrates a book he always does preliminary paintings first. (Those "first drafts" are always striking, fully as good as most people's finished works.) So, whenever he did a painting for *Thirteen Moons on Turtle's Back*, he would show it to me. I'll never forget the first time he did that, for as soon as I saw that painting of the elder carving the pole, I knew there was a problem of authenticity.

It was not, as some have thought, that an eastern woodlands Indian was carving what looked like a totem pole—a custom that many think was found only along the northwestern coast of the continent. In fact, Andree' Newton, the daughter of my late friend Mdawelasis, is herself a wood carver and often has to explain to people that she is *not* copying the traditions of the Tlingit or the Kwakiutl. Here in the northeast, many of our Native nations used to carve effigy poles, perhaps six to ten feet long, that would be placed upright in front of people's homes. "They were," Mdawelasis said, "sort of like mailboxes are today, to show where someone lives." Sadly, European missionaries saw such carvings as works of the devil. In most Native villages the old carved poles were destroyed and people forbidden to make new ones. One of the few Native groups that preserved that carving tradition were the Abenakis of Odanak, the community from which Mdawelasis came.

In any event, having seen an actual pole being shaped, I knew there was a problem with Thomas's depiction. He showed it being carved in an upright position—with the carver reaching up, a hammer and chisel in his hand. It was my first of what would turn out to be many collaborations with Thomas, so I hesitated a moment before speaking.

"It's a beautiful painting," I said, "but some of the details are not right."

To my relief and delight, his reaction was to ask me—with great eagerness—to point out the errors so that he would correct them. Thus it was that the pole ended up being shown in a horizontal position—so that the carver would both save energy and lean into his work. And the hammer and chisel were replaced by a traditional tool, a beaver tooth fastened into a wooden handle that an Abenaki carver would use for the fine details that make a carving come alive—just as those fine details do for a story.

Fine details. Those have come to me, as have the ideas for so many of my stories, by careful attention. So allow me to end this essay with that word Mdawelasis spoke to me those many years ago. It's a short word, but its meaning is long. Kina. Listen.

CHAPTER 3

Survival through Stories: An Introduction to Indian Literatures

P. Jane Hafen

American Indian written expression presents paradox. The literary traditions of indigenous peoples are, in a real sense, timeless. Basic features and stylistic devices, such as the ritual of oral storytelling, trickster figures, sacredness of place, and fluid time remain largely unchanged. Yet American Indian writings have also been subject to historical transformations that have come with European contact: writing, translation, English language expression. Resisting colonialism and the imposition of stereotypes is also a literary technique of survival.

Additionally, American Indian literary traditions have been concerned with the particularity of individual tribal experience. American Indian writers exist in complex relation to multiple traditions: the mainstream Western literary canon, the particular oral traditions of their peoples, the political discourses of the time in which they live, and, as Robert Warrior (Osage) has pointed out in *Tribal Secrets* (1993), an indigenous intellectual tradition that has taken shape around both the spoken and the written word, while preserving and creating a distinctive tribal discourse of survival.

Naming

Nomenclature for indigenous peoples has developed since the first European contact. As an objective body, Native people were seen by Europeans as redskins, uncivilized, savages, and, due to Columbus's navigational error, Indians, later distinguished as American Indians. Naming indicates power. As individual tribal peoples, most native peoples refer to themselves by their particular tribal identifications: I am Taos Pueblo, N. Scott Momaday is

Kiowa, James Welch is Blackfeet, Joy Harjo is Muscogee Creek. Luci Tapahonso is Navajo, but also referred to as Diné, the name that tribe calls itself. "Native American" became politically apt during the 1970s, but as Sherman Alexie (Spokane/Cœur d'Alene) says in "The Unauthorized Autobiography of Me,"

> I have never met a Native American. Thesis repeated: I have met thousands of Indians.
>
> November 1994, Manhattan: PEN American panel on Indian Literature. N. Scott Momaday, James Welch, Gloria Miguel, Joy Harjo, me. Two or three hundred people in the audience. Mostly non-Indians, an Indian or three. Questions and answers.
>
> "Why do you insist on calling yourselves Indian?" asks a white woman in a nice hat. "It's so demeaning."
>
> "Listen," I say. "The word belongs to us now. We are Indians. That has nothing to do with Indians from India. We are not American Indians. We are Indians, pronounced In-din. It belongs to us. We own it and we're not going to give it back."
>
> *(One Stick Song 13)*

As a collective whole, more Indians call themselves Indians than "Native Americans"; however, the tribal name is still preferable and also establishes tribal sovereignty.

Diversity

Primary to understanding American Indian literatures is an awareness of the diversity of peoples in the Western Hemisphere. Distinct language groups comprised of particular cultures and geographic varieties represent many ways of looking at the worlds. Within each particular culture are complex social structures, adaptive techniques and origin stories which reflect the moral universe of each people and, quite often, their geographic circumstances. These complex aspects can be explained as *tribalography*. As Choctaw writer LeAnne Howe explains:

> I must tell you what my term *tribalography* means and how it achieves a new understanding in theorizing on Native studies. This is a tall order for a storyteller, but here goes. Native stories, no matter what form they take (novel, poem, drama, memoir, film, history), seem to pull all the elements together of the storyteller's tribe, meaning the people, the land, and multiple characters and all their manifestations and revelations, and connect these in past, present, and future milieus (present and future milieus mean non-Indians). [. . .] *Tribalography*

comes from the Native propensity for bringing things together, for making consensus, and for symbiotically connecting one thing to another. (42)

Because the endeavor of American Indian literatures is holistic, derived from particular experiences, cultures, histories, and traditions, as Howe notes, most Indian authors use a variety of literary genres.

As part of tribal diversity, the U.S. government has recognized more than 560 indigenous nations as political entities within the boundaries of the country. This fact introduces some of the intricate relationships that American Indians have with the United States. In the Declaration of Independence, indigenous peoples are referred to as "merciless Indian savages" and later defined by the Supreme Court as "domestic dependent nations." Unlike other minority populations, American Indians have a unique history and relationship with the government. For example, Indians are the only minority required to show documentation of their minority status. This proof developed from historical treaty rights and status where individuals were obligated to demonstrate membership in a tribal nation. An individual's "Indianness" is measured in fractionated blood quantum (4/4, 1/4, 13/16, etc.) and requires a "Certificate of Degree of Indian Blood." However, due to more recent court rulings, each tribe may define its own qualifications for membership. Some tribes, like the Cherokees of Oklahoma, require only proof of descent—one has to show s/he descended from a documented member of the tribe. Other tribes require blood quantum and language facility or residency to be members of an Indian nation.

Trickster Narratives

Each tribal group, in addition to being a political entity as previously mentioned, has its own origin story. Those stories often reflect the geographic circumstances of a particular tribe. For example, many of the tribes from the southwest have stories that describe emergence through the earth. Many of the woodland culture groups have earthdiver stories where an animal, a turtle, muskrat, or something similar, dives to the bottom of the ocean and retrieves a piece of earth. Some plains groups have origin stories where a being falls through a hole in the sky.

A consistent character in many origin stories is a trickster character—a coyote, a rabbit, a spider. Generally speaking, a trickster story socializes moral behaviors by demonstrating what happens when excess is allowed to rule. Because the trickster is often outrageously humorous, graphic acts and language are often the norm. These stories contrast with the portentous creation stories of the Hebrew Scriptures/Bible where life is determined by original sin rather than a humorous and gluttonous raven. Clearly, having trickster characters function in creation stories creates a different worldview than stories that emphasize sin. Alfonso Ortiz (San Juan Pueblo) and Richard Erdoes have an edited collection of traditional stories in *American Indian Trickster Tales*.

Trickster characters also appear in contemporary fiction. Tosamah, the Kiowa preacher in *House Made of Dawn*, offers an extreme sermon based on the Gospel of St. John. Gerald Vizenor (White Earth Ojibwe) models trickster narratives himself in his own fictions, the Bearheart chronicles and Almost Browne stories. Louise Erdrich (Turtle Mountain Ojibwe) has embodied the Ojibwe trickster figure of Nanabozho in her character of Nanapush. Nanapush appears throughout Erdrich's opus of North Dakota novels. He finally meets his demise in *The Last Report on the Miracles at Little No Horse* after chasing a moose, being dragged in a canoe by the moose and apparently coming back to life for a moment, complete with an erection.

The humor of trickster stories, both traditional and contemporary, points to the persistence of oral narratives in written form and the crucial element of survival humor in storytelling. The enduring presence of trickster characters also illustrates a connection of past, current, and future cultural values.

Identity, Narrative, and Time

The issues of identity, who has the right to define Indian identity and how individuals relate to non-Indian and Indian communities, permeate Native literatures. An early novel, *The Surrounded* (1936) by D'Arcy McNickle (Cree/Flathead), introduces tropes of alienation and identity. Not only must the main character, Archilde Leon, experience discrimination and misunderstanding from the non-Indian world, but he must also face complications among his own people. Alienation followed by reconciliation to a tribal community through language and ritual is a theme about identity in Momaday's Pulitzer Prize winning novel, *House Made of Dawn* (1968). Leslie Marmon Silko (Laguna Pueblo) retells a similar story in *Ceremony* (1977). The reconstruction of story is also a trope Silko uses throughout much of her work.

More recent fiction that explores identity issues is the work of prolific writer Sherman Alexie. In the novel *Indian Killer* (1996), Alexie uses the main character of John Smith to assess the confusion of someone who is born Indian but raised outside the culture by non-Indian parents. This situation reflects a historical reality of assimilation practices where, prior to the Indian Child Welfare Act of 1978, children could be removed from tribes and placed outside their cultures or sent to boarding schools with the express purpose to "Kill the Indian, Save the Man." In a very personal narrative, Alexie confronts identity in *The Absolutely True Diary of a Part-Time Indian*. This book won the 2007 National Book Award for Young Adults. Although it is a novel, its details reflect Alexie's own life as the main character copes with poverty, racism, and exceptional intellect. The novel concludes with a semi-apology to the Spokane Tribal Community but acknowledges that the tribe will always be part of the character's identity.

Although Alexie's young adult novel has a single narrator and protagonist, many Indian writings do not. For example, Momaday's *House Made of Dawn* has four distinct sections, three with third person narrators, the Jemez Pueblo sections and the Kiowa section, and the Navajo section with first person, Ben Benally, as narrator. Even though the story revolves around Abel, his alienation and reconciliation come through his community and his history. The protagonist is the tribe and Abel's part in it.

James Welch (Blackfeet-Gros Ventre) also explores identity issues through alienation and reconciliation in *Winter in the Blood* (1974). The unnamed main character must come to terms with his own personal history and with his relationships. He comes of age and to an awareness of himself. In an inspired historical parallel, *Fools Crow* (1984), Welch recreates nineteenth century Blackfeet circumstances and reconstructs language to outline how the main character, Fools Crow, must also come of age and face the coming changes to Blackfeet society. An example of Welch's language usage is a literalization of terms, such as calling the Rocky Mountains the "Backbone of the World." Even though the novel's primary language is English, sprinkled with occasional Blackfeet words, Welch's usage presents a Blackfeet perspective. Like Alexie reclaims "Indian," Welch not only reclaims worldview through English, but he also reclaims Blackfeet history. The climax of the story occurs when Fools Crow has a vision of the apocalyptic events that will transform the Pikuni (what the tribe calls itself) to the Blackfeet, a tribe in the modern world. Fools Crow sees how the tribe will face starvation, a decimating smallpox epidemic, and an attack from the U.S. Army. More than 170 Blackfeet, mostly women and children, were killed when the army mistakenly attacked while seeking another group of Indians who had caused trouble with the white settlers in Montana on 23 January 1871. These real historical events are rendered in Welch's story from the Native point of view and experience. Welch emphasizes not the tragedy of disease, starvation, and massacre, but the survival of the Blackfeet even in the most dire circumstances: "He [Fools Crow] had been brought here to the strange woman's lodge in this strange world to see the fate of his people. And he was powerless to change it. [. . .] As he sat in hopeless resignation, he heard the sound of children laughing" (358). Fools Crow then sees the children in a school, dressed in clothing from the white world. The school is symbolically surrounded by a barbed wire fence: "'Much will be lost to them,' said Feather Woman. 'But they will know the way it was. The stories will be handed down, and they will see that their people were proud and lived in accordance with the Below Ones, The Underwater People and the Above Ones'" (359–60). Welch demonstrates Fools Crow becoming aware of his identity within the Blackfeet community; he shows the key to survival is storytelling even with his own metanarrative of the retelling of Blackfeet history; and he reclaims an indigenous point of view that had not previously been represented. His resources included historical documents and studies, and the stories of his grandmother who had survived the Maria River massacre.

LeAnne Howe also tells stories that cross time barriers. Both of her novels, *Shell Shaker* (2001) and *Miko Kings: An Indian Baseball Story* (2007), use fluid time to reclaim history. In *Shell Shaker* events from early Choctaw encounters with Europeans in Mississippi parallel current events in Oklahoma. The tribal emphasis or "cultural bias" also shows how historical Choctaws attempted to colonize the Europeans to Choctaw ways of seeing the world yet were ultimately removed to Indian Territory (Oklahoma). Time is the central subject of *Miko Kings*. Using multiple narrators, Howe shows how the concepts of time can be relative and how the stories can change. The baseball metaphor is apt because the game is run outside of a time constraint and the construction of the game is counter clockwise. Howe also utilizes multiple narrators in her stories to emphasize the tribe as a communal protagonist. Using multiple narrators also implements non-linear storytelling as characters offer their perspectives from what is current to them.

Like all the authors mentioned so far, Howe is also a poet. In *Evidence of Red* (2005), she writes a number of short narratives and an especially pointed critique in a poetic dialogue between Indian Mascot and Noble Savage. By directly confronting two of the major stereotypes of Indians, Howe shifts from object to subject position; instead of allowing popular culture to continue its objectification of Indians through mascots and Noble Savage, Howe gives them new voice through sexual metaphor. She reclaims the most egregious stereotypes by taking ownership of them.

Another writer with versatility is Joy Harjo. Not only has she created numerous volumes of poetry and short narratives, but she has also musically interpreted them with her band Poetic Justice and her own saxophone playing. Clearly the saxophone is a modern musical instrument, invented by Adolphe Sax in 1841, yet Harjo's mastery of the instrument as a mode of indigenous expression demonstrates adaptability and survival techniques. Although some contemporary theorists might label Harjo's performances as "hybrid," she clearly puts her own Muscogee Creek interpretation on ideas, concepts and expressions.

Sense of Place

Each of the authors mentioned thus far have, in addition to writing their tribal experiences, tied their works to geographic place. More than ambience or setting, the placing of the stories represents cultural ties to the land. Nearly all the narratives begin with setting rather than character and then, quite frequently, the place functions as a character. Not only does geographic locale mirror the cultural markers in stories, but it often becomes a trope for identification. In *House Made of Dawn*, Abel returns to Jemez Pueblo; in *Ceremony* Tayo returns to Laguna Pueblo; Sherman Alexie's character Arnold Spirit is torn by his ties to Wellpinit, Washington; Fools Crow sees the landscape change before his very eyes, but remains defined by that particular home in Montana; Oklahoma is the red earth of Howe's novels.

Another major American Indian author who imbues her writing with a sense of place is Louise Erdrich. Her series of novels is a complex intertwining of characters and families connected to an imaginary reservation but with events and descriptions that resonate with the nature of the northern Great Plains and the woodlands culture of the Ojibwe. She describes her own sense of developing character and place:

> In a tribal view of the world, where one place has been inhabited for generations, the landscape becomes enlivened by a sense of group and family history. Unlike most contemporary writers, a traditional storyteller fixes listeners in an unchanging landscape combined of myth and reality. People and place are inseparable. ("Where I Ought to Be" 1)

Erdrich's novels are set primarily in the twentieth century. They witness tremendous changes among Ojibwe peoples, including land losses and cultural adaptations through conversion to Christianity and popular influences. These tribal peoples cannot remain unchanged, yet they maintain a sense of who they are as Ojibwes, and they remain tied to the land, even as their place names are adapted by the ever-encroaching dominant society.

"Anishinaabeg" is the traditional name the Ojibwe peoples called themselves and utilizes the image of Ojibwe-specific puckered moccasins:

> White people usually name places for men—presidents and generals and entre-preneurs. Ojibwe name places for what grows there or what is found. [. . .] If we call ourselves and all we see around us by the original names, will we not continue to be Anishinaabeg? Instead of reconstituted white men, instead of Indian ghosts? Do the rocks here know us, do the trees, do the waters of the lakes? Not unless they are addressed by the names they themselves told us to call them in our dreams. Every feature of the land around us spoke its name to an ancestor. Perhaps in the end, that is all that we are. We Anishinaabeg are the keepers of the names of the earth. And unless the earth is called by the names it gave us humans, won't it cease to love us? And isn't it true that if the earth stops loving us, everyone, not just the Anishinaabeg, will cease to exist? (Erdrich *Last Report*, 359–61)

The earth and tribal peoples have a symbiotic relationship; they are mutu-ally self-defining. Forgetting reciprocal dependence leads to destruction. Survival as indigenous peoples is predicated on the land. Erdrich is refuting assimilation and the Vanishing American through adherence to the earth. Yet, through the stories and the places, the Ojibwe continue to exist as one of the largest indigenous cultures in North America. Erdrich depicts the modulations and accommodations through her Ojibwe characters as they struggle to survive.

Native Literary Criticism

Even as authors, many more than can be discussed here, have established their own voices in traditional literary genres, contemporary Native writers have also affirmed a literary criticism that emphasizes tribal issues. Often these writers work in various genres, but their critical voices establish what Robert Allen Warrior (Osage) calls an "intellectual sovereignty." Gerald Vizenor (White Earth Chippewa) utilizes postmodern discourse to create challenging intellectual tribal fictions, but perhaps his most significant influ-ence is in his theoretical discussion of trickster narratives in *Narrative Chance* (1989). Although his conceptual vocabulary is occasionally ponderous, he molds the critical discourse to fit the writings of his discussion rather than allowing the analysis to predominate. Louis Owens' (Choctaw/Cherokee) mystery novels complement his literary critiques *Other Destinies* (1992) and *Mixed Blood Messages* (1998), which is also a memoir. Craig Womack's groundbreaking *Red on Red: Native American Literary Separatism* (1999) not only argues for a tribally based criticism, in this case Muscogee and

Cherokee, but also offers a model for discussing queer theory in an indigenous context.

Native literary critics who challenge the academy to assess Native literature from the inside out include Elizabeth Cook-Lynn (Dakota) who, with anthropologist, Beatrice Medicine (Lakota) and William Willard (Cherokee), founded the journal *Wicazo Ša Review*. This journal, currently edited by James Riding In (Pawnee), has a specific political agenda devoted to tribal sovereignties and tribal voices. Cook-Lynn's *Why I Can't Read Wallace Stegner and Other Essays* sets a standard for evaluating works by both non-Indians and Indians. Her more recent book, *New Indians, Old Wars*, continues her arguments for tribal sovereignties. Paula Gunn Allen's (Laguna-Sioux) definitive gendered interpretations in *The Sacred Hoop* (1992) and *Off the Reservation* (1998) seem to have more impact than her creative writings.

Significant to American Indian children's literature is the growth of electronic media. Debbie Reese (Nambe) writes and administers a website American Indians in Children's Literature (http://americanindiansinchildrensliterature. blogspot.com/). Additionally oyate.org, managed by Beverly Slapin and Doris Seale (Santee/Cree), maintains current discussions and critical assessments. The website complements their publication *The Broken Flute: The Native Experience in Books for Children*.

Using an essay by Simon J. Ortiz (Acoma Pueblo) as a starting point, Womack, Warrior and Jace Weaver (Cherokee) extend the argument for tribal sovereignties in *American Indian Literary Nationalism*. A distinguished poet and writer of short narratives, perhaps Ortiz puts it best in discussing survival, resistance, story, and place in the context of tribal national identity:

> It has been this resistance—political, armed, spiritual—which has been carried out by the oral tradition. The continued use of the oral tradition today is evidence that the resistance is on-going. Its use, in fact, is what has given rise to the surge of literature created by contemporary Indian authors. And it is this literature, based upon continuing resistance, which has given a particularly nationalistic character to the Native American voice. (10)

Encompassed in the oral tradition is a grand narrative impulse in many of the stories and literatures discussed here and elsewhere. Ortiz's description of the literature complements Howe's ideas of tribalography and what Alexie calls "reservation realism." Resistance to colonization has been ongoing since the early European encounters on this hemisphere. That Indians still exist more than 500 years later despite disease, violence and institutional attempts at assimilation is evidence of tenacity and a strong sense of tradition. Of course that does not mean traditions have not changed or that many have not been lost, but in adaptive strategies, Ortiz again observes:

> Many Christian religious rituals brought to the Southwest (which in the 16th century was the north frontier of the Spanish New World) are no longer Spanish. They are now Indian because of the creative development that the native people applied to them. Present-day Native American or Indian literature is evidence of this in the very same way. And because in every case where European culture was cast upon Indian people of this nation, there was similar creative response and development, it can be observed that this was the primary element of a nationalistic impulse to make use of foreign ritual, ideas, and material in their own—Indian—terms. Today's writing by Indian authors is a continuation of that elemental impulse. (8)

Indigenous authors have taken English and made it their own language and used it for their own unique expression of tribal nationalism. In each case of literary study, consideration should be given to tribal origin, place, stories derived from oral practices, and survival strategies.

Conclusion

American Indian Literatures are complex and unlike other ethnic literatures. Their history and development reflect a unique relationship Native peoples have with the U.S. government and the status of sovereign tribal nations. Therefore, one of the literary major concerns is tribal identity that is often defined through the community and represented by multiple narrators but must also address the impositions of the government. Identity is also established by geographic place that represents a political history and linguistic relationship with the land. The holistic telling of stories through a variety of genres conflates past and present as emphasized by oral traditions and trickster figures. Indigenous authors find power through their own voices by resisting and reclaiming the images and stereotypes that have been imposed on them through a colonial system. Despite violence, disease, institutional attempts at assimilation, through the imposition of the English language, Indian authors have survived to tell their own stories.

Works Cited

Alexie, Sherman (Spokane/Coeur D'Alene). *Indian Killer*. New York: Atlantic Monthly P, 1996.
———. *One Stick Song*. Brooklyn: Hanging Loose Press, 2000.

Allen, Paula Gunn (Laguna Pueblo/Sioux). *Off the Reservation: Reflections on Boundary-Busting Border-Crossing Loose Canons*. Boston: Beacon, 1998.

———. *The Sacred Hoop: Recovering the Feminine in American Indian Traditions*. Boston: Beacon, 1992.

Cook-Lynn, Elizabeth (Dakota). *New Indians, Old Wars*. Urbana: U of Illinois P, 2007.

———. *Why I Can't Read Wallace Stegner and Other Essays*. Madison: U of Wisconsin P, 1996.

Erdoes, Richard, and Alfonso Ortiz (San Juan Pueblo). *American Indian Trickster Tales*. New York: Viking, 1998.

Erdrich, Louise (Turtle Mountain Ojibwe). *The Last Report on the Miracles at Little No Horse*. New York: HarperCollins, 2001.

———. "Where I Ought to Be: A Writer's Sense of Place." *New York Times Book Review*, 28 July 1985: 1, 24–25.

Harjo, Joy (Muscogee), and Gloria Bird (Spokane). *Reinventing the Enemy's Language*. New York: Norton, 1997.

Howe, LeAnne (Choctaw). *Miko Kings: An Indian Baseball Story*. San Francisco: Aunt Lute, 2007.

———. *Shell Shaker*. San Francisco: Aunt Lute, 2001.

———. "The Story of America: A Tribalography." In *Clearing a Path: Theorizing the Past in Native American Studies*. Ed. Nancy Shoemaker. New York: Routledge, 2002. 29–48.

McNickle, D'Arcy (Cree/Flathead). *The Surrounded*. 1936. Reprint, Albuquerque: U of New Mexico P, 1992.

Medicine, Beatrice (Lakota). *Learning to Be an Anthropologist and Remaining Native*. Urbana: U of Illinois P, 2001.

Momaday, N. Scott (Kiowa). *House Made of Dawn*. 1969. Reprint, New York: Perennial, 1989.

Ortiz, Simon (Acoma Pueblo). "Towards a National Indian Literature: Cultural Authenticity in Nationalism." *MELUS* 8.2 (1981): 7–12.

Owens, Louis (Choctaw/Cherokee). *Mixedblood Messages: Literature, Film, Family, Place*. Norman: U of Oklahoma P, 1998.

———. *Other Destinies: Understanding the American Indian Novel*. Norman: U of Oklahoma P, 1992.

Silko, Leslie Marmon (Laguna Pueblo). *Ceremony*. New York: Viking, 1977.

Slapin, Beverly, and Doris Seale (Santee/Cree). *The Broken Flute: The Native Experience in Books for Children*. Walnut Creek: AltaMira P, 2005.

———. *Through Indian Eyes: The Native Experience in Books for Children*. Philadelphia: New Society Publishers, 1992.

Tapahanso, Lucy (Diné). *Blue Horses Rush in: Poems and Stories*. Tucson: U of Arizona P, 1997.

———. *Saanii Dahataal, the Women Are Singing*. Tucson: U of Arizona P, 1993.

Vizenor, Gerald (White Earth Chippewa), ed. *Narrative Chance: Postmodern Discourse on Native American Indian Literatures*. Albuquerque: U of New Mexico P, 1989.

Warrior, Robert Allen (Osage). *Tribal Secrets: Recovering American Indian Intellectual Traditions*. Minneapolis: U of Minnesota P, 1995.

Weaver, Jace (Cherokee), Craig S. Womack, and Robert Warrior. *American Indian Literary Nationalism*. Albuquerque: U of New Mexico P, 2006.

Welch, James (Blackfeet-Gros Ventre). *Fools Crow*. New York: Viking, 1986.

———. *Winter in the Blood*. New York: Harper, 1974.

Womack, Craig S. (Muscogee/Cherokee). *Red on Red: Native American Literary Separatism*. Norman: U of Oklahoma P, 1999.

CHAPTER 4

Oral Narrative and Ojibwa Story Cycles in Louise Erdrich's *Birchbark House* and *Game of Silence*

Elizabeth Gargano

In a 1985 interview, Louise Erdrich describes her fascination with the sacred stories of traditional Ojibwa culture, separate tales, which nevertheless form an interrelated whole. These stories, she acknowledges, have served as an esthetic model for her fiction. Such interrelated oral stories generally revolve around a central and unifying figure, often a powerful manito from the spirit world or a human being with magical powers. In Erdrich's words:

> One tells a story about an incident that leads to another incident in the life of this particular figure. Night after night, or day after day, it's a story telling cycle. It's the sort of thing where people know what they're going to say. They're old stories, but the stories have incorporated different elements of non-Chippewa [non-Ojibwa] or European culture as they've gone on, so that sometimes you see a great traditional story with some sort of fairytale added to it.
>
> *Conversations* 4

Erdrich describes a rich and enduring tradition that achieves a dynamic balance between continuity and innovation. The storytelling tradition can open at any point to include new elements. Hospitable to contemporary experiences, it maintains a profound cultural relevance and significance; it continues to serve its Ojibwa audience by reflecting their experience back to them and imbuing such experience with sacred meanings, while also situating it within familiar cultural patterns.

In her two novels for children, *The Birchbark House* (1999) and its sequel *The Game of Silence* (2005), Erdrich creates histories that are also cultural texts in this specific revitalizing sense. In both novels, she employs a cyclical narrative structure and interweaves the daily experiences of her human protagonists with traditional stories of such powerful spirit-mentors as Nanabozho, the great trickster-creator. Erdrich's creative juxtapositions shed new light on the lives of the human characters, while also illuminating the regenerative powers of traditional Ojibwa storytelling.

In recent years, such critics as Hertha Wong, James Ruppert, and Catherine Rainwater have explored the Ojibwa roots of Erdrich's use of the story-cycle form in her rich body of fiction for adults. Hertha Wong, for example, emphasizes the "polyvocality" of "Native American oral traditions" as a source for Erdrich's use of interwoven but separate narratives in her first novel *Love Medicine* (Wong 173). James Ruppert's "Mediation and Multiple Narrative in *Love Medicine*" argues that the novel "celebrate[s] [Native American] culture by [means of] a continuing recreation of the multiple facets of identity through multiple narrative" (230). Catherine Rainwater reminds us that Erdrich's novel *Tracks* "draws on a variety of oral storytelling strategies" (145), while *The Bingo Palace* embodies a "collective narrative voice" that combines the "authority and humility" of the "traditional oral storyteller" (152). In contrast, the story cycle aspects of Erdrich's children's fiction have received relatively little attention. In her illuminating essay, "Sea of Good Intentions: Native Americans in Books for Children," Melissa Kay Thompson emphasizes the historically and psychologically accurate content of Erdrich's children's novel, as opposed to the Native American stereotypes in so much children's fiction. Understandably, other critics have also focused on the content of Erdrich's novel, rather than its form. Lisa Hermien Makman, for instance, contends that Erdrich's depiction of an actively working child protagonist typifies multiculturalism's emphasis on child labor as integrated into the fabric of culture.

As I argue in this essay, however, an appreciation of Erdrich's skillful incorporation of Ojibwa story-cycle elements is crucial to understanding both *The Birchbark House* and *The Game of Silence*. Drawing on the conventions of oral storytelling, Erdrich repeatedly interrupts both novels' forward momentum with self-contained traditional tales that emphasize cultural continuity while also serving to explain and contextualize present action. Rather than foregrounding a linear, plot-driven narrative, Erdrich subtly interweaves events into a natural and spiritual landscape where change is cyclical and at times illusory. Even the most dramatic actions are woven like bright threads into nature's dense and variegated tapestry. Further, Erdrich's haunting and lyrical narratives affirm a collective cultural vision beyond the individual consciousness of her fictive protagonist. Incorporating story-cycle elements and subordinating linear narrations to a cyclical narrative structure, Erdrich's novels for children reflect an Ojibwa worldview that affirms gratitude to nature for its gifts, the preciousness of communal knowledge and traditions, and the integration of daily activities with sacred experience. Thus Erdrich's work also implicitly critiques Euro-American assumptions about humanity's supremacy over nature and the importance of individualism, as well as a generalized Western tendency to accept stark divisions between the sacred and secular realms. In sum, Erdrich's novels fuse form and content to a new end, calling readers to understand her child-protagonist's adventures through an active engagement with Ojibwa values and traditions.

I

Set in the 1800s during the era of white incursion into the Native American homeland, *The Birchbark House* chronicles seven-year-old Omakayas's discovery of her vocation as a healer after she helps to nurse her family through a devastating smallpox epidemic. Omakayas learns that she is an adopted child, the survivor of an earlier outbreak of the disease, and that she was saved by a family friend, the mysterious Old Tallow, who serves as an image of female independence and power. In the course of her narrative, then, Omakayas survives a series of demanding ordeals in order to discover a vocation, a mentor, and a new identity. In *The Birchbark House*, the looming threat of white expansion remains muted, allowing Erdrich to describe a relatively self-contained Ojibwa community on the Island of the Golden-Breasted Woodpecker (Madeline Island) in Southern Lake Superior. Yet already, some alien elements are changing the fabric of daily life. Whites are traveling "in larger numbers . . . to Ojibwa land and setting down their cabins, forts, barns, gardens, pastures, fences, fur-trading posts, churches, and mission schools" (*Birchbark* 76–77). Whites also bring the deadly disease of smallpox, which ravages the community and eventually kills Omakayas's baby brother Neewo.

Set two years later, *The Game of Silence* dramatizes an Ojibwa community now under direct attack by the U.S. government. Invalidating a previous treaty, the government orders the Ojibwe to move west into the land of the Lakota and Dakota tribes—a forced migration that may end in a battle between the tribes. While Omakayas strives to come to terms with her personal destiny, readying herself for a vision from her spirit helper, her community struggles to understand the threats that jeopardize its homeland. By the end of the novel, as the family reluctantly travels west, Omakayas faces the terrible loss of their homeland with a new spirit of adventure. In this second novel, the white presence has proliferated on Ojibwa land. Omakayas and her cousin Twilight play with a white friend, "Break-Apart Girl," so-named because her cinched corset and voluminous skirts make her look as if she could break apart at the waist. Black-Gown, the Catholic priest, has established a church, and Ojibwa children increasingly attend the school, learning to decipher the "speaking tracks" (*Game* 131) with which the whites record their treaties and transactions.

Working against the traditional linear structures that have shaped so many Western narratives, Erdrich divides both novels into four seasonal sections, focusing on each season's summons to specific tasks, pleasures, and journeys. During the summer, Omakayas's father, Mikwam, is away, hunting and fishing, while the women pursue the all-important work of house-building, tanning, and farming. In fall, the family harvests wild rice and moves to a sturdy cold-weather cabin. Winter is a season of storytelling and visits, when Mikwam comes home to his family. Spring brings a healing ceremony "to cure winter's illnesses" (*Birchbark* 210), the bubbling sweetness of maple sugar, and a renewed sense of life's possibilities. By subordinating the family's story to the cyclical narrative of the seasons, Erdrich suggests that human activities can best be understood, not as a progressive linear development, but rather as a ritual round of profoundly necessary acts that mirror natural processes. Erdrich's vision is grounded in an all-embracing respect for nature at the heart of Ojibwa culture. Unlike the white settlers with their surprising habit of surrounding their settlements with "mud and garbage" (*Game* 131), the Ojibwe, Omakayas reflects, "didn't throw out the same things that the chimookomanag [whites] found useless" (*Game* 132). Rather than seeing nature as raw material to be utilized and then discarded, Omakayas and her family return what they don't use to its source, as an act of homage to nature. After eating fish, for instance, they throw "the spines and bones back into the water . . . to show respect for the fish so that they would allow people to keep catching them" (*Game* 72).

An Ojibwa understanding of nature not only shapes Erdrich's deployment of narrative structures. It also permeates her framing of point of view. While both novels generally embrace the view of Omakayas, its child protagonist, the narrative escapes a univocal perspective by slipping into the thoughts of surrounding characters and creatures in order to dramatize motives that Omakayas has refused to envision or understand. Thus, after portraying Omakayas's anger at her rambunctious brother Pinch, as well as her exultation that he has gotten himself "in trouble" yet again, the narrative shifts briefly to Pinch's point of view: "It was hard being Big Pinch, harder than his sisters would ever know" (*Birchbark* 83). Eschewing a conventionally unified point of view, Erdrich stages a single foray into Pinch's consciousness in order to contextualize Omakayas's thoughts within a larger familial viewpoint, demonstrating that her individual perspective is merely a fragment within the overarching mosaic of a larger communal vision. Beyond this, however, Omakayas learns to enter into the realm of nonhuman consciousness. She comes to understand the language of animals, of plants, of ghosts and spirits who speak to her in dreams and through the music of birds. As a future healer, Omakayas also learns to listen to the "bear clan" (*Birchbark* 207), who, according to her grandmother's lore know the medicinal value of forest plants. An individual point of view, Erdrich suggests, can be neither isolated nor owned. Rather all viewpoints are subtly interconnected. Thus, the "polyvocality" identified by Wong extends well beyond human speech, as Erdrich's texts also give voice to Omakayas's powerful animal mentors.

II

A circular structure and a flexible concept of point of view reinforce Erdrich's cyclical, communal, and de-individualizing project. Her homage to the Ojibwa story cycle emerges most prominently, however, in her integration of traditional oral tales into Omakayas's narrative. While Erdrich emphasizes the embedded stories' separate identity by setting them apart from the surrounding text and assigning them titles, she also dramatizes their impact on the unfolding lives and sensibilities of her characters. Early in *The Birchbark House*, Mikwam, Omakayas's father, returns from hunting and trading to tell a tale of being captured by hungry ghosts who planned to devour him. Recounted in a vivid virtuoso style, Mikwam's tale leaves open the possibility that he is exaggerating and shaping his experience for entertainment value, deploying traditional motifs from his storytelling tradition. In other words, objectivity and accuracy are not the point here; instead, oral storytelling emerges as a collective art that shapes and contextualizes, rather than merely rendering, experiences.

Furthermore, when shaped into stories, such transformed experiences serve the valuable function of guiding future behavior and events. Soon after Mikwam tells his story, he and his friends discuss the white settlers pouring into Ojibwa territory. Speculating about the whites' motives, Mikwam's friend Fishtail asserts: "Before they were born, before they came into this world, the chimookoman [white people] must have starved as ghosts. They are infinitely hungry" (80). As this new threat to the Ojibwe is contextualized in the language of Mikwam's story of the spirit world, his narrative sheds light on the realistic events of the novel. Mikwam speculates that his ghostly attackers "had perhaps starved to death and so were eternally hungry." Failing to perceive Mikwam's human nature, they identify him as "meat" and argue over which one of them will claim his "bones" *(Birchbark* 65).

In Fishtail's view, the white invaders suffer from a similar obsession, equally deadly. As he exclaims, "Not even when we are gone and they have the bones of our loved ones will they be pleased" (*Birchbark* 80). Prisoners of their own delusion, the invading whites take on the characteristics of living ghosts. They are ready to devour their fellow human beings, driven by their fierce appetite, not for necessary food, but rather for land. Since the concept of the cannibal ghost seamlessly merges sacred realities and daily experience, revealing connections between the powerful world of spirits and the humans who mimic them, Erdrich's narrative is positioned to draw similar parallels between otherworldly stories and the dailiness of life.

As such narrative juxtapositions emphasize, oral storytelling is a flexible instrument, capable not only of preserving old meanings but also of generating new ones in order to explain unforeseen experiences. Placing the white invaders within an Ojibwa worldview not only attaches a moral significance to the whites—the "hungry ghosts"; it also offers strategies for resisting and outwitting them. Just as Mikwam uses trickery to escape the ravenous phantoms in his story, so he later tricks a white trader to secure food for his family. An accomplished chess player, Mikwam challenges the trader to play for supplies. Performing poorly at first, he fools the trader into raising the stakes, just as he once duped the hungry ghosts into letting him escape. Mikwam's victory, when he beats the trader at the white man's game of chess, is presented as only a brief respite from winter's trials. Nevertheless, it represents one more victory in the struggle for survival in a hostile world. If the embedded stories provide guidance for characters in the novel, they also provide a subtle form of guidance for readers as well. The tales enable Erdrich to deepen her critique of Euro-American expansion through the interplay of different forms of narration, rather than by resorting to explicit didacticism.

In even more profound ways, the tales told by Omakayas's Nokomis, or grandmother,[1] signal the integration of daily and sacred experience. Near the beginning of the section titled "Winter" in *The Birchbark House*, Nokomis recounts an evocative story from her own childhood. As a young girl, she had taken her canoe to the dark side of the lake, where the water was deepest—despite her grandfather's warning never to go there. In this forbidden spot, she encounters the ghost of her grandmother, who rises, young and beautiful, from the depths of the lake where she drowned. Later, when the young girl's grandfather comes in search of her, he rediscovers his lost wife and chooses to follow her into the land of the dead. Like young lovers, the grandparents enter the canoe and "paddle away together, into the darkness" (*Birchbark* 138). In the face of mortality, loyalty and love forge a sense of continuity that speaks across generations, through the eternal present of storytelling. As the young wife and her old husband vanish into the recesses of Nokomis's memory, they provide a haunting image of the story's power to bridge the gap between past and present.

Nokomis's story not only commemorates those who have died; it also reminds us that life is inextricably intertwined with mortality. Thus, her tale of a ghostly visitor initiates a season of death and dying, as smallpox strikes the village, brought by a "visitor . . . from the mainland" (*Birchbark* 142). When her family members fall ill, quarantined in their cabin, Omakayas is left unscathed, living in a temporary bark lodge outside the house of death. Like her great-great-grandfather in Nokomis's story, however, Omakayas chooses to follow her family into the shadows of death rather than remain safe but alone: "If they were all to die together," Omakayas reflects, "then let it be so" (*Birchbark* 147). Nokomis's tale of her grandfather's mysterious reunion with his wife's ghost embodies the values of courage, loyalty, and devotion—traits that her granddaughter now enacts. Through such stories, generations are linked in an endless chain, and continuity is maintained as a cultural value.

In *The Game of Silence*, Nokomis continues to forge stories about her own childhood, inspiring Omakayas to face her fears and take action. In a world where disasters loom, growing up seems a dangerous enterprise. When nine-year-old Omakayas dreads the three or four-day sojourn in the forest that she must undergo to experience a spirit vision, Nokomis recounts a time when she herself was lost in the woods as a child. In her story, Nokomis encounters a *memegwesi*, a magical, tiny man with a "little crinkled face" (106). Small as he is, Nokomis nevertheless senses that "there was something huge about him" (*Game* 106). Soothing her fears of him, the spirit man announces, "I am always around. You just haven't tracked me before" (107). Like many magical figures, the little man poses a question that sets a test for Nokomis: "You have found me. Now what are you going to do!" (106). When Nokomis makes the right choice, reverently offering the friendly spirit a pinch of tobacco, he rewards her by promising to "[l]ook after you when times are difficult" (107).

Nokomis's reverence for the world of nature and its mysteries pays numerous dividends. First, she experiences a new self-confidence and strength. Later, during a long and hungry winter, the spirit leads her to a secluded spot where a bear is hibernating, providing food for her family.[2] Following him into the woods, Nokomis falls to the ground more than once "in [her] . . . weakness." In fact, she does not discover the bear until she is "nearly at the end of [her] . . . strength" (*Game* 109). Apparently just a means of passing the time while gathering plants for medicine, Nokomis's story is also a parable designed to teach her granddaughter strength and endurance. Later Omakayas realizes that "Nokomis told stories for a reason. This one . . . about her helping spirit was a clear message . . . that it was time for Omakayas to seek instruction from her own spirits" (*Game* 110). Since Omakayas must seclude herself in the woods to make contact with her own spirit helpers, the reiterated motif of Nokomis's willingness to lose herself in the forest is clearly of crucial importance. As a further aid to her granddaughter's courage, Nokomis creates a song about the *memegwesi*, who now serves as an internalized emblem of reassurance for Omakayas. Through the song, Omakayas is able to retell and reexperience Nokomis's story when she waits for her spirit vision in the woods. Initially frightened of the spirits she may encounter, she reassures herself by singing Nokomis's song of the *memegwesi*: "If she had to see a spirit, Omakayas thought she wouldn't mind seeing the funny little man whom her grandmother had described" (*Game* 227).

If the tale of the *memegwesi* gives reassurance when Omakayas faces her ordeal in the woods, it also helps her face an even greater trial, the forced departure of her family for the west. Dismayed that they must leave the *memegwesi* behind, Omakayas consults Nokomis, who reassures her that "the memegwesiwag have relatives all through this land": "Perhaps he will send word to his cousins across the bay, perhaps he will ask them to care for these people who must leave their home, perhaps they will be waiting for us, watching over us" (*Game* 238). Nokomis's words help Omakayas embark on the family's forced exile with a "calmer heart" (*Game* 238). Finally, the reassuring image of the *memegwesi* returns yet again when Omakayas watches the forest from the family's departing canoe. In the tree trunks, she seems to glimpse, "other spirits, good ones, perhaps relatives of Nokomis's little helper, and she threw her heart out before them" (*Game* 248). If the reassuring figure of the magical little man has ramifications even beyond Nokomis's original intentions in creating the story, he also illustrates how the collective voice of the storyteller transcends a merely individual perspective. By retelling Nokomis's story, Omakayas not only takes on some of her grandmother's hard-won wisdom, but also applies the story's traditional values to new experiences and challenges.

III

Most crucial to the novel's project of interweaving sacred significance and dailiness are Nokomis's *aadizookaans*[3] or "teaching stories." In *The Birchbark House*, Nokomis recounts a traditional Ojibwa sacred story about the cultural hero Nanabozho's creation of the earth. Enfeebled by the horrendous smallpox epidemic and now on the verge of starvation, Omakayas's family is renewed and regenerated by Nokomis's story. Once again, Omakayas herself is inspired to action. In Nokomis's tale—titled "Nanabozho and the Muskrat Make an Earth"—repeated rains have lapped the earth in water. The magical Nanabozho, "the great teacher of the Ojibwe" (*Game* 89), is marooned, perched in the highest limb of a pine tree, as the water rises "to his mouth" (*Birchbark* 172). When Nanabozho asks an otter and a beaver to dive deep and bring up a grain of earth so that he can rebuild the world, both animals try but fail. Finally a tiny muskrat succeeds in bringing up five grains of earth, which Nanabozho casts onto the waters to create a new world.

Unlike previously discussed stories, which show their human narrators encountering and interacting with inhabitants of the spirit world, the *aadizookaan* is a seminal sacred story in the Nanabozho cycle. A narrative of origins, it fuses history and religion, as it chronicles the epic actions of Nanabozho, an ambiguous figure who exists in many incarnations and embodies conflicting attributes. Erdrich describes him as "the great teacher of the Ojibwas, who used his comical side to teach lessons, often through hilarious mistakes" (*Birchbark* 243). In the words of Christopher Vecsey, "The Ojibwas viewed [Nanabozho] as a human, manito, hare, wolf, demigod, hero, trickster and buffoon. He was known to take on many forms and many personalities" (85). Vecsey emphasizes that Nanabozho is both a nurturing creator and a cultural hero, protecting the Ojibwa people from such threats as witchcraft and teaching them the principles of medicine and hunting; at the same time, he embodies destructive as well as creative energies. As a trickster, he can challenge, or even threaten, the principles of Ojibwa society (Vecsey 86). Vecsey's description, of course, is that of an ethnologist, attempting to classify the many appearances of Nanabozho in oral narratives.

A different view emerges in the words of Charles Kawbawgam, an eloquent Ojibwa storyteller of the nineteenth century. In the 1890s, Kawbawgam narrated numerous Ojibwa tales to Homer Huntingdon Kidder, who recorded and published them. Kawbawgam described Nanabozho this way:

> [W]e know only that he was a man like ourselves. Yet he had more power than any other Indian; he could speak to the water and make it stop and to the wind and make it talk. He called the animals his brothers; men he called his uncles; women and trees and all that grows and all that flies he called his brothers and sisters. . . . [H]e could do wonders that no other Indian could do. Yet he lived like others; he had a family and camped through the woods, and when there was famine, he went hungry with the rest.
>
> (quoted in Kawbawgam 30)

In contrast to Vecsey's analytical and somewhat fragmented description, Kawbawgam's is synthetic, emphasizing the unifying thread that runs through Nanabozho's varied incarnations—his fusion of human and divine attributes. Despite his marvelous powers, he remains associated with, and emblematic of, the human condition. This dual nature is central to an understanding of his life and his story. The sacred figure of Nanabozho is a unifying nexus of oppositions: human and animal, sacred and flawed, intensely powerful but subject to at least some of the conditions of human experience. In Erdrich's narrative, storytelling is just such a nexus between oppositional worlds and contradictory impulses. It serves as a gateway between individual experience and collective wisdom.

As Erdrich emphasizes, "Omakayas knew that her Nokomis told her this story for a larger reason. . . . She thought many times of the muskrat diving down, down for that little bit of dirt that made the world" (*Birchbark* 175). Nokomis's story is both hopeful and challenging. If the tiny muskrat can be instrumental in saving and renewing the world, a child too can make a difference. Weak and hungry, Omakayas is inspired by Nokomis's tale to leave the cabin in search of food for her family. As Erdrich notes, "this was the first time Omakayas had ventured into the woods since the day she had entered the cabin. On that day, she had followed the sickness inside and determined to do battle with the evil spirit of the disease. Now she decided . . . she would find food" (*Birchbark* 178). Just as Nokomis's earlier story forecasts a journey toward darkness and death, so her *aadizookaan* precipitates Omakayas's quest for survival and renewal.

Tellingly, Nokomis's story not only inspires Omakayas to seek food for her family; it also, somewhat comically, appears to motivate her pet bird, Andeg, to help out. "As if he had understood Grandma's story," Erdrich writes, "Andeg made his own efforts . . . [he] hunted the woods for seeds and nuts [and found] enough to feed the family for a day or two" (*Birchbark* 175–76). Playful in tone, Erdrich's depiction of Andeg's helpfulness also conveys the message that humans and animals communicate in profound and mysterious ways. Andeg not only seeks to feed the family; he also, in a touching but misplaced mating ritual, expresses his love for Omakayas by bringing her twigs to build a nest. In fact, Nokomis's *aadizookaan,* or teaching story, underlines the deep links between the human and animal world. A creator who fuses divine and human attributes, Nanabozho cannot remake the lost world without the cooperation of his animal companion, the muskrat, who brings him the necessary five grains of earth. In Nokomis's tale, the muskrat dives so deep that he drowns and must be revived by Nanabozho's healing breath. Thus the humanized Nanabozho and his animal collaborator mutually save each other and together recreate the earth, initiating a cyclical interdependence that will recur throughout history.

The parallel is clear when, immediately following the tale, Nokomis dreams of Old Horn—a venerable buck deer—who will sacrifice his life to provide the family with food. She gives Mikwam explicit directions, based on her dream, to locate the deer. Later the family members thank the deer's spirit, expressing their belief that it lives on in a different form. Nokomis's *aadizookaan* not only spurs both humans and animals to concerted action; it also reveals deeper connections between the human and animal realms in order to set in motion a new and redemptive chain of events. Erdrich's cyclical narrative, then, enacts the mysterious processes that it describes. Plot is equivalent to the profound patterning of nature. Stories generate dreams, visions, and even external events.

Like *The Birchbark House*, *The Game of Silence* also builds up to a climactic *aadizokaan* that both teaches Omakayas about her cultural history and shapes her future behavior in profound ways. Nokomis's story "The Little Girl and the Wiindigoo" (*Game* 159) recounts the experience of an orphaned girl ignored by her community until they find themselves under attack by a giant *wiindigoo*, a "terrible monster of the ice and snow" (*Game* 159). A wise old man suggests a solution: everyone will try to smoke a magical pipe and only the person who can "get it to light without a match will be the one with the strength to fight the wiindigoo" (*Game* 161). Although the bravest warriors are unable to breathe fire into the pipe, the motherless girl, with the help of the "spirit who was looking after her" (162–63), causes the pipe to glow with fire at her touch. Having lit the magical pipe, the girl becomes wise and "powerful" (163): she allows the cold to fill her until she grows "into a giant" (*Game* 163) and then fights a "terrible raging battle" (164) with the *wiindigoo*, "a huge man-shaped thing white as frost" (163). After killing the monster, the girl shares some hot tallow soup with him, prying open his icy, jagged teeth and pouring the broth down his throat. Released from the terrible spell of the winter frost, she and the *wiindigoo* return to normal size, and he is revealed as an ordinary man. Generously, the tribe never tells him that he had become a *wiindigoo*, but instead enjoins him to hunt for the little girl, his savior, providing her with food for the rest of her life.

Nokomis's story makes use of the traditional figure of the *wiindigoo* in order to inspire her granddaughter to trust her own powers. Eternally hungry, the *wiindigoo* haunts the winter landscape in times of famine and feasts on human flesh. A complex and multilayered concept, the *wiindigoo* evokes numerous significances. In her glossary at the end of the novel, Erdrich characterizes it as "a giant monster of Ojibwa teachings, often made of ice and associated with the starvation and danger of deep winter" (*Game* 256). In *Traditional Ojibwa Religion and Its Historical Changes,* Christopher Vecsey defines the *wiindigoo* as "a giant cannibal made of ice, symbolizing winter and starving times" (77). Vecsey describes the *wiindigoo* as a single powerful manito; yet, as he points out, lesser *wiindigoos* also appear in Ojibwa tales, magical beings who embody traits of their powerful namesake. In *The Birchbark House,* for instance, Omakayas imagines "the icy breath of giant wiindigos striding over the ground, cracking trees off with every foot crunch" (13).[4] Insidiously, the *wiindigoo* spirit can take possession of human beings in times of famine, causing them to perceive their fellow humans as food. Possessed by the *wiindigoo* spirit or maddened by starvation, these human *wiindigoos* may be driven by their fatal hunger to destroy other human beings.

Nokomis's *wiindigoo* tale affirms the ability of a small girl to rescue her community from the deadly personification of winter. Later in the novel, Omakayas finds herself able to perform a similar feat. When guiding Black-Gown, the Catholic priest, to visit his parishioners in another village, Mikwam becomes trapped on an island of ice in the midst of the now thawing lake. Unaware of his whereabouts, the family is frightened and distraught until Nokomis brings out the pipe that she saves for special sessions of mediation, reflection, and prayer. The whole family smokes the pipe; afterwards Omakayas has a vivid dream of her father's whereabouts, enabling a search party to locate and save him and Black-Gown from the deadly ice and snow. Like the girl in Nokomis's story, Omakayas is empowered by the magic pipe to defeat the terrible *wiindigoo* of "deep winter" with its threat of "starvation" and "danger." On his return home, Mikwam tells his own heroic story of endurance on a spar of ice. As he explains, he and the priest argued about the relative power of their gods to rescue them. Inspired by a traditional sacred story, Omakayas's dream validates Mikwam's side of the argument. Later, Mikobines, a wise older man of the village, reminds Omakayas that the source of her magical dream lies outside of herself in "Gizhe Manidoo" (*Game* 221), "the great kind spirit" (*Game* 253) who watches over the Ojibwe: "Gizhe manidoo gave you a very great gift, but you must remember that this gift does not belong to you. This gift is for the good of your people" (*Game* 221).

Based on a traditional, sacred story, Omakayas's dream is also a narrative, one that ultimately produces a happy ending for the chilling tale of entrapment on the ice that Mikwam will later recount. If Mikwam's story ends happily, Omakayas also recognizes that there is no real end to the storytelling process. In fact, her ultimate accomplishment in *The Game of Silence* is her own realization that she too is a storyteller, producing new variations on traditional themes. In a prescient vision of her future life, she sees herself as an old woman rich in experience, recounting stories to her grandchildren: "the vision she received and the stories she told, the scenes of emotion, good and bad, that she endured, was the story of her life" (*Game* 232). Here, Omakayas's experiences throughout a long life are figured forth, not as events but rather as "stories," shaped by the narrative techniques and cultural values of the traditional teller of oral tales.

A continuing controversy has surrounded Erdrich's fiction for adult readers. While some readers, such as the novelist Leslie Marmon Silko,[5] have faulted her for focusing on supposedly assimilated Native American characters, others have seen Erdrich's fiction as a moving record of Ojibwa history and culture. In *The Birchbark House*, Erdrich eschews an assimilationist approach, but suggests ways that all readers can enter her text more deeply, offering subtle linkages between event and narrative that evoke a complex Ojibwa worldview. In sum, Erdrich pays her child readers the ultimate compliment: rather than adapting her cultural content to an easily accessible linear structure, she opens the door on a richly patterned, profoundly mysterious world—one that readers themselves must strive to experience. Structuring her novel around storytelling motifs and tropes that illuminate the surrounding action, Erdrich requires her audience to read actively.

According to Catherine Rainwater, Erdrich's adult novels serve as "ethnosemiotic encounters" (145). Foregrounding the techniques of oral storytelling, they foster the "self-conscious accommodation of cultural outsiders in the audience, and thus" convert the "'reader' to [a] 'listener'" (145). In Rainwater's view, "written storytelling is directed to an absent audience" (147). In contrast, orality emphasizes the audience's presence. By dramatizing the process of oral storytelling and the characters' direct and immediate responses to individual tales, Erdrich models how readers, both children and adults, can read and interact with Omakayas's story. Including a glossary of Ojibwa terms at the end of her novel, Erdrich invites children of all backgrounds to share in the riches of her narrative, an impulse also affirmed in a prefatory note to readers: "Dear reader, when you speak this name out loud [Omakayas] you will be honoring the life of an Ojibwa girl who lived long ago" (*The Birchbark House*, "Thanks and Acknowledgements"). At the same time, Erdrich's deftly orchestrated novel does not allow cultural outsiders the comfortable illusion that we now "understand" the Ojibwa experience; instead, it invites us to become more aware of our relation to another culture, and to engage with that culture in the context of a complex and troubled history.

Notes

1. Throughout the novel, Erdrich assigns no name to Omakayas's grandmother, but instead chooses to refer to her by the Ojibwa name for "grandmother." Following her, I do the same in this essay.
2. In this second encounter, the *memegwesi* initially disguises himself as a speaking rabbit, demanding that Nokomis follow his tracks. Typifying an Ojibwa perspective, this transformation not only emphasizes the magical nature of the spirit helper, but also suggests that distinctions between human beings and the animal world are shifting and permeable.
3. Erdrich explains in her note on the Ojibwa language that the novel involves, for her, the work of recovering, and presenting an oral language in written form. Reflecting the fluidity of the recovery process, her two novels of Omakayas employ variant spellings of some Ojibwa words: "adisokaan" in *The Birchbark House* and "aadizookaan" in *The Game of Silence*; "windigo" in *The Birchbark House* and "wiindigoo" in *The Game of Silence*. Unless quoting directly from *The Birchbark House*, I consistently use the spellings in the second novel.
4. As indicated in a previous note, Erdrich uses different variants of the word "windigoo" in *The Birchbark House* and *The Game of Silence*.
5. See Leslie Silko's "Here's an Odd Artifact for the Fairy-Tale Shelf" in *Impact/Albuquerque Journal Magazine* (8 Oct.1986): 10–11. Rpt. in *Studies in American Literature* 10 (1986): 177–84.

Works Cited

Chavkin, Alan, and Nancy Feyl Chavkin, eds. *Conversations with Louise Erdrich and Michael Dorris*. Jackson: U P of Mississippi, 1984.

Erdrich, Louise. *The Birchbark House*. New York: Hyperion, 1999.

———. *The Game of Silence*. New York: HarperCollins, 2005.

Kawbawgam, Charles. *Ojibwa Narratives of Charles and Charlotte Kawbawgam and Jacques LePique*. Ed. Arthur P. Bourgeois. Detroit: Wayne State U P, 1994.

Makman, Lisa Hermien. "Child Crusaders: The Literature of Global Childhood." *Lion and the Unicorn* 26.3 (2002): 287–304.

Rainwater, Catherine. "Ethnic Signs in Erdrich's *Tracks* and *The Bingo Palace*." *The Chippewa Landscape of Louise Erdrich*. Ed. Alan Chavkin. Tuscaloosa: U of Alabama P, 1999. 144–60.

Ruppert, James. "Mediation and Multiple Narrative in *Love Medicine*." *North Dakota Quarterly* 59 (1991): 229–42.

Scheick, William J. "Narrative and Ethos in Erdrich's 'A Wedge of Shade.'" *The Chippewa Landscape of Louise Erdrich*. Ed. Alan Chavkin. Tuscaloosa: U of Alabama P, 1999. 117–29.

Silko, Leslie. "Here's an Odd Artifact for the Fairy-Tale Shelf." *Impact/Albuquerque Journal Magazine*, 8 October 1986: 10–11. Reprinted in *Studies in American Literature* 10 (1986): 177–84.

Thompson, Melissa Kay. "A Sea of Good Intentions: Native American Books for Children." *Lion and the Unicorn* 25.3 (2001): 353–74.

Vecsey, Christopher. *Traditional Ojibwa Religion and Its Historical Changes.* Philadelphia: American Philosophical Society, 1983.

Wong, Hertha D. "Louise Erdrich's *Love Medicine*: Narrative Communities and the Short Story Sequence." *Modern American Short Story Sequences: Composite Fictions and Fictive Communities.* Ed. Gerald Kennedy. Cambridge: Cambridge UP, 1995.

CHAPTER 5

Alive and Well and Reclaiming Their Cultural Voice: Third Generation Native American Children's Literature

Michelle Pagni Stewart

Sad as it seems, General Philip Sheridan's famous saying, "The only good Indian is a dead Indian" reflects what many young readers might find if they search their local bookstore or library for children's and adolescent literature about American Indians. It is not that books *about* American Indians are not available; in fact, as Mary Gloyne Byler remarked in 1973 and again, 20 years later, in 1999, "If anything, there are too many children's books about American Indians" (47). She goes on to explain, "There are too many books featuring painted, whooping, befeathered Indians closing in on too many forts, maliciously attacking 'peaceful' settlers or simply leering menacingly from the background; too many books in which white benevolence is the only thing that saves the day for the incompetent, childlike Indian; too many stories setting forth what is 'best' for American Indians" (47). From the descriptions of the books that she gives, it is apparent that she is describing books about Indians in the past, which are the books that have, until more recently, dominated American Indian children's literature.

Fortunately, American Indian authors have begun writing the stories of their past themselves, giving a much-needed, more culturally accurate and sensitive view of the history of various tribes and peoples. Louise Erdrich's series of books about a young Anishinabe named Omakayas—*The Birchbark House* (1999), *The Game of Silence* (2005), and *The Porcupine Year* (2008)—which are seen as a response, of sorts, to the stereotypical

Native depictions found in Laura Ingalls Wilder's novels, among others, lead the charge for a revision of history and depiction of American Indians found in so many problematic children's texts. Joseph Bruchac (Abenaki) has also written a number of historical fiction novels, including *Sacajawea* (2000), *Hidden Roots* (2004), *The Winter People* (2002), and the recent *March toward the Thunder* (2008). Through these novels and others, then, Native writers seek to reclaim their stories, to tell them from a Native perspective, unpacking the stereotypes inculcated by Hollywood and much "classic" literature, whether written for children or adults.

Because of the work of Erdrich and Bruchac, among others, children's literature has progressed beyond what I call the First "Generation" of American Indian children's literature, books typically written by an outsider depicting the Native culture, most often replete with stereotypes and misperceptions, told through the lens of the dominant discourse. As Naomi Caldwell-Wood, Lisa A. Mitten, and Paulette F. Molin explain, these often well-loved books, when viewed from the perspective of Native Americans, are problematic, written more for the benefit of non-Native audiences than Natives.[1] More and more these days, books about American Indians would be of the Second or Third "Generations," written by an insider (someone knowledgeable of and sensitive to the culture). Second Generation books seek to dismantle the cultural stereotypes and misperceptions found in First Generation books, a task that, similar to what James Ruppert describes in *Mediation in Contemporary Native American Literature,* "create[s] cultural criticism of the dominant society, and make[s] manifest the crimes of the past. . . [while] direct[ing] them [Native writers] more toward Native concerns such as survival, continuance, and continual reemergence of cultural identity" (3–4). In doing so, however, Second Generation books have often led to a more limited view of Native cultures although they warrant reading, for they have much to offer young readers and present a major step forward in understanding Native experiences. Books in the Third Generation move beyond what is often a more essentialized view to deconstruct notions of Indian identity by depicting Indian youth with problems that are based on their Native identity or culture as well as those that transcend it. As important, in this Third Generation of literature, authors typically utilize American Indian literary traditions to encourage readers to recognize the richness of their cultures and give them insight into an insider view and understanding.

In *Mixedblood Messages: Literature, Film, Family, Place*, Louis Owens describes the way Native American characters in novels constitute a contested space, a place of signification in which the authoritative discourses have historically aligned the signifier "Indian" with the stereotypical Hollywood image, complete with beads and buckskin, sacred pipes, and headdress regalia.

Children's and adolescent literature also constitutes a contested space since the stereotypes Owens describes continue to dominate the images of American Indians that young people are exposed to in texts about Native cultures. Too often, those images reflect the dominant culture's idea of the signifier rather than a culturally accurate depiction of a young person from a specific tribal culture, someone whose experiences are neither stereotypical nor monolithic. Particularly problematic is the fact that, in contrast to some literature from other ethnic groups, books of the First Generation continue to be published, read, and taught, placing a burden on Native authors to unmask the stereotypes and reclaim the signifier so as to bring to voice the Native experience that has so frequently been silenced by history, films, and literature. In this essay, I explore in depth Joseph Bruchac's *The Heart of a Chief* (1998) and Cynthia Leitich Smith's *Rain Is Not My Indian Name* (2001), contemporary American Indian children's novels of the Second and Third Generations, respectively, as a means to define and exemplify the generations before discussing several other Third Generation novels. These novels, whether of the Second or Third Generation, seek to reclaim the contested space and signifier of "Native American." Even as these writers recognize that they are paving the way for those outside of the culture to gain an awareness of the culture and move beyond prejudiced or stereotypical views, views that are instilled in the collective American consciousness, they have much to undo, necessitating not only a revising of the signifier but a reclaiming of it as well.

Contemporary American Indian fiction

In the introduction to Paulette F. Molin's *American Indian Themes in Young Adult Literature*, Arlene Hirschfelder echoes ideas found in Molin's analyses, that more authors need to write about contemporary American Indians, saying "One can easily make a case that Native people are perhaps one of the least understood of all those who make up the tapestry of American life, owing in part to the paucity of literature about their lives today" (Molin xiv). Cynthia Leitich Smith, who writes about contemporary Native Americans, agrees: "Native people in books for young readers appear almost exclusively in historic contexts. Though historic books are welcome, their numbers have been so proportionally high that many children believe Native Americans went the way of the tyrannosaur or that we all live as we did 500 years ago" ("Social" 8). In fact, Smith identifies contemporary fiction as the "most underrepresented type of Indian-themed book" ("Native"), demonstrating a large void for current American Indian authors to fill, a gap affecting the way young readers—both Native and non-Native—come to discern what it means to be "Indian" in the twenty-first century.

That is not to say that a book has to be contemporary fiction to be deemed Third Generation,[2] but it is true that historical fiction books—because of the necessity of making readers aware of the historical misrepresentations and lack of awareness of a Native view of these events—may not deconstruct notions of Native identity to the extent that contemporary fiction can. Historical fiction must rearticulate descriptions of American Indians as inculcated in movies, television, and even children's literature that continues to be standard fare in classrooms, books including Elizabeth George Speare's *The Sign of the Beaver* and Lynne Reid Banks' *The Indian in the Cupboard*, texts that relegate Indians to sidekick and reinscribe the romantic savage, both stereotypical images largely uncontested within the narratives. Thus, when Native authors decide to write fiction, they know they have a lot to undo, and they must work against a publishing industry and other gatekeepers who continue to print and promote books that will not let go of the stereotyped, objectified signifier, complete with headdress, teepee, and sidekick status.[3] So even as contemporary Native American authors seek to undo the misrepresentations that history, movies, television, and literature have ingrained in the social consciousness, other books—many of which are highly reviewed by critics and promoted by publishers—continue to reinforce the problematic Native signifier.

While both Bruchac and Smith are bringing to the forefront what it means to be a contemporary Native American, the messages of Bruchac's novel are less subtle compared to Smith's, in part likely due to the younger targeted audience of the former, an audience that may cognitively need a more explicit discussion of these sometimes "invisible" representations of the signifier, invisible because they are so mainstream and accepted that many do not even see these stereotyped markers of culture. Smith's novel also employs more overtly complex aspects of American Indian literary style than does Bruchac's novel because she is targeting an older audience, one that is more likely to be able to comprehend cognitively some of what distinguishes Native American literary traditions from Eurocentric ones, traditions such as multiple perspectives, shifting time periods, and trickster characters, and other means of recapturing oral tradition in written form. Yet, as Smith herself has explained, a problem inherent in writing for children using these characteristics of American Indian literature, a style more often found in American Indian books written for adults, is that when an author does utilize these stylistic devices, unknowing reviewers may misunderstand what the author is doing, which translates into less-glowing reviews and, more important, a misperception of the rich literary traditions underlying the stories.

In "A Different Drum: Native American Writing," Smith explains how fellow writers and reviewers have suggested she make changes to her writing to make it "right." She gives a few examples, such as when she was told she was "wrong" for relying on the number four in her picture book *Jingle Dancer* rather than the Western-centric, ubiquitous three or when she depicted a circular journey for the protagonist in *Rain Is Not My Indian Name* since, as she was told, the "'the right way to do it' was to create 'a straight arrow through the story'" ("Different" 410). What this criticism fails to recognize is that American Indian culture and literature value the number four for its naturalness (four directions, four seasons, etc.) and completion and see journeys, like life and nature, as being circular rather than straightforward. As Smith's essay indicates, relying on Native structures and beliefs may complicate one's ability to be published, read, and recognized, which is why those books of the Third Generation represent such an important step in the progression of American Indian children's literature: not only are the books moving beyond the more restricted, "safe" ideas found in Second Generation literature, but they better reflect the richness of American Indian beliefs and literary traditions.

Second versus Third Generation Literature—Bruchac and Smith

As explained earlier, any book about a contemporary American Indian is most likely of at least the Second Generation. An example of this is Joseph Bruchac's novel *The Heart of a Chief*, which tells the story of Chris Nicola, a young Penacook, and makes clear to readers a young Native American's conflicts—often as invisible to the dominant culture as contemporary American Indians themselves. Bruchac brings out a number of significant issues, such as the fact that Chris' class is reading Elizabeth George Speare's *The Sign of the Beaver* (cited on Oyate's "Books to Avoid" list) and that his friends call themselves the Rainbow Coalition because they are of such diverse cultural backgrounds (one has a Norwegian father, one an African American mother). Issues of relevance to contemporary American Indians play an important role in the novel from alcoholism (albeit his dad begins drinking when his mom dies—deconstructing the stereotype of the drunk Indian), the conflict of the Penacook tribe over whether they should build a casino and where, and Indian mascots. Although there are some stories within stories, more often they are given indirectly rather than set off as stories within stories. In fact, Chris's grandfather gives him the kind of information that would be found in an American Indian origin story when he explains why deer and rabbits have eyes on the sides of their heads (13–14), but he simply tells Chris the information rather than relaying it through a story.

Yet what makes Bruchac's novel Second Generation is that—at least in the first two-thirds of the book—many explanations of Native American culture, value, and history are given in a more explicit way. For example, when Belly Button's dad hands Chris some sweetgrass, he tells the young Indian, "You know. . . we say that sweetgrass chases away bad things" (51) as if Chris himself would not know that (in fact, Chris mentions sweetgrass twice earlier in the novel). Chris himself narrates some heavy-handed explanations, such as when he says, "Sometimes old people call a younger person grandchild when they're not really related by blood" (60); or "When we end a phone conversation we don't say good-bye. It's an English word and there is no word for good-bye in Indian. Usually we just wish the other person a good journey" (64–65); or "Everything has to be part of that cycle, which is just like our old Penacook idea of the sacred circle of life. If things don't remain in that circle, they don't stay in balance"(146). Although each of these explanations feels a bit forced, something an American Indian would not have to explain, Bruchac—in the tradition of storytelling—begins the book with a prologue suggesting Chris is telling the story *to* someone (whose cultural background is not clear), which might account for some of the explanations and certainly reminds readers that storytelling is an important vehicle for learning, as Bruchac has explained, "It is only through our own stories that people—Indian and non-Indian alike—can begin to understand the true American Indian heritage. . . . Stories were never 'just a story,' in the sense of being merely entertainment. They were and remain a powerful tool for teaching" (*Our Stories* 35).

As the novel progresses, Bruchac incorporates important issues in a more subtle way, such as when he makes a point about mascots because Chris is part of a group making a presentation on the controversial topic, and most of Chris' group is not Native American and does not understand why Thanksgiving is not seen in the same way by American Indians as it is by other Americans:

Think of what it's like for an Indian kid to go to a school where they're dressing the other kids up in phony Indian costumes with eagle feather headdresses made of paper and cardboard. You feel like they're making fun of your whole culture. . . . [And] that's the worst part. They don't know that it hurts our feelings. They tell that story about landing on Plymouth Rock and starting their new colony. They don't mention why there was plenty of room for the Pilgrims to make their settlement there. English slavetraders brought smallpox to the Indians two years before the Pilgrims landed on the coast. When they got off the Mayflower the Pilgrims saw nothing but empty villages because all the Indians had died. And the Pilgrims themselves would have starved if an Indian named Squanto hadn't helped them. And you know what? Squanto could speak English because he'd been taken as a slave to England years before that. And then when he found his way back to America, everyone in his village had died from smallpox. (109–10)[4]

Here, Chris gives his white classmates a lesson in American Indian history and in what it feels like to be objectified because of a school mascot, such as theirs, the Rangerville Chiefs. Bruchac also incorporates these elements of the objectification of Indians in discussing Chris's sister's Pocahontas doll, to which Auntie gives a makeover, "pad[ding] the waist so that, as Auntie put it, 'She looks like a woman and not some danged ant.' Then they dumped the corny buckskin miniskirt. 'She dress this way,' Auntie said, 'her knees gonna be all scarred from the blackberry bushes'" (35). As the novel progresses, the explanations become less frequent and more smoothly integrated into the text: in the first 100 pages, there are more than a dozen "explanations" ranging from who Jim Thorpe is to how Indians respect the land, to how they give thanks for food, but there are only about three such explanations in the last 50 pages. As the reader becomes more in tune with what it means to be someone like Chris—not any Native American, but a young Penacook with an alcoholic father and dead mother, being raised by relatives, having formed a bond with his gym teacher (an Asian American whose parents were interred during World War II), and having been asked to join the wrestling team, who makes his community and the local media aware of the harmful nature of the Indian mascot and who helps his tribe move forward in building a casino without sacrificing valuable land to do it—Bruchac's novel demonstrates how far contemporary American Indian literature for children has come.

Cynthia Leitich Smith's *Rain Is Not My Indian Name* makes that even clearer for, like Bruchac's novel, Smith's deals with what it means to be an American Indian youth today. Even as she handles some of the same issues found in Bruchac's novel, Smith incorporates them without her characters being what she describes as "mistaken for guides on a Native American tour." As she explains in "Native Now: Contemporary Indian Stories," "it's a mistake to summarily force passages of social studies in fiction. Doing so compromises the realism of the characters' perspectives and disrupts the plot structure with details unnecessary to advance the story." For example, early in the novel, Rain explains how schools teach about Indians and what it feels like to be an outsider:

> At school, the subject of Native Americans pretty much comes up just around Turkey Day, like those cardboard cutouts of the Pilgrims and the pumpkins and the squash taped to the windows at McDonald's. And the so-called Indians always look like bogeymen on the prairie, windblown cover boys selling paperback romances, or baby-faced refugees from the world of

Precious Moments. I usually get through it by reading sci-fi fanzines behind my textbooks until we move on to Kwanza. (13)

When the Flash, a reporter for the *Hannesburg Weekly Examiner*, persists in trying to get cultural information from her aunt, Rain recognizes that some rituals should not be explained to outsiders: "I could guess that the harvest was part of Ojibway traditional life—past, present, and future. That being the case, it most likely had some spiritual importance. Aunt Georgia was hinting to the Flash that it might be best for an outsider to leave the details alone" (58). Smith also makes brief allusions to the lost generation (20) and Indian boarding schools (21), but neither is explained in a way that would ring false coming from Cassidy, a character for whom this information is common knowledge.

What is most refreshing about Smith's novel—and something that marks it Third Generation—is the fact that Rain's conflicts are more those of any adolescent, regardless of culture, something that is too infrequently the case when dealing with ethnic literature because of what publishers and teachers expect to see in ethnic literature, which continues to limit the fictional representations we find in children's and adolescent literature. Although it is true that some of Chris's conflicts in Bruchac's *Heart of a Chief* are those experienced by many children such as his dad's alcoholism, in part a response to his mother's death, feeling like an outsider at a new school, being picked on by a bully, and losing a friend to another group of young people, his conflicts, much as Donnarae MacCann argues, are often interstitial conflicts—those between white and Native or those between old and new ways (146). While Smith's protagonist Rain does deal to some extent with what it means to be "Indian" when she discusses her heritage with Flash and when she does not want to join Indian camp, neither of these conflicts is based on her being ashamed of her culture or having the kind of conflict so often found with mixed blood characters. Instead, she is avoiding contact with her peers because she blames herself for her friend's death and wants to punish herself by remaining outside of the group. In addition, Rain's interests—photography and science fiction—are not easily identifiable "Indian" signs thus allowing Rain to transcend the racial signifier. In fact, when Rain indicates she should ask if she can take pictures of the Indian camp (39), she implicitly acknowledges that photography has often been used against Native Americans (disrespecting rituals, for example) and thus asks us to at least acknowledge if not reconsider the contested space.

Furthermore, the style of Smith's novel is also very Native American, marking it a Third Generation novel. In an interview on her web site, Smith discusses her writing style and what makes it Native American; she says,

Mainstream U.S. (and to a lesser extent European) novelists tend to write children's and young adult novels in a very linear way "as if an arrow were shooting through the manuscript." They tend to be about the triumph of individuals. Depicted families tend to be smaller. Community is not reflected in most stories. In contrast, Native novelists tend to be less linear, more circular (though this can be overstated), and offer more stories of extended families and communities. . . . The two novel styles are an extension of the cultural value systems that inspire them.

In fact, her use of both journal entries and the narrative story line provides multiple perspectives, giving the text a speakerly quality, to use Henry Louis Gates' concept, a shift between the private discourse of the journal and the "public" discourse of the narrative.[5] Because all but five of the twenty journal entries are flashbacks,[6] this dialogic structure also results in shifts in time or what P. Jane Hafen in her introduction to American Indian literatures in this book calls "fluid time." Although shifts in chronology and disruptions to the linear narrative are typical in Native American literature written for adults,[7] the technique is less frequently seen in American Indian children's literature. Another kind of polyvocality comes from the fact that we also hear other voices: Rain's grandfather's in his postcards and e-mail, Queenie's in her poem for Galen, Mrs. Owens' in her letter to the editor, and the newspaper voice of the engagement announcement for Fynn and Natalie. Smith's dialogic narrative structure, then, acts as a multivoiced text, so that her book, while moving chronologically through the main narrative, moves more circularly in the journal pieces, a structure that more closely aligns with American Indian literary style, even as Smith revises the signifier of Indian, paving the way for American Indian children's literature that deconstructs the politics of representation and essentializing stories.

Other Third Generation Novels

Although there is still clearly much work to be done with revising and reclaiming the American Indian historical perspective given through fiction, Native authors, like Bruchac and Smith, are not limiting their stories to those of history since to do so will only reinscribe the myth of the vanishing—or vanished—Indian. Contemporary Native writers are also exploring genres that might not be immediately associated with American Indian culture, such as gothic novels. Bruchac has written a number of novels that incorporate elements of the gothic while simultaneously developing stories about contemporary Indian identity and issues, such as *Skeleton Man* (2001), *The Return of Skeleton Man* (2006), *The Dark Pond* (2004), and *Whisper in the Dark* (2006). The latter two, especially, suggest a movement into the Second if not Third Generation as they utilize myths of their respective native cultures, Abenaki (*The Dark Pond*) and Narragansett (*Whisper in the Dark*) while simultaneously developing the stories of Armie in the former and Maddy in the latter. Armie Katchadourian is a young Shawnee-Armenian who, while away at boarding school (that of a prepatory education rather than an Indian boarding school in the tradition developed by Richard Pratt) discovers a dark pond in the woods that keeps luring him to its dangers. He is both fascinated and frightened by the pond even after he meets Mitch Sabattis, an Abenaki graduate student who is studying zoology. The novel commingles the frightening story of the pond with the coming-of-age story of Armie who learns to fit in with the other boys at school and accept the absence of his parents. In *Whisper in the Dark*, Bruchac takes the genre a step farther, incorporating not only the Narragansett stories of Chauquaco Wunnicheke, the cannibal known as "Knife Hand," but also aspects of horror films and stories known to both Native and non-Native readers, such as those by Stephen King, H. P. Lovecraft, and Anne Rice. Maddy, injured in a car accident that kills her parents, has come to live with her Aunt Lyssa and befriended Roger, whose mother is a professor of gothic literature at the local university and whose friendship with Maddy begins to blossom into romance by the end of the novel. Throughout *Whisper in the Dark*, Bruchac plays on and plays with aspects of horror fiction, developing the connection between Maddy and Roger and Maddy and the reader while also giving young readers insight into native beliefs and contemporary Native experiences.[8]

Bruchac is not the only American Indian author to explore the gothic genre while simultaneously telling a story of a young Indian protagonist. Drew Hayden Taylor, in *The Night Wanderer* (2007), which he labels "A Native Gothic Novel," has created a novel that clearly fits into the Third Generation. What marks Taylor's novel Third Generation is both the content and the style, both of which convey aspects of American Indian conflicts and beliefs while deconstructing notions of the historical Indian who is consigned to the past. *The Night Wanderer* centers on the conflicts of an Anishinabe, Tiffany Hunter, whose conflicts have less to do with her Native identity than with her adolescent angst, conflicts that will be familiar to many an adolescent, whether Native or not: she is doing poorly in school and trying to hide that from her father whom she blames for her mother abandoning her, and she is dating a young man whom her father and friends disapprove of and who, as the novel progresses, likes Tiffany more for the discounts her tribal status card can get him than for her company. Tiffany wants nothing more than to get off the reserve and away from what she considers her meddling father and grandmother, even contemplating suicide at one point in the novel.

She is clearly a teen of the times: she listens to Nickelback and plays Xbox. She is, as the narrator reminds us, a typical teen who "ponder[s] the questions that teenagers of all eras frequently ponder" (109), who "was doing [what] had in one way or another been done by the youth of every culture in every part of the world" (129). As such, Tiffany is not marked by her Native identity as much as by her adolescent identity.

At the same time, however, Tiffany is not ostracized from her Anishinabe culture. As a youngster, Tiffany had recognized that the other children at school did not know about contemporary American Indians, but she herself is not as close to her Anishinabe identity as her grandmother is:

> When she was young, some of the kids at school had asked her if she shot a bow and arrow, lived in a tepee, or rode a horse. Frustrated, Tiffany would tell them contrary to popular belief, not all Native people carry arrowheads or sweetgrass with them everywhere they go. No more than all Australian Aboriginals have a boomerang in their back pockets. She knew this for a fact because she had seen it on television. (114–15)

Ironically, Tiffany fails to realize that her own knowledge of others comes from the television, which is likely where her peers received their own misperceptions of American Indians. Clearly, though, Tiffany has knowledge of her Native culture even if she is not seeped in it: she gives Tony and later Pierre the *weekah* root because her grandmother told her it is a way to cure one's ailments, and she says "though she was proud of her Native heritage, she found the annual powwow events quite culturally satisfying enough, thank you very much" (29). Yet toward the end of the novel, as she begins to understand her place in her family better, she tells Pierre, "Sometimes I don't know what being Anishinabe means" (201), an important moment in her identity formation, both as a teenager and as an Anishinabe. She does not deny her Native heritage, but her understanding of who she is and how much she is loved by her father and grandmother is overshadowed by her narcissistic teenage woes.

As important in identifying Taylor's novel as Third Generation is the style of *The Night Wanderer*, a style marked by aspects of orality and Native beliefs more likely to be found in Third Generation literature because the novel is more circular and less Western in format—and thus more likely to be misunderstood or poorly reviewed by readers of an outside perspective. As the narrative makes clear early on in the novel, "no matter how long ago the past occurred, it colored the present and influenced the future" (5), something that Taylor highlights in the novel's structure. Throughout the 27 chapters, almost a dozen different narrative perspectives are given although most often the narration reflects the thoughts of Tiffany or Pierre L'Errant, the mysterious "European" man who comes to stay with the Hunters. Some chapters are filtered through a single character's perspective while others shift to another character's perspective in the midst of a chapter. And, while this may be an editorial typo, the final two chapters are both numbered 26, suggesting that Tiffany's and Pierre's stories have meshed, just at the point where Tiffany has returned home and realized she needs to return to school and to be a more active part of her family—the point where her journey is truly beginning—and where Pierre's journey ends.

Past and present also commingle along with reality and mythic time through the novel's incorporation of the stories of Owl, a young Anishinabe from "a dozen generations or more before" who, it becomes apparent, is in fact Pierre, someone whose stories at time reflect a history of American Indians as a whole rather than that of a single tribal culture. Yet Taylor deconstructs his Anishinabe story, taking young Owl from the days of first contact with fur traders to the moment of his becoming a vampire, in which the young Anishinabe is saved from disease and given eternal life because "the thing that had changed his life" ironically objectifies him in a way perhaps not much different from what classic literature and film has done, saying, "You come from a new land, a new people. I am intrigued. I will let you become the first of your kind to join my kind. If you survive long enough, maybe you will return home" (180). Seeing him as Other, but subject to its will, the vampire consigns Owl to eternal hell, forcing him to take the lives of innocents, to bring death to others, deconstructing the image of the savage Indian by making Owl a blood-thirsty vampire. Yet even here, Taylor complicates the part of his novel that might seem, especially to Stephanie Meyer fans, an already known story, for *The Night Wanderer* also melds the vampire story with Native stories. As Tiffany explains early in the novel: "wendigos. . . were cannibal spirits that ate anything and everyone, spirits that took over a body and made people do crazy things" (16). When Granny Ruth tells Pierre the various stories of the wendigo legends, she describes them as, in one story, "cannibals whose souls are lost. . . [in another story as] humans who, during winter when food was scarce, had resorted to cannibalism" (170). Most important, though, she explains that wendigos can only be killed by burning them, an act that both destroys and frees them, something she hints Pierre himself would benefit from. In this interchange between Granny Ruth and Pierre, then, she cleverly—albeit perhaps unknowingly—connects Pierre with a wendigo rather than a vampire. And from a Native perspective, Pierre L'Errant would align more with a wendigo as he hungers for not just blood but also flesh and has clearly eaten people in his history and, as far as the novel suggests, the present. Yet Tiffany never recognizes Pierre as a wendigo and instead calls him a vampire, something he does not correct.

Again, Taylor has constructed a story that is simultaneously Native-centered and not Native-centered, moving it beyond the more limited demarcations of the Second Generation that, in trying to correct misunderstandings of the past, must first undo the stereotypes and misperceptions so that authors like Taylor are freer to explore genres and stories of all kinds. As such, Third Generation novels can be more cross-coded, shifting between contemporary, universal ideas, such as when Tiffany describes herself as "banished like some discount fairy-tale princess" (20), and then, a page later, having Granny Ruth clarify something culturally specific when she says, "'What is this Ojibwa?'. . . 'I ain't Ojibwa. That's just what them white people want to call us. That ain't even one of our words. I'm Anishinabe'" (21). Although at the novel's end Tiffany does not fully know what it means to be Anishinabe, she realizes she does not want to die and seems pleased to be returning home. In a way, then, Taylor has also invoked the well-known paradigm of American Indian literature called "homing in," defined by William Bevis, who argues that many American Indian texts demonstrate "homing in" when the protagonist—who at the opening of the novel was distant from home physically, emotionally, and ideologically—successfully "homes in" when he reconnects with the people, the place, the history, and the rituals of his tribal culture. While Pierre does return home physically, his death ironically allows him to "home in" in ways that his wendigo spirit was not allowed to previously. Tiffany, too, seems to be a step closer to appreciating her family and her Anishinabe identity. So in some ways, both characters represent a kind of "homing in": Tiffany's last scene involves her kissing her grandmother to send her to bed, ready—even if not prepared for her history test—to go to school in a few hours, and Pierre's last scene entails him waiting for the sun to rise, something he had not seen in hundreds of years, a natural instance that "was glorious" (214–15).

Where Do We Go From Here?

With Louise Erdrich's children's novels and Sherman Alexie's recent award-winning *The Absolutely True Diary of a Part-Time Indian* gaining accolades and bringing attention to American Indian literature for children, it would seem that American Indian children's literature is becoming a more accepted part of the canon. Yet the books analyzed here are not garnering the same attention as Erdrich's and Alexie's books even though they, too, are well-written, interesting novels. Are they perhaps being overlooked because publishers and the non-Native reading public, when seeking depictions of American Indians, still wish to see them as relegated to the past, as not having a story if it is not completely packaged with the accoutrements of their idea of culture? Certainly, American Indian authors seek to reclaim the Indian signifier, to revise the racist histories and attitudes that continue to be perpetuated by books written by those who purport to be well-intentioned and to have done extensive research, but whose books reveal otherwise. Novels of both the Second and Third Generation can help to undo the past and reclaim Native American culture, history, and voice—if only we will listen. As important, though, novels of the Second and Third Generation can remind readers of all ages that the myth of the vanishing Indian is just that, a myth, that American Indians of a variety of cultural groups and experiences people the world, and their stories are as important to understanding Indian identity and culture as are those from the past.

In *Mixedblood Messages*, Louis Owens distinguishes between what he calls the territory, the place of containment in which Native Americans are consigned to the known and unchanging territory that the dominant culture is comfortable with, and the frontier, the zone of the trickster that is fluid, constantly shifting as American Indians reimagine themselves and their sense of identity (26–35). The concepts of the territory and the frontier can be likened to the Second and Third generations, respectively. Texts of the Second Generation work to establish an American Indian identity from within, especially as it rearticulates what it means to be a person from a variety of Native tribes, times, and experiences, whereas texts of the Third Generation—because of the work done in the Second Generation—need not be centered solely on the notions of American Indian identity. As Owens says of the frontier, these texts belong to the "always changing zone of multifaceted contact within which every utterance is challenged and interrogated, all referents put into question" (*Mixedblood* 26). Rain and Tiffany's conflicts are not those of someone caught between two worlds, nor are they solely a product of their American Indian heritage. Neither Smith nor Taylor overexplains the Native backdrop of their stories as though the primary audience were outsiders. Yet an outsider audience can find knowledge of American Indian beliefs and history—or at least can find a place to begin to access those concepts.

In Thomas King's *Green Grass, Running Water,* four American Indian characters—named Lone Ranger, Ishmael, Robinson Crusoe, and Hawkeye—seek to "fix" what is wrong with the world (starting with Hollywood westerns!), but they recognize early on that it is "too big a job to fix it all at once" (King 133–34). With respect to children's literature, it seems Native authors find themselves in a similar situation: there is so much to undo with respect to the ingrained attitudes and depictions of American Indians throughout children's and adolescent texts and films that the best they can do is to start somewhere. But if Second and, even more significantly, Third Generation texts offer readers—both young and adult alike—a chance, as Catherine Rainwater suggests in *Dreams of Fiery Stars: The Transformations of Native American Fiction*, to "revise ethnocentric, appropriative, and other destructive types of readerly habits" (23), then they are making a giant leap forward for American Indian children's literature. These novels by Bruchac, Smith, and Taylor make clear what Native children and adolescents themselves already know: Indians are alive and well and reclaiming their cultural voice and identity.

Notes

1. Caldwell-Wood and Mitten, in "Selective Bibliography and Guide for 'I' is Not for Indian: The Portrayal of Native Americans in Books for Young People," decry these fictional works as "terrible when examined with the criteria of whether the Native American(s) depicted in them are accurately and even humanly portrayed." Molin, in *American Indian Themes in Young Adult Literature*, says the books are disappointing, especially since Native adolescents and children have a need to read "strong, accurate portrayals of contemporary Native peoples in young adult fiction" (3).
2. In fact, in a paper delivered at the 2006 Children's Literature Association Conference held in Mahattan Beach, California, I argued that Louise Erdrich's *Birchbark House* falls more into Second Generation whereas *Game of Silence* is more Third Generation. This also demonstrates that an author does not determine the generation of a novel as much as the content and style do.
3. Debbie Reese, in her 1998 *Horn Book* article, gave a name to this oft-seen stereotype, the "TV Indian" since it comes to us from the movies and television. In children's literature, this stereotype, unfortunately, gets further solidified in countless alphabet books that use "Indian" to depict the letter "I" or in concept books reiterating the "Ten Little Indians" counting rhyme.
4. Interestingly, Michael Dorris made a similar argument in his piece titled "Why I'm Not Thankful for Thanksgiving." See *Through Indian Eyes: The Native Experience in Books for Children*, edited by Beverly Slapin and Doris Seale.
5. For Gates, a speakerly text is one that oscillates between first and third person, between oral and written voices (22). Gates, in discussing speakerly texts, analyzes the two narrative voices found in Ishmael Reed's novel *Mumbo Jumbo*, arguing the second narrative serves a dual function, ironically commenting on both the other narrative and the writing of it (216). In many ways, the journal entries in *Rain Is Not My Indian Way* serve the same function—they comment on what is happening in the narrative while simultaneously telling a story in their own right.
6. Two of the journal entries are timeless (one explains her heritage and discusses how her parents met; the other one discusses friendship) and three others involve the day of the narrative story line.
7. Paula Gunn Allen explains this concept in *The Sacred Hoop*.

8. I discuss Bruchac's two gothic novels in more depth elsewhere (a paper given at the 2008 Children's Literature Association Conference held in Newport News, Virginia, and a version forthcoming in *Studies in the Novel*), which is why I do not develop the argument further here. I also did not want to focus too much on a single American Indian author since I want to demonstrate that a number of authors are writing literature of the Third Generation and within the gothic genre.

Works Cited

Alexie, Sherman. *The Absolutely True Diary of a Part-Time Indian.* New York: Little, Brown, 2007.

Bevis, William. "Native American Novels: Homing In." *Recovering the Word: Essays on Native American Literature.* Eds. Brian Swann and Arnold Krupat. Berkeley: U of California P, 1987. 153–85.

Bruchac, Joseph. *The Dark Pond.* New York: Scholastic, 2004.

———. *The Heart of a Chief.* New York: Dial, 1998.

———. *Hidden Roots.* New York: Scholastic, 2004.

———. *Marching toward the Thunder.* New York: Dial, 2008.

———. *Sacajawea.* New York: Scholastic, 2000.

———. *Skeleton Man.* New York: HarperCollins, 2003.

———. *Our Stories Remember: American Indian History, Culture, and Values Through Storytelling.* Golden, CO: Fulcrum Publishing, 2003.

———. "Take Two Coyote Stories and Call Me in Your Next Life Time." *A Broken Flute: The Native Experience in Books for Children.* Eds. Doris Seale and Beverly Slapin. Walnut Creek: AltaMira P, 2005. 209–11.

———. *The Winter People.* New York: Puffin, 2004.

———. *Whisper in the Dark.* New York: HarperCollins, 2006.

Byler, Mary Gloyne. "Introduction to American Indian Authors for Young Readers." *American Indian Stereotypes in the World of Children: A Reader and Bibliography.* Ed. Arlene B. Hirschfelder. Metuchen, NJ: Scarecrow P, 1982. 47–54.

Caldwell-Wood, Naomi, and Lisa A. Mitten. "Selective Bibliography and Guide for 'I' is not for Indian: The Portrayal of Native Americans in Books for Young People." 22 January 1999. http://info.pitt.edu/~lmitten.alabib.htm.

Erdrich, Louise. *The Birchbark House.* New York: Hyperion, 1999.

———. *The Game of Silence.* New York: HarperCollins, 2005.

Gargano, Elizabeth. "Oral Narrative and Ojibwa Story Cycles in Louise Erdrich's *The Birchbark House* and *The Game of Silence.*" *Children's Literature Quarterly* 31.1 (2006): 27–39.

Gates, Henry Louis, Jr. *The Signifying Monkey: A Theory of African-American Literary Criticism.* New York: Oxford UP, 1988.

King, Thomas. *Green Grass, Running Water.* Toronto: Harper Collins, 1993.

Larrick, Nancy. "The All-White World of Children's Books." Reprinted in *The Black American in Books for Children: Readings in Racism.* Eds. Donnarae MacCann and Gloria Woodward. 1st ed. Methuhen: Scarecrow P, 1972. 156–68.

MacCann, Donnarae. "Native Americans in Books for the Young." *Teaching Multiculture Literature in Grades K–8*. Ed. Violet J. Harris. Norwood, MA: Christopher-Gordon Publishers, 1992. 137–69.

Miranda, Deborah A. Foreword. *A Broken Flute: The Native Experience in Books for Children*. Eds. Doris Seale and Beverly Slapin. Walnut Creek: AltaMira P, 2005. 1–3.

Molin, Paulette F. *American Indian Themes in Young Adult Literature*. Lanham, MD: Scarecrow Press, 2005.

Owens, Louis. *Mixedblood Messages: Literature, Film, Family, Place*. Norman: U of Oklahoma P, 1998.

Rainwater, Catherine. *Dreams of Fiery Stars: The Transformations of Native American Fiction*. Philadelphia: U of Pennsylvania P, 1999.

Reese, Debbie. "Mom, Look! It's George, and He's a TV Indian!" *Horn Book Magazine* (Sept/Oct 1998): 636–38.

Ruppert, James. *Mediation in Contemporary Native American Fiction*. Norman: U of Oklahoma P, 1995.

Seale, Doris, and Beverly Slapin. *A Broken Flute: The Native Experience in Books for Children*. Walnut Creek: AltaMira P, 2005.

———. *Through Indian Eyes: The Native Experience in Books for Children*. Philadelphia: New Society Publishers, 1992.

Smith, Cynthia Leitich. "A Different Drum: Native American Writing." *Horn Book Magazine* (July–Aug 2002): 409–12.

———. "Native Now: Contemporary Indian Stories." *Book Links* (December 2000–January 2001. 11 November 2008. http://www.ala.or/aboutala/hqops/publishing/booklinks.

———. *Rain Is Not My Indian Name*. New York: Harper Collins, 2001.

———. "Social Justice in Native American Literature for Youth." *Journal of Children's Literature* 31.1 (2005): 7–9.

Taylor, Drew Hayden. *The Night Wanderer: A Native Gothic Novel*. New York: Annick Press, 2007.

Thompson, Melissa Kay. "Native Americans in Books for Children." *Lion and the Unicorn* 25.3 (2001): 355–74.

SECTION II

African American Literature

CHAPTER 6

The Cadence of Language: An Interview with Julius Lester

Yvonne Atkinson

*I*first met Julius Lester at an academic conference on American Literature. He was one of the presenters in a session that focused on the works of Joel Chandler Harris. Three papers were presented during the session. I recall that Lester's paper explained how as a child he had "discovered" Harris's work in a public library. Lester went on to tell how finding people of color and stories he knew in a book introduced him to a world of possibilities. In fact stories told and heard by African Americans became a significant element of Lester's body of work. Of the other two papers presented in that session I remember them as being of the nostalgic-happy-darkies-singing-in-the-fields sort. In those papers there was no mention that Harris collected stories from Blacks; rather, the focus was a minstrelized evaluation of the authenticity of Harris's depictions of enslaved people. In those papers Harris became author rather than collector, and he was praised for his "genuine" depictions of the good ole days of the South. After all three papers were given, Lester questioned the other presenters about their research. They assured him that they were great fans of Harris and that he, Lester, was taking everything too seriously. Lester then took them to task for their indulgent approach to Harris's works. He carefully explained to them the history of enslavement in the United States and the history of the misappropriation of African American artifacts. Further, he elucidated the danger of perpetuating stereotypes, especially by academics. He did not back down.

When Michelle Pagni Stewart and I were contemplating this book, and we had settled on the idea of author interviews, Julius Lester was my first choice— both as someone who writes prolifically for children and someone who stands up for what he believes in. I contacted him, and he agreed to be interviewed via e-mail.

According to Lester's biography found on his web site, he was born on January 27, 1939, in St. Louis, Missouri. He has published 43 books and received numerous awards: the Newbery Honor Medal, the Lewis Carroll Shelf Award, National Book Award Finalist, National Jewish Book Award Finalist, National Book Critics Circle Award Finalist, Boston Globe/Horn Book Award, Coretta Scott King Award. Moreover Lester is an academic who taught at the New School for Social Research in New York and the University of Massachusetts, where he was a professor in the Judaic and Near Eastern Studies Department and an adjunct professor of history. He also received the University of Massachusetts finest awards: The Distinguished Teacher's Award, the Faculty Fellowship Award for Distinguished Research and Scholarship, as well as the Chancellor's Medal. He retired from the university in 2003.

Atkinson: To what extent do you consider yourself an "ethnic" writer? Is that even your mission in writing literature?

Lester: I do not define myself as an "ethnic" writer. I am a writer, and I write what interests me. I write what I know. I write what I care about. Much of what interests me, much of what I know and care about flows naturally from my background as a black person who grew up in the Midwest and the South in the 1940s and 1950s as the son of a Methodist minister who liked to tell stories and who was a good preacher whom I enjoyed listening to for the cadences and sound of his voice.

But I am also someone who grew up studying music, fell in love with the music of Johann Sebastian Bach when I was seven. I am also someone who found my first inspiration to be a writer in the life and work of the English poet, Shelley.

I could go on, but my point is that defining me by my ethnicity is to miss the breadth of my interests and accomplishments. My ethnicity has certainly informed my life and my writing because I grew up under racial segregation, but my ethnicity does not represent my totality.

Atkinson: What made you decide to write for children?

Lester: I don't separate what I write for children from everything else I write. I write for all ages from preschool to old age. Whatever age you are, there is a book written by me for you to read.

However, writing for children has special pleasures because contemporary adult fiction has moved away from storytelling and has become the playground of academic critics. I am a storyteller. I love stories, and children love stories, so writing for children came very naturally.

Atkinson: What is your inspiration for your stories?

Lester: There is no one answer that covers the 40+ books I've published. However, as a general rule I would say that I do not get inspired. That is a wonderfully romantic notion, but the process of writing for me is prosaic.

Some books have come from an editor calling me up and presenting an idea. Most books come from a question I have and the only way I can find an answer is to write. *To Be a Slave* came from my wondering just that— what was it like to be a slave? I would say most books come from this kind of wondering about what a certain experience is like. My novel, *When Dad Killed Mom,* came from reading a newspaper article about a man who killed his wife, then killed himself, and left two children orphans. What was it like for the children? Where were they when they learned their father had killed their mother? What was the first night after the murder like? The one following? In the novel the father does not kill himself, which raises a whole set of different questions, such as, how do you relate to your father after he's killed your mother? Where does your love for your father go? Writing is hard work, and inspiration seldom plays a role.

Atkinson: What do you hope children will learn from your books? Do you have an overt didactic plan for your books?

Lester: This question is always asked of authors of children's books, but I've never been asked this about my adult books. My aim in whatever I write is to touch the heart of the reader.

Atkinson: How important is it for you to teach outsiders about your culture? Do you ever just write without feeling a need to explain or clarify cultural meanings in your text? Do you worry, then, that what you mean might be misconstrued by some audiences?

Lester: I don't look at people who are not black as being outsiders. I am not qualified to know who might or might not be "outsiders" to my "culture." A black person who grew up in prep schools might be more of an "outsider" than a southern white person from Mississippi. And, I've had blacks misconstrue books I've written as well as whites. There were black parents who had more trouble with *Sam and the Tigers*, my refashioning of "Little Black Sambo," than there were whites. In other words, whites are not necessarily "outsiders" by virtue of race and blacks are not necessarily "insiders" by virtue of race. We are all outsiders to groups not our own.

I don't think of my books as teaching about my culture. I write about a variety of experiences, some of which are unique to black history. I don't think of such books as teaching as much as I do sharing, as an invitation to others to enter that experience. While in a book like *To Be a Slave*, for example, I am certainly presenting factual information with which people, black and white, may not be familiar, even more I am trying to communicate what the emotional experience of being a slave was like. My hope, my aim, as I said previously, is to have an impact on the heart of the reader.

Atkinson: Do you ever worry that, in your efforts to create real, round— and thus flawed—characters, some people may criticize what you have done or misinterpret that character as representing the entire culture? (For example, if a Native American author were to create a character who is an alcoholic, would that feed into the stereotype of the drunken Indian?)

Lester: No. All I can do is write as well as I can, knowing what I know at the time of writing. How well that Native American author creates an alcoholic character will determine whether it feeds "into the stereotype of the drunken Indian."

The narrative voice in my retelling of the Uncle Remus tales is quite different than the Uncle Remus stereotype created by Joel Chandler Harris.

Atkinson: How would you characterize contemporary children's literature? Are parents and teachers trying too hard to be gatekeepers—that is, controlling what kids read and are exposed to? Is this a positive or a negative effect for children? Or, are there ethnic topics that are (or should be) taboo in children's literature?

Lester: I think we are living in a golden age of children's literature in terms of the quality and variety of books offered.

There is an inherent paradox in writing children's literature, which is that the audience we write for does not buy books. We write for children but it is parents, teachers and librarians who decide which books children have access to. Parents and teachers and librarians are, by definition, gatekeepers. It is their responsibility to choose the books children can read. Are some overzealous? Sure, especially the ones who try to ban my books. ☺

Atkinson: Have your children's books ever been criticized for being too ethnic or for their cultural content? What about the reverse—have you ever been criticized for not being "ethnic enough"? How do you respond to this criticism?

Lester: Yes and yes. Yes and yes. To the latter, I respond by saying what I said earlier, namely, that my ethnicity does not represent my totality as a human being, and my responsibility as a writer is to the range and richness of human experience, not just one aspect of it. There are some who say I am not black enough, but these are people who have a political definition of what it is to be black. I grew up under racial segregation when whites defined what it meant to be black. In the 1960's blacks began a redefinition. I was not going to exchange being defined by whites to being defined by blacks. I define who I am, no one else.

As to the former, there were blacks who criticized me for my retelling of *Little Black Sambo* and also for retelling the Uncle Remus tales. My response was simply, "But they are wonderful stories. I've freed them from their racist history."

Atkinson: You can be perceived as speaking for an entire culture. How does that affect your writing—or does it?

Lester: I don't think I am perceived that way. Because I am Jewish and also black, I think people don't know what my culture is. And, in the appendices of most of my books, I write about my research and methodology so that the reader understands how what I've written may differ from the culture and where it may not. Since so much of my work is based in the slave experience, or the tales and culture that were expressed in slavery, I think it is clear that I am speaking for that experience, which I am entirely comfortable with. Since before writing *To Be a Slave*, I've felt that the spirits of dead slaves were lined up inside me patiently waiting for me to tell their stories. I've done my best.

Atkinson: What hurdles do ethnic authors of children's literature have to face? How has this served as a catalyst for what you do, or as a hindrance?

Lester: The primary hurdle is editors who think they know more about the black experience than I do. I go into detail about this in my book *Writing for Children and Other People*. I've had some legendary battles with editors, battles which I won. Fortunately, such experiences have not been the norm.

Works Consulted

Julius Lester Web site. 27 February 2009. http://members.authorsguild.net/juliuslester/bio.htm.

CHAPTER 7

"Way Down in the Jungle Deep, the Lion Stepped on the Monkey's Feet": An Introduction to African American Literature[1]

Yvonne Atkinson

Literary genres can be defined as categories of artistic composition, marked by distinctive styles, forms, or content. The distinctive style and form of African American oral traditions is one of the markers of African American literature. Toni Morrison in "Unspeakable Things Unspoken" said, "The most valuable point of entry into the question of cultural (or racial) distinction, the one most fraught, is its language—its unpoliced, seditious, confrontational, manipulative, inventive, disruptive, masked and unmasking language" (11). An analysis of the process of acquisition of the enslaver's language by enslaved Africans explains the development of a written discourse based in African oral traditions.

It was commonly believed that Africans brought to America as slaves were blank slates, with no history, culture, or language. It was assumed that Africans' minds were empty just waiting to be filled by their masters. This belief is the basis for the terminology used to describe slavery as a school and the slave owners as masters. In truth, Africans brought to America as enslaved people came with oral and literary traditions that, because of the system of slavery in America, were not erased or replaced with Western European traditions. In slavery Whites segregated Blacks; Blacks were required to live and work separately from Whites. Blacks also chose not to associate too closely with Whites. For the most part, Whites were considered to be "the enemy" and, therefore, were allowed close enough to be observed, but from a safe distance. The separation of Black and White was not only a physical separation; it was also a social and cultural separation. One of the ways Blacks could establish a clear boundary between themselves and their persecutors was through language. Amiri Baraka explains in *Blues People*: "It is absurd to assume, as has been the tendency, among a great many Western anthropologists and sociologists, that all traces of Africa were erased from the Negro's mind because he learned English. The very nature of the English the Negro spoke and still speaks drops the lie on the idea" (9). Language not only became a line that divided one group from the other, it also became the vessel containing the remnants of Traditional African[2] cultures.

Trudier Harris explains why language became the bearer of cultural traditions, "In a country where, as late as the 1830s, there were laws prohibiting the teaching of slaves, it was necessary for the oral tradition to carry the values the group considered significant. . . . Thematic folk expressions and folk beliefs had their parallels in the structural patterns that later shaped . . . [African American] literature" (2). Not only are the structural patterns of African American literature shaped by Traditional African oral traditions, but the written language is also influenced by the homelands of the enslaved. According to Geneva Smitherman, the enslaved Africans "Africanized" the language of their oppressors (2). While for the most part using the lexicon of their oppressors, the enslaved Africans retained and incorporated their native language grammars, mechanics, and styles into their spoken language, creating a new language: Black English (2).

In "Discourse, Ethnicity, Culture, and Racism," Black English is said to be "the most pervasive and dominant discourse variety used . . . [by] Americans of African descent. Although other subcultural groups have their own intragroup discourses, the variety of English spoken by American descendants of African slaves has the longest history and has had the most significant impact on public culture in the US" (Van Dijk, Ting-Toomey, Smitherman, and Toutman 148). The authors describe the Africanization of English in the following way:

> US based Pidgin English—dates from 1619 when the first cargo of African slaves landed at Jamestown on the Dutch vessel *The Good Ship Jesus*. This Pidgin English was used initially as a transactional language in communication between master and slave. However, the Pidgin quickly became the lingua franca. . . . Africans in enslavement appropriated the foreign tongue and made it work for them as a counter-language, a symbolic bond of solidarity. This was accomplished by superimposing upon the white man's

tongue discourse styles and linguistic-cultural practices that were known only to those born under the lash. (148–49)

Geneva Smitherman further states in *Talkin and Testifyin* that Black dialect is "an Africanized form of English reflecting Black America's linguistic-cultural African heritage and conditions of servitude, oppression and life in America. Black Language is Euro-American speech with an Afro-American meaning, nuance, tone, and gesture" (2). African Americans also "Africanized" written English by adapting the rules of Black English oral discourse to written English, giving the written language the ability to mask and/or change meaning. Language became trickster. While trickster figures are evident in a number of cultures, each trickster is culturally specific because one of the traits of the trickster is that while it breaks rules, it also defines and maintains culture. Some qualities of African American tricksters are (1) the trickster is neither good nor bad; rather the trickster just is; (2) the trickster is not hidden or cloaked; rather, the trickster is readily recognizable; (3) the responsibility of being tricked is not on the trickster; rather the fault is on the one who is tricked. In fact, as John Roberts explains, "Enslaved Africans . . . found in their social relationship to and material and physical treatment by the slavemasters sufficient justification for [viewing] the . . . trickster as folk hero" (34).

Further the trickster figure from African American culture is dissident in that it disrupts, erases, and questions boundaries; it is masking in that it veils by immersing meaning in cultural context, and it is rhetorically skillful in that one must pay close attention for understanding. In African American literature, language becomes trickster: "Tricksters shake things up, splinter the monologic, and shatter the hierarchies" (Smith xii). Margaret Atwood defines the trickster as, ". . . subversive in that he disrupts conventions and transgressive because he crosses forbidden boundaries, yet he displays no overtly high and solemn purpose about these activities" (Reesman 7). Jeanne Campbell Reesman, looking specifically at the African American trickster tradition, lists this figure's qualities as "satire, parody, indeterminacy, double-voicedness, open-endedness, and chance . . . " (xv). Written English in African American literature has all of these qualities. African American oral traditions encourage language to be rebellious, revolutionary, and seditious. The "peculiar institution" of slavery reenforced these traits of oral tradition because of the need to mask meaning in order to cross forbidden boundaries. Meaning, based on content, can be indeterminate for those who do not have cultural knowledge.

An example of this trickster language's masking ability is in the lyrics of W. C. Handy's "St. Louis Blues":

> Feel tomorrow lak ah feel today
> I'll pack up my trunk, and make ma git away
> Saint Louis woman wid her diamon' rings
> Pulls dat man 'roun' by her apron strings
> 'Twern't for powder an' her store-bought hair
> De man she love wouldn't gone nowhere, nowhere
> Got dem Saint Louis Blues I'm as blue as ah can be
> Like a man done throwed that rock down into de sea.[3]

This is a song about the Great Migration, when African Americans left their homes in the rural South for employment opportunities in northern cities. This is a song about transition and liminality, about crossroads. In African American folklore, the crossroad is a dangerous place. Yusef Komunyakka, Pulitzer Prize–winning poet, described the crossroads as expressed in African American oral tradition, in the 1997 Introduction of *Ploughshares: A Literary Journal* as ". . . a real place between imaginary places—points of departure and arrival. It is also a place where negotiations and deals are made with higher powers. In the West African and Haitian traditions of Legba, it is a sanctified place of reflection. . . . The crossroads is a junction . . ." (5). "St. Louis Blues" is a testimony about what happens at a crossroads. In the song, a couple has been separated by the Great Migration. The woman is at home, somewhere in the rural south, and the man has gone north to St. Louis to find work. The woman knows her man is involved with another woman in the city. She says she is going to go to the city and get her man back. She tells how her man was lured away by diamond rings, powder, and store-bought hair: all trappings of the commoditized world of city living. These people are at a crossroads. They are changing from rural sharecroppers to city factory workers. The woman not only knows her world is changing and she is being forced to change, but also understands that the changes taking place may not be for the best. She is going into the unknown where the system of value has deemed her less valuable. The diamond ring, powder, and store-bought hair are the trappings of beauty as interpreted by the dominant culture: White America. Her man's attraction to this artificial beauty indicates the dangerous and unknown arena she will enter when she goes to St. Louis to reclaim his attention and affection.

Because the underlying story of the crossroad is the foundation of the song "St. Louis Blues," knowledge of African American culture reveals the masked undercurrents of the crossroad, one of the major motifs of African American folklore. While this "crossroads" trope is evident in a number of folktales and myths, African American oral traditions place a particular emphasis on the dangers inherent at crossroads, both figurative and literal. Toni Morrison's *Beloved* is a story about crossroads. The setting of the story is liminal: the time period is after emancipation but before true freedom; the Ohio of *Beloved* was one of the strongholds of the underground railroad, yet slavery penetrated this sanctuary because of the Fugitive Slave Act; and interestingly, the Ohio River, while a marker of freedom—once it was crossed, an enslaved person was in a free state—was also a boundary, a barrier that obstructed or denied access to freedom. Sethe and Paul D. are caught in liminality. While they are living in freedom, their slave past still entraps and haunts them holding them firmly to Sweet Home, the physical and psychological site of their enslavement. Until they can "lay it down" (move beyond slavery and enslavement), they cannot be free (*Beloved* 86). *Beloved* is a story about negotiating liminal space, a story about finding a way out of no way.

The tropes of language as trickster, trickster figures, crossroads, and liminality from Black English oral traditions are some of the identifying characteristics of African American literature. African American literature is identifiable, then, not because the characters are Black, or because the author is Black; rather, the literature is African American because it "reflects Black America's linguistic-cultural African heritage and conditions of servitude, oppression and life in America" (Smitherman 2). It is written, oral-Africanized-English, with all the nuances of spoken Black English: the language and the style. The style of Black English is recreated in written text by the use of tropes taken from oral traditions. Three most significant tropes from African American oral traditions—Signifyin[4], Witness/Testify, and Call and Response—can be also be used to indentify African American literature.[5]

According to Smitherman, some of the properties of Signifyin are,

> Indirection, circumlocution; metaphorical-imagistic (but images rooted in the everyday, real world); humorous, ironic; rhythmic fluency and sound; teach but not preachy; directed at persons or persons usually present in the situational context (siggers do not talk behind yo back); punning, play on words; introduction of the semantically or logically unexpected. (121)[6]

Signifyin in written text could be in the narrative, dialogue, or even in a particular setting. An example of Signifyin in dialogue can be found in Angela Johnson's novel *Heaven* when Marley says, "Uncle Jack hasn't seen me since I was born. He was in Ohio a few years ago. He said nobody was home for two days. Butchy figures that was the weekend Momma and Pops dragged us to Cleveland to the museums, fireworks, and a rib burn-off"

(11–12). The "rib burn-off" is the Signifyin moment: indirect, metaphorical-imagistic, humor, irony, etc.[7] "Rib burn-off" indirectly refers and speaks to the tradition of barbecuing, specifically rib cook-offs, in African American communities. The term "rib burn-off" also creates the ironically humorous image of the outcome of this BBQ experience.

Another aspect of Signifyin is that it is used as a gatekeeping mechanism: it is an "in-group" activity. This is clear when one considers the indirectness, "circumlocution; metaphorical-imagistic" aspect of the trope (Smitherman 121). One must have "group" knowledge in order to comprehend the underlying significance of Signifyin. If a person is not part of the group, meaning is lost, and that person is excluded. Johnson's "rib burn-off" is a key that opens the gate for her readers, an invitation to become one of the in-group that is made up of the characters in the book and the readers. Rhetorically, this invitation facilitates the readers' connection to and empathy with the characters of the text. Because the trope of Signifyin is also gatekeeping, the reader who understands the underlying and layered meaning of rib burn-off is part of the group, and those who do not are identified as outsiders. This phrase also can/will "put-you-in-the-mind" if you have experienced a rib burn-off. "Put-you–in-the-mind" is a phrase from Black English that means a person is taken back, through memory, to another place and/or time to relive a moment. A "put-you-in-the-mind" experience is, like most other tropes in Black English, a group-building, boundary-marking experience. Those who experience this shared moment are part of the group, and therefore are comforted by the fact that they are not alone.

Another trope from Black English oral traditions that is group-building is Call and Response. In *In the African American Grain*, John Callahan says, "African American writers use the call-and-response tradition as a bass line in their pursuit of voice, and their work" (xii). He goes on to say, "As it evolves in black American oral tradition, the call-and-response pattern registers the changing relationship between the individual musician or storyteller and the community" (16). According to Maggie Sale in "Call and Response as Critical Method: African-American Oral Traditions and *Beloved*,"

> Antiphony or call and response, function, improvisation, and audience performance can all be thought of as part of the group or communal nature of art.... Call-and-response patterns provide a basic model that depends and thrives upon audience performance and improvisation, which work together to ensure that the art will be meaningful or functional to the community. (41)

Lawrence Levine further elaborates on Call and Response when he says, "the overriding antiphonal structure of the spirituals placed the individual in continual dialogue with his community, allowing him at one and the same time to preserve his voice as a distinct entity and to blend it with those of his fellows" (qtd. in Callahan 16). Call and Response is a form of collaborative improvisation (Callahan 19).

Smitherman defines Call and Response as a form of "spontaneous verbal and non-verbal interaction between speaker and listener in which all of the statements ('calls') are punctuated by expressions ('responses') from the listener" (104). Smitherman explains that call and response "is a basic organizing principle of folk to achieve the unified state of balance or harmony which is fundamental to the traditional African world view" (104). She goes on to say,

> Some calls from the speaker might elicit a co-signing response from one person, an encouraging type of response from someone else, a completer response from still another listener. Whatever is being said at that particular moment will affect different listeners in different ways. The dynamics of black communication allow for individual variations within the structure. Thus all responses are "correct"; the only "incorrect" thing you can do is *not respond* at all. (108)[8]

In written texts, the immediacy of the moment is lost, except in dialogue. For example, in *Heaven* when Marley is trying to work out her feelings for the people she thought were her parents who in reality are her aunt and uncle, she says to Bobby,

> "I hate them, Bobby."
> Bobby takes off his paint-spattered shirt and covers [his daughter] Feather with it.
> "Must be hard to hate people you've loved for most of your life."
> I get up and walk over to the black shiny wall. He's started a painting. It's going to be a slow, steady painting. Bobby's going to take his time. He says that he once worked on a painting for a year and changed it about twenty times. He had to put it away.
> I lean against the black wall.
> "Happening wall, Bobby."
> Bobby says quieter, "Must be hard to hate people you've loved. . . ."
> I turn to face the wall. "For most of my life." (60)[9]

Marley's "For most of my life" is the response to Bobby's call. He elicits her response by his unfinished statement, and her response indicates validation of his statement. While in written text, the immediacy of Call and Response is negated, what is left is the need for balance and completion.[10] This need allows the transference of Call and Response from an oral discourse to a written discourse.

Johnson's two books, *Heaven* and its prequel *First Part Last*, are also a form of Call and Response because *First Part Last* was written as a Response to an incident: in an interview, Johnson talked about why she wrote the *First Part Last:* she was sitting on a bus and she noticed a young man with a baby. Why wasn't he in school? Was the baby his? Where was the mother?[11] She started to wonder about his story. She was Called on to Respond to these questions, prompting her to tell Bobby's story. The trope of Call and Response is further evident in the back and forth of the "Then" and "Now" chapters of *First Part Last*. The "Then" chapters are Responses to the Call of the "Now" chapters. Their back and forth movement provides a balance in the storytelling event.

The final trope from Black English oral traditions important to understand when looking at African American literature is Witness/Testify. Witness/Testify is much like Call and Response in that it can be verbal and it is interactive between speaker and audience. The difference between the two is that Witness/Testify's function is to create empathy, which in turn creates a safe place for discussions of intimacy. In the Traditional Black Church where the discourse of Black English is used, taught, and venerated, Witness/Testify is an integral part of church services. Time is set aside for Witness/Testify. Someone in the congregation will Testify, and the congregation becomes her/his Witness. Most of the time a parishioner will stand and begin with some form of the traditional opening of, "Giving honor to God who is the head of my life, to my pastor, ministers on the rostrum, and my church family" and then launch into his or her Testimony. The Testimony could be about something wonderful or something bad that has occurred; it could be a song that reflects the feelings of the singer. The Testimony is not given to "fix the situation" or find some form of closure; rather, the Testimony is a sort of sharing in a safe environment. The congregation is not supposed to judge the teller or the Testimony being told. The congregation is supposed to listen with open hearts. Then, through verbal and nonverbal gestures, they let the speaker know that they understand and have been through something similar in their lives. This understanding and empathy let the speaker know that he or she is not alone. The shared empathy of Witness/Testimony is community building. It reinforces the idea of group solidarity that is so important in African American culture.

Shoogy gives her testimony to Marley in Angela Johnson's *Heaven*. Shoogy tells Marley that during a beauty pageant she "gave up and lay down on the stage and started crying" (68). She goes on to tell Marley that after that, she began cutting herself and she "cut off all her hair with nail clippers" (68). She tells Marley this story because she wants her friend to know she understands Marley's anger, frustration, fear, and uncertainty because she has felt that way too. Marley understands and responds, "I don't think I'm going to have a screaming fit. But lately, all of a sudden, my head will start hurting, and I can feel my whole body get so stiff, I feel like it's going to break apart" (69). While Shoogy and Marley's situations are not the same, their feelings about the situations are similar. Sharing these feelings allows Shoogy to expose a painful part of herself with her friend, and by doing so she demonstrates her trust and love. Marley, by Witnessing Shoogy's Testimony, learns about an important aspect of her friend's life, and she learns that she is not alone. Marley is also given hope because if Shoogy got through "her screaming fit," then Marley can make it through her situation.

The trope of Witness/Testify can also be seen in Johnson's *First Part Last*. Bobby gives the reader his testimony:

> I tried not to run, but I did.
> I tried not to cry, but when I looked down at my shirt it was soaked; with me wanting to believe it was sweat. By then, though my nose was running and I couldn't even see the faces of the people, I ran into the street.
> And I must have been screaming. . . .
> Must have looked crazy and desperate, but it was better for me to run all the way to the hospital from my mom's 'cause the note on the door said meet her there, something had happened to Nia.
> The whacked part was I didn't start trying to make a deal with God till I was almost running through the doors. And when I see my mom's face I know I got to catch up.
> So I start begging.
> I say how it's supposed to work out 'cause we thought about it. We made a mistake but we aren't stupid. We are going to do the right thing.
> Then I guess I start babbling about how Nia looks when she sleeps and how she smiles and eats and laughs, but I have to stop 'cause even though I don't think about God or go to church, maybe this isn't the way you make deals with him.
> Maybe he doesn't listen if you scare everybody in the emergency room and hold on to your mom that tight while you're screaming and crying more than you ever have in your whole damned life. (119–20)

Bobby's Testimony lets the reader Witness this intimate moment. As Witnesses, we listen with our hearts. Because we have grown to know Bobby and Nia through his narrative, we empathize with his emotional upheaval. We stand Witness to his Testimony. We as readers are members of his community, and we have been allowed to participate in Bobby's grief and in turn remember a time in our lives when we experienced grief. These shared emotions acknowledge our humanity.

Both Johnson's *Heaven* and *First Part Last* tell universal stories, but the way they are told is characteristically African American. African American literature is a gestalt of Western European literary traditions, Traditional Western African oral traditions, and the experiences of those who survived enslavement. Knowledge of African American culture allows the reader insight. More importantly, understanding guards against misappropriation because when the text is viewed as a narrative based in Black English oral traditions, its cultural and historical connections are acknowledged.

The genre of African American literature can be identified by its categories of artistic composition, marked by distinctive styles, forms, and/or content based in the distinctive style and form of African American oral traditions. Because African American literature is based on oral traditions, the literary theories that focus on Western European literary traditions are not a good fit for African American literature. When African American literature is approached with an eye to what makes it African American, we empower the narrative to speak with the richness of the cultural and literary traditions from which it comes.

Notes

1. "Way down in the jungle deep. . . ." is the traditional opening line of "The Signifyin Monkey" which is a time-honored toast from African American oral traditions.

2. Traditional Africa refers to the Africa at the time of slavery in America.

3. Lyrics to W. C. Handy's "Saint Louis Blues" can be found at http://www.theonlineblues.com/w-c-handy-saint-louis-blues-lyrics.html.

4. This is not to be confused with Henry Louis Gates Jr.'s literary theory of Signifyin(g). While Gates says he is basing his theory on Black English oral traditions, "It is in the vernacular that, since slavery, the black person has encoded private yet communal cultural rituals. *The Signifying Monkey* explores the relation of the black vernacular tradition to the Afro-American literary tradition" (ix); he does not adhere to definitions of Signifyin taken from scholars of Black English or African American oral traditions.

   Gates further says, "The black tradition is double-voiced. The trope of the Talking Book, of double-voiced texts that talk to other texts, is the unifying metaphor within this book. Signifyin(g) is the figure of the double-voiced" (xxv). While I agree with the idea that "double-voiced texts that talk to other texts" are part of Black English oral traditions, I disagree that this is a form of Signifyin as defined in Black English oral traditions. Gates' theory, in fact is more like Call and Response and Witness and Testify. For this essay, I will use definitions of Signifyin, from Black English oral traditions. See "Signifying,

Loud-Talking and Marking" in *Mother Wit from the Laughing Barrel* (pages 310–328) for a definition and examples of Signifyin from the Black English oral traditions.

5. There are other aspects of Black English oral traditions that are evident in African American literature, but Signifyin, Witness/Testify, and Call and Response are the principal tropes and the others are extensions of them.

6. For more functions for Signifyin, see Carol D. Lee's *Signifyin as a Scaffold for Literary Interpretation,* 12–16.

7. Claudia Mitchell-Kernan describes Signifyin as a "way of encoding messages or meanings which involves, in most cases, an element of indirection" (Dundes 311).

8. Smitherman defines forms of Call and Response: "*Co-signing* (affirming, agreeing with speaker) . . . *Encouraging* (urging speaker to continue in direction he has started) . . . *Completer* (Completing speaker's statement, sometimes in response to "request "from speaker, sometimes in spontaneous talking with speaker" (107).

9. This is also Signifyin. It is an "act of talking negatively about somebody through stunning and clever verbal put down" (Smitherman 82). Bobby is putting down Marley with his reminder that she is hating people whom she has loved and been loved by.

10. See *Muntu: African Culture and the Western Word* by Jahn Janheinz for a discussion of balance and completion as part of traditional African worldview.

11. Angela Johnson. "Author Program In-Depth Interview: Insights Beyond the Side Shows" (<www.teachingbooks.net/content/JohnsonA_qu.pdf>).

Works Cited

Angela Johnson. "Author Program In-Depth Interview: Insights beyond the Side Shows." www.teachingbooks.net/content/JohnsonA_qu.pdf.

Atwood, Margaret. "Masterpiece Theater." *Trickster Makes This World: Mischief, Myth and Art.* Lewis Hyde. *Los Angeles Times Book Review*, 25 January 1998.

Baraka, Amiri. *Blues People: Negro Music in White America.* New York: William Morrow and Company, 1963

Callahan, John F. *In the African-American Grain.* Illinois: U of Illinois P, 2001.

Dundes, Alan, ed. "Signifying, Loud-Talking and Marking." *Mother Wit from the Laughing Barrel.* UP of Mississippi, 1990. 310–28.

Harris, Trudier. *Fiction and Folklore in the Novels of Toni Morrison.* Knoxville: U of Tennessee P, 1991.

Janheinz Jahn. *Muntu: African Culture and the Western Word.* New York: Grove Press, 1961.

Johnson, Angela. *First Part, Last.* New York: Simon Pulse, 2004.

———. *Heaven.* New York: Simon Pulse, 2000.

Komunyakka, Yusef. "Crossroads." Introduction. *Ploughshares: A Literary Journal* 72 (1997): 5–7.

Lee, Carol D. *Signifying as a Scaffold for Literary Interpretation.* New York: NCTE, 1993.

Morrison, Toni. "Unspeakable Things Unspoken: The Afro-American Presence in American Literature." *Michigan Quarterly Review* 28 (1989): 1–34.

Reesman, Jeanne Campbell. *Trickster Lives: Culture and Myth in American Fiction.* Georgia: U of Georgia P.

Roberts, John. *From Trickster to Badman: The Black Folk Hero in Slavery and Freedom.* Philadelphia: U of Pennsylvania P, 1989.

Sale, Maggie. "Call and Response as Critical Method: African-American Oral Traditions and *Beloved.*" *African American Review* 26.1 (1992): 41–50.

Smith, Jeanne Rosier. *Writing Tricksters: Mythic Gambols in American Ethnic Literature.* Berkeley: U of California P, 1997.

Smitherman, Geneva. *Talkin and Testifyin.* Detroit: Wayne State UP, 1977.

Van Dijk, Teun A., Stella Ting-Toomey, Geneva Smitherman, and Denise Toutman. "Discourse, Ethnicity, Culture, and Racism." *Discourse as Social Interaction.* Thousand Oaks: Sage Publications, 1977.

CHAPTER 8

Trauma and National Identity in Haitian-American Young Adult Literature

Katharine Capshaw Smith

Various, multifaceted, and provocative, African American children's literature in the twentieth and twenty-first centuries resists simplistic encapsulation. The explosion in contemporary picture book titles has prompted critics like Michelle H. Martin to posit that we are currently in "the same sort of 'Golden Age' that mainstream Anglo children's literature underwent in the late-nineteenth century" (xi). Certainly the last 30 years have produced world-class African American authors like Virginia Hamilton, Walter Dean Myers, and Angela Johnson. But as critical attention has turned to texts produced for children by black authors before the 1970s, dozens of exciting artistic voices have emerged, each attesting to the significance of childhood within African American communities and to the crucial position of children's literature in crafting a community's sense of history and identity. Lost voices from the 1910s, 1920s, and 1930s, like Arna Bontemps, Effie Lee Newsome, Silas X. Floyd, Jane Dabney Shackelford, Rose Leary Love, and many, many others, have called on us to reshape our construction of an African American children's literary tradition. Whereas critics outside of black children's literature may be aware of a few threads of that tradition—Langston Hughes's poetry, for example, or Mildred Taylor's historical novels—within the critical conversation scholars have been amazed by the sheer variety of forms and subjects available historically to black child readers. From nature poetry to political tracts, from feminist drama to jazz-inspired picture books, African American children's literature as a field continues to enrich its readers. Just as black culture is by no means monolithic, its children's literature takes on a multitude of shapes, tones, and subjects.

Caribbean American experience forms an important thread in the fabric of black children's literature. Whereas the African American critical dialogue has attended to writers for adults like Jamaica's Claude McKay and Michelle Cliff, similar attention to Caribbean migrant authors (to the United States) writing for a child audience has been slower to appear, although critics like Cynthia James and Mawuena Kossi Logan have helped ameliorate the critical neglect. Within the field of Caribbean literature, however, attention to works for children is burgeoning. And a thriving interest in the migrant experience within ethnic literary traditions offers a useful lens for examining the liminal quality of Caribbean American texts for young people. Importantly, analysis of Caribbean American migrant children's literature must be rooted in awareness of particular Caribbean national traditions, as well as in knowledge of comprehensive African American and American literary histories. For a migrant text, we must ask questions like: How does the text emerge from a particular Caribbean history or literary tradition? How does the text react aesthetically to the task of bridging a specific Caribbean experience with American culture? And, finally, does the text participate in African American literary modes or patterns? Can or should we place the text within the category of African American children's literature? In what follows I will ask these questions of two young adult books by writers of Haitian descent, Edwidge Danticat's *Behind the Mountains* (2002) and Jaira Placide's *Fresh Girl* (2002), in an attempt to explore the features of contemporary Haitian-American children's literature.

A brief history of Caribbean migrant literature will help us become more aware of the currents that shape contemporary children's texts. In the past 40 years, Caribbean postcolonial literature for adults has undergone a shift in representing emigration. Literature of the 1950s, 1960s, and 1970s rendered an experience of exile, with characters (and the writers themselves) leaving a Caribbean home culture for the "motherland," often with educational goals. George Lamming's *In the Castle of My Skin* (1970), Samuel Selvon's *Lonely Londoners* (1956), and V. S. Naipaul's *Miguel Street* (1959), as well as many others, explore such an expatriate sensibility. Recently, as Carine M. Mardorossian has studied, Caribbean literature describes an experience of migrancy, with characters motivated by economic or political circumstances to leave the Caribbean for the United States or Canada. A literature of migrancy does not oppose the homeland to the new host culture, but rather emphasizes the migrant's unsettled identity in relationship to both sites. Characters often draw parallels between the two cultures rather than oppositions, with the result being the migrant's awareness of her continually unfinished sense of place.

This major shift in imagining transnational experience—from exile to migrancy—is not without its own limitations since the new migrant literature has been imagined, in some ways, monolithically. Critics sometimes unreflectively identify authors' biographies with their literary characters, as in the cases of Julia Alvarez and Jamaica Kinciad. As Mardorossian notes, "It is thus ironic that while the shift from exile to migrant literature helped challenge an unproblematical reliance on the category of experience as the basis of explanation in literary criticism, the same kind of undertheorized relation to experience seems to have resurfaced in critical approaches to the new migrant aesthetics" (18). Granted, the work of Alvarez, Kincaid, Danticat and others draws on the authors' lived experience of migration, but readings of their texts often rely heavily on autobiographical interpretations. Plus, the definition of migrant experience has focused almost exclusively on hybridity, an approach that enables critics to consider the potential for postcolonial resistance in the cultural multiplicity of migrant characters. The hybrid migrant, forming a new transnational identity by fusing elements from her heritage with experience in the United States or Canada, has become nearly a critical cliché, according to Mardorossian. Certainly some writers, like Julia Alvarez in particular, embrace a potentially liberational indeterminacy when characterizing migrant experience, but too often critics apply this model to the literature of *all* contemporary writers who have emigrated from the Caribbean to the United States.

Young adult literature of migrancy configures personal and national identity in multiple ways. By focusing on Danticat and Placide, I hope to complicate assumptions about how Haitian migrant texts configure hybridity, particularly because hybridity is *the* dominant critical currency in examining the way texts bridge Caribbean experience and American culture. As in most migrant texts, Danticat and Placide's characters reveal a continuous sense of displacement; both books also resist a binary opposition of the home country and the new site. But unlike in traditional configurations of migrant hybridity, the synthesis between the homeland and host culture eventually deteriorates. A balance, exchange, or equanimity between the two sites becomes impossible because the home culture bears with it the palpable weight of trauma. In her celebrated adult texts, like *Breath, Eyes, Memory* (1994), *The Farming of Bones* (1998), *Krik? Krak!* (1995), and *The Dew Breaker* (2004), Danticat explores various configurations of Haitian identity, often emphasizing the legacy of sexual and political violence. While Mardorossian sees in *Breath, Eyes, Memory* Danticat's embrace of a complex folk culture (a gesture that recalls early Caribbean nationalist writers) as a solution to sexual trauma and to the difficulties of biculturalism, in her young adult novel, *Behind the Mountains*, Danticat redefines the term hybridity: instead of emphasizing Haitian-American migrant hybridity, Danticat imagines *Haitian* identity as syncretic, and thus emphasizes the aesthetic possibilities residing in the perpetually unfinished state of Haitian identity. For Haitian characters in America, any experience of multiplicity, possibility, or incompletion points toward a core Haitian identity, rather than a fusion of America with Haiti. Alternately, Placide's first young adult novel, *Fresh Girl* (2002), begins as a more typical hybridized migrant novel as Mardi incorporates "American" and Haitian qualities; however, in speaking the unspeakable about traumatic Haitian experience, *Fresh Girl* expunges through testimony the stigma of a Haitian past and moves its protagonist toward the American possibility of personal reinvention. Both novels resist conventional theorizations of hybridity, particularly as those theorizations tend to imagine hybridity as a somewhat open-ended intersection between cultures. For both authors, Haiti is too powerful to be fused with American experience.

What interests me the most about both of these novels is their use of childhood as a perspective on migration. The novels of exile writers, like George Lamming's *In the Castle of My Skin* (1970), employed the *Bildüngsroman* as an analogue to cultural evolution, a model that also placed the child at the center of issues of national identity by emphasizing the child's education and progress. But migrant literature uses childhood as a conduit for discussions about *reluctant* movement since emigration stems often from social rupture, economic deprivation, and political violence. Children, imagined as less empowered to determine the course of their lives, and more subject to victimization (developing into, in some cases, icons of victimhood), become an ideal model for writers to explore this forced migration. And inevitably the construction of migrant subjectivity stems from the unhappy displacement. This is the case for Danticat and Placide's texts: in *Behind the Mountains*, the central character, Celiane, spends the first half of the book in rural Haiti and in Port-au-Prince living with her mother and brother; after Celiane is injured in a political bombing, the family joins the father in Brooklyn, New York, and Celiane spends the remainder of the book adjusting to the household's new location. In Placide's novel, Mardi has left Haiti in the wake of political violence to join her parents in New York. Set years after the move, *Fresh Girl* explores the effect of repressed sexual trauma on Mardi's identity, as the teenager negotiates the demands of her Haitian family and the pressures of her American classmates, all while shouldering the burden of rape. Both Celiane and Mardi experience traumas of displacement and of physical/sexual violence. While their responses to a bifurcated identity are quite different, both Celiane and Mardi must bear the weight of their own Haitian history.

That weight is not exclusively negative, however, as both novels emphasize the sustaining value of Haitian family and cultural traditions. With the palpable legacy of Haiti in mind, any typical configuration of hybridity as fusion or as parallelism becomes impossible for Celiane and Mardi, and in response both novels posit new possibilities for migrant identity.

Mardorossian identifies Danticat as "anchored in a nationalist ethos" (21) and as "the rightful heir of black consciousness movements whose genesis can be traced back to movements like Negritude and Haitian 'Indigenism'" (27). Instead of envisioning fragmentation as a condition of migrancy, Danticat imagines a solidification of Haitian identity as the solution to the trauma of displacement. Celiane overcomes fragmentation rather than inhabits it. What distinguishes Danticat, though, from conventional Indigenists is her reinvention of that rooted identity. One might expect that Celiane would take solace in her grandparents' rural lifestyle, and imagine pastoral life as an ideal untouched by politics and violence. And to some extent that is the case, as Celiane rhapsodizes over the landscape, takes comfort in her grandfather's folk tales, and explains that "where I live, people don't talk about politics all that much. Or maybe they do and I am not allowed to go to those places where people gather to do it" (36). However, a timeless folk ideal is impossible in Haiti, especially for children who are inevitably touched by political violence and social flux, and Danticat's radical assertion in the face of the absence of a static folk identity is to offer Celiane solace in a Haitian character that is at its heart *fluid*. If Celiane, as in the traditional models of migrant literature, embraces multiplicity and hybridity, it is a Haitian multiplicity rather than a hybridity based on a fusion American experience.

The crucial way in which Danticat roots her characters in Haitian hybridity is to render migration the cornerstone of Haitian identity. But she does not privilege migration to America, as one might expect, but rather the movement from the country to Port-au-Prince, which becomes a kind of Genesis story of modern Haitian experience. In her essay, "We Are Ugly, but We Are Here," Danticat explains, "My grandmother was an old country woman who always felt displaced in the city of Port-au-Prince where we lived and had nothing but her patched-up quilts and her stories to console her" (138). At the risk of drawing in autobiographical details, we can note that Danticat herself has witnessed the Haitian subject's loss of the rural and her perpetual unfinished adjustment to urbanity, qualities which will come to characterize Haitian identity in *Behind the Mountains*. Celiane makes sense out of the movement to New York by analogizing that experience to migration to Port-au-Prince. Early in the novel, Celiane's mother explains of Port-au-Prince, "'People get lost in the city'" with people who "feel lost, as though they are looking for themselves" (25). When Celiane actually gets lost trying to find her bus in New York, the experience becomes the culmination of an identity expressed through Port-au-Prince: she "understand[s] now" (108) what it means to be adrift.

Celiane's experience of political violence propels her away from a simple construction of Haitian identity. While she may believe and hope that children are not implicated in politics, her experience emphasizes that young people cannot be isolated from social and national identities. Significantly, Celiane experiences violence in the space between the urban and the rural; while traveling by camion (a work truck without sides) to her rural home from her aunt's house in Port-au-Prince, a bomb explodes at a busy crossroads. Celiane and her mother are injured, and the girl spends several days unconscious and unidentified at a local hospital. The bombing results from political upheaval surrounding the turbulent 2000 Haitian elections. When Celiane remembers the bombing, she associates the experience with Haitian identity in terms that recall her mother's description of loss in the city: "Some nights I dream that after the bombing I am lost and never found again, that I forget my name, and am unable to tell anyone who I am. Other nights I dream that it is Manman [mother] who is lost and who forgets her name and is never found" (63–64). Violence ruptures Celiane's sense of certainty about identity, opening up the frightening possibility of anonymity and rootlessness. This phenomenon exactly mirrors the negative potential in traditional paradigms of hybridity: liminality can bring with it profound loss and disconnectedness. However, Danticat differs from other migrant writers by placing that sense of liminality in Haiti rather than in the United States. Indeterminacy results from Celiane's more complex understanding of her positionality and national identity, an identity she assumes regardless of her age; however, that indeterminacy bears positive as well as negative potential, as we will come to see.

Once the text establishes that a collision between folk culture and urbanity is at the heart of modern Haitian hybridity, it envisions New York as a secondary incarnation of Haitian urban dislocation. Celiane's grandfather offers a proverb about Port-au-Prince that eventually becomes applied to New York. The grandfather tells the tale of a man who leaves the rural community and finds ice in the city, and then tries to bring it up the mountain: "The man came back to the village several times and tried to find a way to define ice to his friends, who had never seen it, but all he had to show for his encounter with the ice was a wet shirt. 'So ice is a wet shirt,' his friends told the man to keep him from feeling bad" (67). In describing a distance between imagined rural staticity and an enlargement of experience in the city, the proverb hints at the divide between a historic folk identity and a modern urban experience defined by the marvel of coldness, of difference from the rural. Interestingly, Celiane uses the grandfather's story to suggest that even rural Haitians participate in the new identity of urban dislocation: "I think the lesson of the story is that even though Granpè Nozial hadn't been to the city with us to see what we had been through, he could understand it because he could see the result in Manman's leg" (67). Even Haitians who do not migrate to the city, who might seem to embody a nostalgic rural staticity, actually participate in a national identity fraught with indeterminacy, violence, and risk. There is no timeless rural ideal; there is no idealized modernity. Instead, Haitian identity rests in the interstice between the two, in the recognition of loss on both fronts.

Though the proverb describes Port-au-Prince, the novel continually defines New York through images of ice, whether in Celiane's vision of New York from the plane above "a city filled with ice crystals and light" (83), or in the prevailing cold: "Even though the sun was shining, it did nothing to warm me. Instead it seemed allied with the chill, transforming itself into something I never knew existed, a cold sun" (90). All experience of New York echoes the dislocation at the heart of Haitian identity, the loss of the folk culture, and the unsettled emotional and economic climate of Port-au-Prince. New York becomes a second version of the Haitian capital, and a means not of creating a new hybrid sense of American-Caribbean self, but a vehicle through which Celiane can concretize her Haitian identity.

Danticat's novel continues to resist a conventional treatment of migrant hybridity by privileging Haitian points of reference over American. When Celiane, her mother, and her brother arrive in New York, a friend greets them not with "Welcome to America," but with "'Welcome to the Tenth Department'. . . (Haiti is made up of nine geographical regions or 'departments,' and those living abroad, in the Diaspora, are considered part of a tenth one)" (86). Late in the book Celiane and her family listen to Aristide speak on the radio at his inauguration, praising the "tenth department" of Haitian migrants: "Honor and respect and bravo for the Tenth department Haitians living abroad. There is no place like home" (141). The United States becomes a province of Haiti, reflecting powerfully Danticat's "nationalist ethos" (Mardorossian 21).

Celiane and her family live and socialize within a Haitian community, one that brings her back to Port-au-Prince: "The mass was in Creole. There were so many Haitians in church that if not for the cold, I would have thought we were at mass with Tante Rose in Port-au-Prince. . . . At Saint Jerome's, Haiti did not seem so far away. I felt that if I reached out and touched anyone at the mass, I could be back in Haiti again, as though every person there was carrying a piece of Haiti with them in the warmth of their skin, beneath their winter coats" (94–95). The turbulent 2000 election in the United States becomes an echo of elections in Port-au-Prince, and George Bush's inaugural address becomes an inroad to talk about "what Haitians have contributed to this country" (121). Lincoln's birthday leads to a discussion of America's late recognition of Haitian sovereignty. Actually, one might expect that school would be the context for Celiane to encounter and incorporate an American identity, but Danticat places her in a Creole-speaking class in New York and she encounters only Haitian students. She and her family listen to a Creole language radio station, and Celiane amuses herself with speaking English, but prefers Creole. In an interview, I asked Danticat about how Celiane imagines herself; Danticat replied, "she simply sees herself as Haitian, as a Haitian immigrant. But like all many young immigrants, her view of herself will probably change. In a few years she'll probably end up calling herself Haitian-American, like a lot of us" (202). It is suggestive, then, that Danticat focuses on Celiane's early experience, solidifying Celiane's Port-au-Prince identity through migration to New York rather than exploring a fusion Haitian-American identity that might evolve over time.

To return to the topic of the character of Haitian hybridity, while Celiane certainly fears the anonymity and rootlessness at risk in a liminal identity, great positive rewards also surface in the book's depiction of the meeting ground between the rural and urban. Aesthetics becomes the primary site for the novel's exploration of the positive dimensions of Haitian hybridity. Celiane's brother, Moy, is a painter, and Celiane is a diarist (the novel is in the form of her diary). For Danticat, a productive fusion of verbal and visual art characterizes a hybrid Haitian perspective. She told me in the interview,

> The public space for Haitian art includes walls and moving vehicles, like the tap taps. [Typically pickup trucks or vans, tap taps are a form of public transportation in Haiti, and are intricately decorated with painted images and slogans.] Sometimes when you see a tap tap, you think you're looking at a moving cathedral, practical stained glass. The themes range vastly too in tap tap art, from religious symbols to basketball and rap stars. So taps taps, I think, are the people's museum. They merge art and life in the most poignant way. They also have commentary and advice sometimes. I wanted the reader to SEE very well that aspect of Haitian life because if you go to Haiti, especially the capital, that's one of the first things you're likely to encounter. You're right in seeing the tap tap as a common medium for Moy and Celiane. It's a kind of thing that the two of them could have easily collaborated on. I see popular visual art especially the way it's used in Haiti as a kind of cousin to written art. Celiane and Moy do too. Just as you might tell a story with your voice. The tap taps also tell a story. (199)

By fusing word and image in order to convey a populist Haitian perspective, tap taps emblematize syncretic Port-au-Prince experience, one in which the folk sayings of the countryside meet the urban space of the motor vehicle and the improvisational energy of visual arts. Danticat's writing itself also employs beautiful imagistic descriptions that reveal an interdependence of the visual and literary (sometimes she explicitly links painting and Celiane's vision: mountains "look like blue and gold, like one of the paintings that Moy's artist friend, Bos Dezi, makes to sell at the tourist market in the capital, Port-au-Prince" [5]). Just as Celiane's rural grandfather is touched by the violence in the capital, her mother—a character reluctant to leave the country for Port-au-Prince—speaks in folk sayings that invoke the visual: "Manman likes to speak in pictures . . . They are called proverbs. I like proverbs because you have to stop and think to interpret them. They make a picture for you and you must discover for yourself how to interpret it" (8). Syncretism characterizes Haitian artistic production, and Celiane is implicated; she must interpret the hybrid culture that surrounds her.

Not only does Danticat employ a fusion aesthetic, but the end of the novel—in which Moy tells the story of migration from rural Beau Jour to Brooklyn in a series of paintings—emphasizes the syncretic Haitian identity, as Celiane gives meaning to the art by titling it "Behind the Mountains," after a proverb, and vowing that "Moy and I will write a book together. Moy will tell our story in images. And I will tell even more of our story with words" (160). As an artist, Celiane sees the world through the Haitian tap-tap aesthetic, another strategy that anchors her to Haiti, and to Port-au-Prince specifically. And isn't Port-au-Prince the perfect city to represent this kind of concomitance? According to Rafael Lucas, "Port-au-Prince . . . is simultaneously the capital of sorrow and the Caribbean Babylon, the mythical city with 'problematic' spatiality where the rich quarters, the squalid shantytowns, the overpopulated suburbs, and the fearsome barracks rub up against one another" (61). But for Danticat, this admixture of perspectives and experiences can produce tangible rewards, particularly in creating new, vibrant forms of art. The indeterminacy and instability of Haitian migrant (country to city) identity does not exclusively invoke violence and trauma. For Celiane and her family, migration to Port-au-Prince engenders a new aesthetic identity that will sustain Celiane's sense of self in America. *Behind the Mountains* reconfigures perceptions of migrant hybridity by placing it squarely in a Haitian context, and transforming the secondary migration into simply an echo of the first. Celiane is most Haitian when feeling lost in an urban context, and most Haitian when discovering the aesthetic potential of breaking barriers between forms. Her greatest achievement is in embracing the rewards of the fluid, dynamic city space by calling for the fusion of art and literature.

While Danticat foregrounds Haitian syncretism and minimizes exchange with America, Jaira Placide's *Fresh Girl* addresses the question of American-Caribbean identity by grappling directly with the main character's attempts to assimilate. The novel depicts the trauma of forced migration by initially posing a conventional perspective on American-Caribbean hybridity. Although Mardi is not technically a Haitian national since she was born in America, she moved to Haiti as a small child, only to be uprooted at age 12 during the violence surrounding elections in 1994. Mardi is wounded by her experience in Port-au-Prince. She was raped by armed men at age 12 and did not tell her family. The novel largely explores her responses to repressed trauma since her symptoms resemble those of posttraumatic stress syndrome. In our first image of Mardi, she lies on the bathroom floor in the middle of the night, awakened by a nightmare of the rape, and tries to calm herself by putting together an elaborate puzzle:

> I'm making this, me. It's me who's putting together all the animals in the kingdom. I put together a 250-piece puzzle in less than an hour. And the lights aren't even on. My legs are cold on the broken-tiled bathroom floor. . . . It's two o'clock in the morning. I'm tired but I don't want to go back to sleep. What if I dream about the soldiers again? What if I dream about Ike at school? What if I wake up dead? I get up and wash my hands. I scrub and scrub with the Brillo pad. The backs of my hands hurt, but I feel better. (1)

By putting together the puzzle in the dark, Mardi attempts to overcome the fragmentation resulting from the rape.

But instead of success (eventually she imagines that the lion has escaped the puzzle and threatens her family), Mardi finds that she can control the psychic pain only by inflicting physical pain on herself. When she feels most uneasy about her past, she sleeps on a bed of rocks, and in other sections of the novel she cuts, bruises, stabs, and burns herself. Clearly Mardi's experience accords with that of actual trauma survivors who, according to Judith Herman, "relive in their bodies the moments of terror they can not describe in words" (Francis 79). The depiction of Mardi's repression and self-violence is significant also in extending the accomplishment of writers like Danticat. As Donette A. Francis argues about Danticat's books for adults, "poor Haitian women's bodies . . . become sites of national trauma and the erosion of the Haitian body politic" (77). In *Fresh Girl*, Placide acknowledges the signification of children's bodies in documenting Haiti's violent history; this is a profound moment of thematic crossover for the field of Haitian children's literature, since Placide refuses to isolate falsely the Haitian female child's experience from the Haitian female adult's experience.

In addition to marking the burden of a Haitian history, Mardi's memories of sexual trauma also become the site of her early Haitian-American hybridity. From the first page of the novel, Mardi fuses her memory of the historic terror with her fear of an American boy who harasses her, Ike. Mardi dreams about Ike in terms that echo the *macoute* attack, and when Ike corners her she enacts this fusion: "My hand grabs hold of a wooden stick leaning against a wall. I swing it at Ike. When I keep missing him, I start hitting myself in the face and yell, 'Stop! Leave me alone! Enough! Stop!' I realize what I'm doing but can't stop" (150). Since present-day American harassment and historic trauma combine, Mardi participates (at this point in the novel) in the conventional pattern for migrant literature, one in which exchanges between the host culture and home culture take shape to define the subject's liminality.

Mardi's school setting, however, sets the stage for her assimilation into American culture and her movement away from Haitian history and identity. Haitian children are stigmatized within the school, as American children call them boat people and allege that they have "Haitian Body Odor" (33). Interestingly, Haitian children who hope to erase their cultural signification hurl the worst insults at Mardi, and are "the first ones" (33) to invoke stereotypes. "Maybe teasing me somehow proves how American they are—or how Haitian I am" (33), Mardi writes in her diary, as she discovers that within a school setting, one cannot abide in both cultures. Her Haitian classmates erase their own cultural identification, and Mardi feels the pressure to divest herself of Haitian cooking, clothing, manners, and folk knowledge.

Perhaps because the text constructs hybridity as the dual burdens of Mardi's rape and Ike's abuse, eventually Haitian-American identity becomes something to be overcome, expunged through testimony. Unlike the ending of Danticat's *Breath, Eyes, Memory* where the protagonist returns to Haiti and finds in folk culture a means toward healing the inherited trauma of rape, the conclusion of *Fresh Girl* works to expel Haitian (and American) violence for the possibility of American reinvention. Mardi's grandmother says, "You and Serina are the lucky ones. You're both young and can change, especially you, Mardi, maybe because you were born here. You're the American. You're born with choices" (107). And even though Mardi's family remains a crucial site of emotional sustenance, the last third of the book pushes Mardi toward a new openness with her family that suggests her desire to overcome hybridity and position herself as American. Mardi's uncle witnesses one of Mardi's confrontations with Ike, a moment which allows him to understand her uncomfortable present and unbearable past. Ultimately, Mardi tells her aunt and uncle about the rape; in a long passage that reads as a flashback, Mardi relives the rape, recounting it in present tense. Her aunt replies to the story, "'Nothing is bad in you, no —no experience can turn you into something without your permission" (176–77), a reaction that enables Mardi to revise her image of herself as spoiled by the past, as not a "fresh girl" in the United States.

After telling about the rape, Mardi is able to confront and silence Ike, and dispels a romanticized attachment to Santos, a boy originally from the Dominican Republic. (Her attachment to Santos is thematized as a fantasy reunification of the island of Hispaniola). But the culmination of Mardi's reinvention comes when she stands in at the edge of a pond, and thinks, "I look down at my hands and rub them together, liking the feel of them. I lift my skirt and touch my legs. My skin is smooth, not broken. I touch my face. My eyes are big, my nose is wide, and my lips are smiling" (209). Water, of course, is intimately linked with Haitian migration. As Lucas notes, "The sea represents a frontier space and a way out ('nager pour sortir' 'swim to leave'—the *boat people's* solution). There we find beings in the margins . . . those who want to 'marronner'—that is, to escape the infanticide, devouring country" (71). A few pages earlier, Mardi sits by the water with her uncle Perrin, a political dissenter who had left Haiti on a boat, unlike Mardi who migrated by plane; he explains that "There's always something out there, the survivors trying to cross. . . . It's life and death, that water" (198). Mardi takes a step toward "life" as an American in the water, hoping to eradicate the pain that she identifies with her Haitian history.

The most powerful statement of Mardi's progress toward an American identity comes in the last paragraphs of the novel, as Mardi prepares to leave her family for a summer camp in upstate New York. She recognizes that her grandmother and aunt will return to Haiti if Haiti's president is reinstated, but she herself expresses no desire to relocate there. Instead, Haiti becomes associated with memory and nostalgia:

> I look around the kitchen. In the dark my eyes can still recognize the big cooking spoons, the I LOVE HAITI wooden machete souvenir, the local bodega calendar of a topless woman, the three pictures of fruits, the floral plastic tablecloth, toaster, blender, Brillo, Palmolive, and the patchwork-quilt rag that hangs on the refrigerator door. I have good eyes. I can even see the fading crack on the wall in the shape of Hispaniola. (213)

In this passage, elements associated with island life—fruits and flowers—become plastic and unreal, and the tools of her self-mutilation, like Brillo, become mere kitchen accessories. The most tangible evidence of her Haitian history becomes minimized into a tourist souvenir; the machete is the conventional weapon of the macoutes, evoking those who raped and brutalized Mardi. (The Tonton Macoutes, a volunteer secret police initiated by François "Papa Doc" Duvalier, terrorized the Haitian population through violence and torture.) From the distance of her American kitchen, Mardi can transform that history into a tourist artifact, and the ton ton macoute's instrument of violence is divested of power. Fragmentation, the "fading crack" of the island, retreats, and movement into a new vision of Americaness by expelling Haitian trauma dominates. This is not to say that the book disparages all elements of Haitian cultural identification; the grandmother, aunt, and uncle are characterized as generous and loving people, and their attachment to Haiti offers Mardi sustenance. But as a young person grappling with her sense of place within America, Mardi finds that American reinvention is a welcome solution to the anguish of a liminal identity. As much as her family loves and nourishes Mardi, she herself focuses on the rape as a defining moment in her sense of national identity. Associating cultural indeterminacy with victimhood and passivity, Mardi expels a traumatic past and clings to a new American self.

Marie-José N'Zengou-Tayo notices that Haitian-American adult writers employ "children as a mouthpiece for Haitian popular migration" (74), and in children's literature responses to hybridity and migration are more contested, more various than one might expect. For Danticat and Placide, Haitian identity dominates, excluding the Haitian-American "hybridity" so often assumed in appraisals of the new literature of migrancy. The association of Haitian identity with trauma—whether of migration to the city from the country or of sexual/political violence—bears such weight that its tangibility is immutable. In studying Haitian-American children's literature, critics are able to expand configurations of cultural and ethnic identity.

Finally, these books make apparent not only the complexities involved in figuring a national identity, but also the linkage of women's stories of violence to children's stories. In many cases the stories are not separable, and often they have been separated in critical appraisals of Caribbean migrant literature. Danticat writes in her essay "We Are Ugly, but We Are Here":

> Two years ago, a mother jumped into the sea when she discovered that her baby daughter had died in her arms on a journey which they had hoped would take them to a brighter future. Mother and child, they sank to the bottom of an ocean which already holds millions of souls from the middle passage, the holocaust of the slave trade that is our legacy. (141)

Mother and daughter stories of migration and trauma are linked, across generations and across time. In fact, Danticat's and Placide's texts mark an important moment in the development of both Caribbean migrant literature and African American literature. For migrant literature, these texts return the voice of the child to the cultural conversation.

But in terms of placing the texts within an African American tradition, Danticat and Placide refuse to isolate children's experience from larger issues of cultural and national identity and trauma. In a telling exchange at the end of *Behind the Mountains*, Moy and his father discuss the boy's coming of age: "'Okay, so you are a man,' he finally spoke up. 'But you will find that it's not so easy being a man.' 'It has not been so easy being a boy, either,' Moy said" (152). By acknowledging the challenges and complexities of black childhood, Danticat and Placide participate in a long tradition within African American culture of refusing to segregate children from adult social and political concerns. Whether it be the Harlem Renaissance's appeals for children to become race leaders, or the Black Arts Movement's call for children to take political action, the black American community has rarely isolated children from the greater concerns of the community. Adults may want to insulate children from political and social circumstances, but young black people are politically positioned, African American children's literature attests, and are entirely capable of taking action in response to their environments. I asked earlier whether or not we are able to place Caribbean migrant texts for young people within the category of African American children's literature. Absolutely. Not only do they participate in black American literary traditions like the awareness of child sophistication, but they help us uncover the variety of experiences and histories that make up black American culture. One should also be aware that *Behind the Mountains* and *Fresh Girl* form just one pattern within a growing body of Haitian-American literature. Haitian folk tales, historical fiction like Danticat's *Anacaona, Golden Flower* (2005), and novels of suburban life like Joanne Hyppolite's *Ola Shakes It Up* (1998) all attest to the multiplicity of perspectives on Haitian-American experience.

Works Cited

Danticat, Edwidge. *Behind the Mountains*. New York: Scholastic, 2002.

———. "We Are Ugly, But We Are Here." *The Caribbean Writer* 10 (1996): 137–41. 9 January 2009. http://www.thecaribbeanwriter.org/ContrMainFrame. php?volsec=10036.

Francis, Donette A. "'Silences Too Horrific to Disturb': Writing Sexual Histories in Edwidge Danticat's *Breath, Eyes, Memory*." *Research in African Literatures* 35.2 (2004): 75–90.

Lucas, Rafael. "The Aesthetics of Degradation in Haitian Literature." *Research in African Literatures* 35.2 (2004): 54–74.

Martin, Michelle H. *Brown Gold: Milestones of African-American Children's Picture Books, 1845–2002.* New York: Routledge, 2004.

N'Zengou-Tayo, Marie- José. "Children in Haitian Popular Migration as Seen by Maryse Conde and Edwidge Danticat." *Winds of Change: The Transforming Voices of Caribbean Women Writers and Scholars.* Ed. Adele S. Newson and Linda Strong-Leek. New York: Peter Lang, 1998.

Mardorossian, Carine M. "From Literature of Exile to Migrant Literature." *Modern Language Studies* 32.2 (Fall 2002): 15–33.

Placide, Jaira. *Fresh Girl.* New York: Random House, 2002.

Smith, Katharine Capshaw. "Splintered Families, Enduring Connections: An Interview with Edwidge Danticat." *Children's Literature Association Quarterly* 30.2 (2005): 194–205.

CHAPTER 9

For *All My Children,* or Approaching African American Children's Picture Books

Neal A. Lester

I guess being colored doesn't make me *not* like
the same things other folks like who are other races.
Langston Hughes, "Theme for English B"

Introduction

Some of our first impressions of ourselves, of our world, and of our places in the world emerge from texts—print and nonprint—presented to us as children by adults—teachers, family, and guardians. From seeing Spot run to watching Father and Mother with Dick and Jane, we stumbled into a world of near perfection, where everyone spoke a passionless standard of English, wore clean pastel-colored clothes, and were costumed in pink skin, straight hair, and bright white teeth with matching wide smiles. The innocence of youth gave many of us little reason to question that Cinderella, Jesus, cowboys, Mother Goose, Mickey and Minnie Mouse, and Barbie could only be imaged and imagined as white. Thus, too many persons of color grew up nourished by images often different from our perceptions of our racial, familial, and cultural selves as legitimate beings with rightful places in the world. If we existed as people of color, we existed in and along the margins as others inhabited the center.

If a fundamental purpose of literature is to connect us on some human level while giving us access to experiences that may or may not be our own, African American children's picture books afford that opportunity. If the worst thing we as teachers can do for our children is to shy away from texts and experiences that emerge from different subject groups, then the best we can do for ourselves and our students is to legitimize every child's experiences while introducing all children to new ones. African American children's picture books supplement other progressive means to counter the invisibility and marginality of brown children and brown peoples' experiences especially in the fictional world. African American picture books can particularize narrative constructions, thereby forging and advocating intercultural awareness, sensitivity, and understanding.

Guiding Light

When new teacher Ruth Sherman stirred the pot of national controversy in 1997 by introducing Carolivia Herron's children's book *Nappy Hair* to her third-grade African American and Latino/a students, the reality of that controversy left some white teachers uneasy about approaching any such text that might thrust them into dangerous cultural and racial flames by teaching a text about difference from the perspective of an outsider. Perhaps more important than the fact of the controversy was the reminder that issues regarding race and culture still make whites generally and white teachers more importantly uncomfortable and vulnerable. Rudine Sims Bishop, in her essay "Multicultural Literature for Children: Making Informed Choices," from *Teaching Multicultural Literature in Grades K–8*, offers advice and reassurance to the reluctant educator preparing to teach a multicultural children's text:

> Unfortunately, it is not possible to create a tidy checklist that can be applied to every book from a parallel culture. There are however, at least two general strategies that, if adopted, can raise levels of awareness and make teachers better informed selectors and evaluators of multicultural literature: be aware of various types of multicultural literature [and] read extensively in literature written by "insiders." (43–46)

While I do not want to reinforce the oversimplified and artificial insider/ outsider binary, it is important that those teaching texts about cultural experiences different from their own be keenly aware of potential traps, those that can be easily avoided and those that cannot.

Another World

Specifically, books for children offer an exciting world that complements and interfaces with adult literature and with adult experiences. Since children typically do not write these books, it is clear that the issues and ideas in children's books are filtered through and created by adults' perspectives and views. Surely, discussions of identity, family, values, and dreams connect readers across genres, across generations, across genders, and across cultures

Children's picture books simultaneously construct for us and instruct us on master narratives about class, race, gender, sexuality, and economics. All texts differ, and specific lenses can allow us to read and therefore experience texts in more meaningful ways. Herein is the link that potentially connects us to each other through language and through the ability of language and narrative to construct and give order to our experiences and our named identities.

Days of Our Lives

To arrive at what characterizes a black text is to engage in an exercise of knowing contexts and recognizing patterns of representations. Such patterns, however, do not mean that every seemingly similar text will have these traits and share nothing experientially with representations from and of other groups. In fact, efforts to talk about a group or a group's experiences as either unique or universal undermine the fullness of any given text. Diana George and John Trimbur's definition of culture affords some common ground upon which to base this recognition of patterns, patterns that deconstruct conventional notions of a universal by constructing a different and equally viable whole universe:

> Culture refers . . . to the way of life that characterizes a particular group of people. . . . *Culture* offers a way to think about how individuals and groups organize and make sense of their social experience—at home, in school, at work, and at play. Culture includes all the social institutions, patterns of behavior, systems of belief, and kinds of popular entertainment that create the social world in which people live. Taken this way, culture [is] . . . a people's lived experience—what goes on in the everyday lives of individuals and groups. (2)

Hence, this exercise of providing examples of how to engage fully and effectively an African American children's text is foremost an exercise in reading culture, "in finding patterns that are familiar" (2). "Reading culture means bringing forward for analysis and reflection those commonplace aspects of everyday life that people normally think of as simply *being there*, part of the natural order of things" (3).

I offer here examples of some of my favorite African American children's picture books and suggest ways to talk about and to think about these as they present and represent salient aspects of African American culture: Eloise Greenfield's *Honey, I Love* (1978), Ysaye M. Barnwell's *No Mirrors in My Nana's House* (1998), and Angela Johnson's *Tell Me a Story, Mama* (1989). What threads these texts together for me is that they are in fact authored by African Americans, they highlight the rich nuances and textures of orality and rhythmic storytelling, they challenge stereotypes, they present complex identity issues, they comment on social attitudes and perceptions about race, and they present messages of cultural and racial affirmation. On some level, each book reaffirms a positive message of difference that simultaneously affirms our basic humanity and our connections to others all over the world. Such connections allow us to experience the world more fully and with a greater awareness of a world outside ourselves. Such connections also remind us that we are not alone in any of our experiences. Such connections legitimize our experiences and enable us to see that we are not the center of the universe. Indeed, such connections can give us a more holistic perspective on what is happening in our own world and in the worlds that surround us. Such connections can be both personally uplifting and personally humbling. Acknowledging difference enhances our experiences; it does not necessarily limit our thinking or our experiences.

Eloise Greenfield's *Honey, I Love*

Eloise Greenfield's popular picture book, *Honey, I Love* (1995)—based on the collection of poems by Greenfield and published as *Honey, I Love and Other Love Poems* (1978)—is the celebration of self-acceptance, family, and independence within a familiar African American cultural milieu.

As with any picture book, illustrations provide a first clue to a book's presentation and representation of truth and alternative realities and experiences. Just as we look at images to mirror truths, pictures and illustrations can also reiterate and perpetuate stereotypes and caricatures if illustrators are not sensitive to representations of difference—hairstyles, skin hues, characters' clothing, for instance. When all characters are presented as one skin tone, this sameness tends to undermine genuine diversity efforts. Only when representations seek to represent multiple layers of difference visually and aesthetically can every child reader find him or herself and know difference as personal enhancement. The very stylized early version of Greenfield's collection includes all black and white sketches by Diane and Leo Dillon, lots of fluffy, cloudlike afros and Afrocentric braided hairstyles. Despite the illustrator's lack of variation in skin tones for the brown characters in the 1995 edition, the little girl on the cover has intricately neat cornrows that suggest the book's racial and gender focus. Beads on braids blowing in the wind provide an alternative to straight-haired, blonde images of female beauty that typically dominated the pages of children's picture books, early readers, and commercial advertisements. Greenfield's is not the story of Father, Mother, Dick and Jane, or Goldilocks and the Three Bears, but rather a story of a spunky little brown girl who enjoys being herself. Indeed, Jane Spivey Gilchrist's illustrations in the 1995 version present smiling brown children with brown dolls, both children and dolls bedecked in Afrocentric hairstyles. The family is having fun, and the little girl narrator luxuriates in herself and everyone and everything important to her in her environment: her cousin visiting from the south, the cousin's southern drawl that differs from her own northern rhythms, the frolicking water play on a hot summer day, her friends and their dolls, the family trip to the country, and her mother's comforting presence. There is little need to determine whether this story represents a single-parent home since the book focuses squarely on community that extends beyond a nuclear family: a cousin, a church family, an uncle, and neighbors. That the characters are moving, acting, traveling, visiting, playing, laughing, and smiling further contributes to this narrator's self-pride and passion for life in her present existence. Here, Greenfield draws on a rich tradition of black women whose humor was their weapon of survival in a world that could not and would not accept them on their own terms. Daryl Cumber Dance offers further context of humor and women's oral traditions being passed from generation to generation:

I'm happy that my daughter and her peers are sharing this tradition [of self-affirmation through humor] which is an education in life, in being black women, in dealing with the world, in deflecting the threatening blows, in relating to men, and loving . . . themselves as blackbrownbeigecreamdamn-nearwhite women with straightcurlybushy-kinkylongdamneardowntowaist-mediumshort hair and breasts and hips of varied and sundry descriptions. I am happy that she is learning that laughter is not simply funny; it's serious medicine; it's righteous therapy. She who laughs . . . lasts. (xxvi–xxvii)

Because this is a designated "Let's Read Aloud" book, an African American lyricism is at the center of this reading experience. In fact, it falls within the tradition of what scholar Henry Louis Gates, Jr. calls a "speakerly text" wherein meaning is as deeply embedded in the sounds and rhythms of the words as in the story narrative itself. Fully engaging with such a text depends on a reader's ability to experience the visual symbols/words on the page as a text's aural and oral performance (Gates 174). This story's uncomplicated poetic rhythms are achieved in the repetition of rhyming couplets: "south" and "mouth," "warm" and "arm," "walks" and "talks," and "coat" and "boat." Elements of black vernacular are clear in the title, "Honey, I Love"—word and a rhythm traditionally associated with black women. Dance comments further on a cultural specificity of black women's language as it relates to humor and self-affirmation: "The literature, popular culture, and folklore of African American women reflect their love of musical, rhythmical language; their tremendous range of tonal inflections; their delight in rhyme, colorful metaphor and simile, and pure sound; and their affinity for verbal play and name-calling" (xxiii).

Indeed, such terms of community and endearment among black women like "Honey, hush!" or "Honey chile" and more contemporary variations like "Girl, stop!," "sho'nuff," "shut yo mouff," or "Girlfriend" provide a linguistic vibrancy and a richly textured cultural, racial, and gender familiarity. The repetitious "I love" is punctuated with words or phrases that privilege spoken word over the potentially more restrictive "standard English": "'cause" rather than "because," "she don't want" instead of "she doesn't want," and "I love Me" instead of "I love myself." Clearly, the language has nothing to do with the intelligence level of this child but rather with the linguistic rhythms with which this protagonist is familiar and the words and rhythms that surround her and largely define her within her celebrated community.

Greenfield's black vernacular is celebrated with a chantlike lyricism. Teachers should be keenly aware of instances where blacks' alleged "nonstandard English" and pronunciations have been linked to racist stereotypes and even to the popular nineteenth-century American minstrel entertainment where whites in blackface and later blacks in blackface mocked blacks' alleged buffoonish behavior and clumsy, unintelligible speech. This minstrel-like dialect is irregular rhythmically and focuses on exaggerated words and repetitive sounds purely for the sake of eliciting laughter and cultural and social condescension from audiences. Greenfield's book challenges this tradition of a privileged standard English by infusing this narrative with authentic alternative rhythms that construct and sustain African American identities and cultures from youth to old age. Contextually then, Greenfield's language, linguistic rhythms, and book's title follow closely in the tradition of Daryl Cumber Dance's anthology of African American women's humor, *Honey, Hush!*, a testament of cultural strength and intimacy. As a text grounded in the richness of spoken black vernacular, Greenfield's invites oral performance that enables readers to experience the fullness of its celebration. The poetic rhythms further recall the accessibility of such Maya

Angelou poems as "Still I Rise" and "Phenomenal Woman"—poems that also luxuriate in black women's self-affirmation individually and collectively.

Ysaye M. Barnwell's *No Mirrors in My Nana's House*

An advertisement, "What's wrong with this picture?" from the New York-based Black Owned Communications Alliance (BOCA)—appearing in a national black readership magazine, calling for more representation of African Americans in media communications—shows a young black male child draped in a towel that he has transformed into a cape around his shoulders as he stands looking into a bathroom mirror. Instead of seeing his little black boy image in the mirror, the image that stares back at him is a reflection of a white adult male, Christopher Reeve–looking superhero. On the one hand, one might read this visual narrative as this little black boy's defiance, his daringness to construct himself as an action hero no matter that the image that stares back does not reflect his true self-image. On the other hand, the advertisement attacks the invisibility of little black boys and little black girls who need images of themselves reflected not just in this bathroom mirror but in other figurative social mirrors that surround us and them. Since as playwright Anna Deveare Smith contends in her introduction to *Fires in the Mirror* (1993), that "the mirrors of society do not mirror society," the spiritual health of African American children, according to the profoundly simple message of Ysaye M. Barnwell's *No Mirrors in My Nana's House* (1998), must be nurtured by family and communities of individuals who celebrate as a beauty ideal any and every brown/ black person.

Many adult stories exist about little brown girls trying to accept themselves as they are. For instance, Toni Morrison's *The Bluest Eye* is the shared tragedy of those consumed by self-delusion and self-hate because they do not inhabit the fictitious and seemingly perfect white world of Father, Mother, Dick, and Jane. As the embodiment of a whole community's racial self-loathing—what W. E. B. Du Bois, in *The Souls of Black Folk* (1903) calls "double consciousness," that is, always looking at oneself through the eyes of those who look at blacks with pity and contempt (215). Pecola Breedlove prays not for self-acceptance but for transformation into a white Other:

> It had occurred to Pecola some time ago that if her eyes, those eyes that held the pictures, and knew the signs—if those eyes of hers were different, that is to say, beautiful, she herself would be different. Her teeth were good, and at

least her nose was not big and flat like some of those who were thought so cute. If she looked different, beautiful, maybe Cholly would be different, and Mrs. Breedlove too. Maybe they'd say, "Why, look at pretty-eyed Pecola. We mustn't do bad things in front of those pretty eyes. . . ."

Each night, without fail, she prayed for blue eyes. Fervently, for a year she had prayed. Although somewhat discouraged, she was not without hope. To have something as wonderful as that happen would take a long, long time.

Thrown, in this way, into the binding conviction that only a miracle could relieve her, she would never know her beauty. She would see only what there was to see: the eyes of other people. (40)

Arguably, Pecola does not get her bluest eyes and is forever trapped in a spiritual and emotional paralysis. Indeed, the superlative in any case is relative to others' subjective assessments of what is blue, what is bluer, and what is bluest. Any absolute superlative is thereby illusory at best. Unfortunately among African Americans, Pecola Breedlove is not an extreme example of this futile self-image battle; in fact, the rest of her African American community—her neighbors, her would-be friends and peers and their parents, and even her mother—have absorbed the pains of self-hatred based on what they do not have physically, aesthetically, and economically. Pecola's story grows broadly out of the painfully familiar 1940s and 1950s doll and human drawings experiments of psychologists Kenneth and Mamie Clarke, who found that black children preferred playing with white dolls and imagined all things white, such as skin color, as all things right and best in the world:

It is clear that the Negro child, by the age of five is aware . . . that to be colored in contemporary American society is a marker of inferior status. . . . The negation of the color, brown, exists in the same complexity of attitudes in which there also exists knowledge . . . that the child himself must be identified with that which he rejects. . . . These results seem most significant from the point of view of what is involved in the development of a positive, constructive program for more wholesome education of Negro children in the realities of race in the American culture. They would seem to point strongly to the need for a definite mental hygiene and educational program that would relieve children of the tremendous burden of feelings of inadequacy and inferiority which seem to become integrated into the very structure of the personality as it is developing. (Clarke and Clarke 350)

When the doll test was repeated by [Brooklyn] Urban Academy high schooler Kiri Davis in the seven-minute short film *A Girl Like Me* (2005) the results of racial preference and white idolization by black children remained unchanged.

Sweet Honey in the Rock member Ysaye M. Barnwell's picture book *No Mirrors* responds to the challenge of having black children accept themselves for who and what they are—special human beings with a special place in the cosmos: "And the beauty in everything/ was in her eyes/ like the rising of the sun." Based on the composition by Barnwell, the book/compact disc combination and this song performed by the internationally acclaimed black women's a cappella group highlight rich black cultural rhythms, commenting on both race and gender and providing a context for a celebration of black female beauty and self-love. Both philosophically and aesthetically, *No Mirrors* is an effort to arm both brown children and their parents with this tool of cultural and racial affirmation.

Thematically, the book challenges prevailing beauty aesthetics that typically exclude females of color. While the society outside the familiar eyes of this young narrator's Nana's house bombards people of color generally and black girls particularly with lessons in invisibility or negativity, this moment of profound intimacy and affirmation between a grandmother and her granddaughter captures the strength of self-definition individually and communally through a focus on mirrors and self-reflection through the eyes of those who love and nurture the spiritual, psychological, and emotional health of this young narrator. At the center of this book are challenges to the European beauty aesthetic of females: long straight hair, pale or light skin, and thin nose.

In contrast to the social mirrors that distort images of race and gender, the *No Mirrors* narrator accepts her black skin, flat nose, and baggy clothes. This narrator's urban living space—"cracks in the wall," "dust that would fall," "noise in the hallway," and "trash and rubbish" is lived in and real and reaffirms her connections with family and community. Accepting that the less-than-desirable realities of one's environment do not have to define one's sense of self negatively is yet another lesson of self-acceptance.

The reality of human imperfection unites us all, but human imperfection and less-than-ideal experiences do not have to cancel out the joys in our lives. The lesson of *No Mirrors* falls squarely in line with Giovanni's here, that self-acceptance and self-pride gleaned from a supportive family and extended community can help shield this young black female—both as a child and later as an adult—from cultural and aesthetic assaults from the outside worlds: "The world outside was a magical place/ I only knew love and I never knew hate."

Further Synthia Saint James' multicolored construction-paper-cut-out illustrations of brown characters in different sizes and shapes and with different skin tones and hairstyles demonstrate important attention to representing diversity within this subject group. The stylized faceless brown representations offer inclusivity visually and aesthetically. The bold colors underscore the boldness and simplicity of the profound lesson for any child and for any adult: the power of self-acceptance. Images of family, friends, movement, sound, play, quiet, and solitude create a world of unlimited possibilities for this young child who sees love and strength in her Nana's eyes. While the text implies that the world can threaten this child's self-assurance and self-direction outside the safe space of family and familiarity, this child is instructed to seek renewal and legitimacy by looking literally and figuratively—almost hypnotically—into her Nana's eyes: "Chil' look deep into my eyes/ Chil' look deep into my eyes/ Chil' look deep into my eyes." Nana's eyes cast the spell that will sustain and rejuvenate in a world that seeks to tear down and deny legitimacy. Nana's lessons of self-love and beauty as reflected in her granddaughter's young eyes give back to Nana a reflection of her own aged beauty and cultural accomplishment. Hence, this book and, its accompanying song performance of the lyrics by Sweet Honey in the Rock, subvert the myth of invisibility to which others might relegate blacks socially, politically, and historically, as articulated in 1947 by Ralph Ellison in *Invisible Man*: "I am invisible, understand, simply because people refuse to see me. . . . When they approach me they see only my surroundings, themselves, or figments of their imagination—indeed, everything and anything except me" (3). *No Mirrors* is then not about deliberate or accidental distortion but about positive constructions of the "me" in any child living in a safe and nurturing environment.

And while it is important that each and every child see himself or herself reflected literally and metaphorically in the mirrors created and provided for them, it is equally important that all children see mirrors of difference as personal and social enhancement and not as personal or social threat. Barnwell's book then establishes a link between generational commitments to cultural survival. Both adults and children from presumably culturally affirming environments will pass this fundamental lesson and adult imperative along to future generations: that all children be loved and valued for what they are and who they are, and what they have every right to grow up to become.

Angela Johnson's *Tell Me a Story, Mama*

In her Nobel in Literature lecture delivered in Stockholm in 1993, Toni Morrison highlights the importance of intergenerational talking and sharing stories. Strategically, the speech sets up a conflict between youngsters and an old blind black woman whose reputation in her community for wisdom supersedes her blindness. In the story that Morrison creates and shares, youngsters approach this blind woman and initially seem bent on mocking her and disproving her celebrated reputation. Morrison ultimately offers the possibility that the youngsters do not intend to test the woman's wisdom but rather to get the older, wiser one to talk with them, to share her stories with them.

Indeed, humans have an inclination to create, to listen to, and to share stories. We write, speak, sign, or sing them; act them out, draw, or paint them; dance them, flute them, or piano them. As performance, talking creates community with a speaker and an audience; education evolves through a mutual creating and sharing. Shared stories become even more interlocked and layered and help us construct our identities as shared identities. When we listen to a radio, watch news broadcast, or read a newspaper, others' stories are created and shared. These stories are then shared in letters, e-mails, text messages, phone calls, and visits. Each opportunity to interact with another human being is another opportunity to share and create a story. Thus, these youngsters' final plea to the old blind woman of Morrison's narrative: "You are an adult. The old one, the wise one. Stop thinking about saving your face. Think of our lives and tell us your particularized world. Make up a story. Narrative is radical, creating us at the very moment it is being created." This power to transform lives through creating narrative and the inherent narrative intersectionality among individuals and communities is at the center of Angela Johnson's *Tell Me a Story, Mama*.

As a variant call-and-response performance ritual here between a mother and her child, Angela Johnson's *Tell Me a Story, Mama* demonstrates the interconnectedness of our lives through stories and the immediacy of storytelling. This little girl's efforts to prolong her bedtime ritual—her request of "Tell me a story, Mama"—occasion an opportunity for a mother and child to construct themselves and each other in one moment that is past, present, and future. The child's request is really an opportunity for her to command an authority over a past and present that is her mother's, her aunt's, and her grandmother's all through the shared vehicle of memory and storytelling. These recollections constitute nine different stories that render her mother brave, defiant, yet a respectful youngster who is now an adult instilling these same values in her young daughter. This little girl's storytelling allows her mother an opportunity not just to witness her child's mastery of storytelling craft but it also allows the mother and the child a shared moment of narrative creation. Johnson's book connects human mortality and the immortality of any shared story created and recreated through memory and storytelling performance.

Johnson's woman-centered story accentuates the strength of the black women who nurtured this young girl's mother even as the young narrator is being nurtured by her mother in the familiar bedtime moment. Indeed, *Tell Me a Story, Mama* presents black women as s/heroes nurturing their families and valuing as gifts the power of memory and the excitement of childhood inquiry. This mother's stories have given her little girl direction for personal growth and have supplied her with valuable female role models.

The text does not present a child asking to have a story read but rather a child requesting that a story be told. This narrative moment of Johnson's text then reverses expected parent/child roles and reiterates the spiraling, never-ending possibilities of making connections to past, present, and future through storytelling. Such a conversation, through story, between a parent and a child can only afford numerous possibilities for mutual growth and education and for personal development. Melissa J. St. Amour summarizes this "universal power of storytelling" (48): "We learn in the form of stories; the human brain is a story-seeking, story-creating instrument. The stories that we share are the foundation for our identities; nothing tells us more about a person than the stories he or she chooses to tell" (47). Hence, the mother in Johnson's story who has taught and teaches witnesses and learns from her daughter's narrative.

This book's emphasis on stories and storytelling might well be tied to African American oral traditions, here privileged in the foundation that the child beckons her mother to "tell" her a story rather than "read" her a story. Johnson's book harkens to a tradition that more often than not takes a backseat to reading and writing and the glorified ideal of alphabet literacy in Western civilization. St. Amour acknowledges the value of storytelling and narrative in everyone's identity formation: "The first step in the journey toward literacy and social responsibility is taken through oral language" (49). That this mother has taught her daughter lessons on behavior, human relations, and life values through storytelling is reflected in the younger daughter's skilled storytelling, part of their individual and shared personal, cultural, communal, and familial identities.

Further, *Tell Me a Story, Mama* explodes a number of cultural stereotypes, among them the middle-class ritual of parents reading bedtime stories to children at the end of the day. While this activity may be a reality of many, it is not a reality for all; not all parents are readers, and not all children embrace this passivity of being read to. That the mother is also presumably a single parent counters stereotypes that connect this family arrangement with economic deprivation and social and familial neglect. Clearly, this mother has a job and the desire, energy, and passion to talk to and with her young daughter, consciously teaching and participating in a rich tradition that will presumably extend into the young child's subsequent adult life.

Reinforcing the richness of *Tell Me a Story, Mama* are David Soman's warm watercolors. The calming pastels and smoky grays offer an impressionist style that interfaces with the narrative. Women's hairstyles are non-European, a brown-skinned doll decorates the young narrator's bedroom, and images from the cover to the final page consistently convey the power of human touch—embracing, comforting, reassuring, protecting, and expressing joy. This strength in caressing and touching appears even in the illustration of the mother's finding a puppy in the mother's youth. Characters' faces express emotional range and depth—happiness, concern, worry, confidence, surprise, celebration, and seriousness as the book demonstrates the tradition of storytelling it elevates.

Conclusion

There is no single way to read a text, no single approach to discussing any given text. And any experienced reader knows that even with the same text, multiple life experiences impact our responses at any given time. Whenever I conduct pre- and in-service workshops on multicultural children's literature generally and on African American children's literature in particular, I stress that individual teachers preassess their critical and cultural literacy relative to texts about experiences that are not their own. Importantly, this same advice extends to scholars, librarians, and parents. Certainly, key to any experience with a text culturally different from one's own lived experience is a private and honest self-assessment of one's own attitudes about the subject group. Honesty and openness beget professional integrity and will grant assistance even when we fall into inevitable traps of cultural and critical ignorance or unthinking. Such personal stocktaking will help determine the extent to which the homework we need to do as socially conscious and responsible adults is content-based, context-based, or perception-based. And while a reader need not have experienced the specifics of an African American children's text in order to "get it," it is imperative to facilitate or to participate in the most successful reading experience for all of us that we acknowledge what we do not know or know well, then do our homework before readings such a text.

As a veteran teacher and researcher of both African American literature and African American children's literature for some over 20 years, I highly recommend that teachers, scholars, and parents alike interface children's picture books with adult books when exploring issues of racial identity, racial representation and misrepresentation, and cultural and linguistic rhythms and nuances. Pulling from popular and material culture—magazines, newspapers, music, toys, postcards, greeting cards, television commercials, and dolls, for instance—also provides useful and relevant ways to supplement readings and discussions of African American children's picture books. And while there are ways to talk about a text without "insider" knowledge of frequent patterns, we must remain aware of the dangers of inviting others to approach what poet Langston Hughes in the excerpted lines that open this chapter calls "colored" texts reductively or oversimplistically. In actuality, no text is ever simple. We can, however, identify through example how a marked "black text" might be read, thought about, discussed, and understood. Ultimately, again as the Hughes epigraph positions, when our particular experiences connect with others' particular experiences, we arrive at a shared lived experience that potentially unites us all in what it means to be human. This chapter has sought to simultaneously challenge and to empower those seeking suggestions and strategies when approaching African American children's picture books. Acknowledging, understanding, and embracing difference in this context can actually move us all toward a greater sense of wholeness, toward a better understanding of our own humanity.

Works Cited

Angelou, Maya. "Human Family." 22 November 2008. http://oldpoetry.com/opoem/33281-Dr--Maya-Angelou-Human-Family.

Barnwell, Ysaye M. *No Mirrors in My Nana's House*. San Diego, CA: Harcourt Brace and Company, 1998.

Bishop, Rudine Sims. "Multicultural Literature for Children: Making Informed Choices." *Teaching Multicultural Literature in Grades K–8*. Ed. Violet J. Harris. Norwood, MA: Christopher-Gordon Publishers, 1993. 37–53.

Clarke, Kenneth B., and Mamie P. "Emotional Factors in Racial Identification and Preference in Negro Children." *Journal of Negro Education* (1950): 341–50.

Davis, Kiri. "*A Girl Like Me*." New York: Reel Works Teen Filmmaking, 2005.

Du Bois, W. E. B. *The Souls of Black Folk* (1903). *Three Negro Classics*. New York: Avon Books, 1965. 207–389.

Ellison, Ralph. *Invisible Man*. New York: Vintage Books, 1990.

Gates, Henry Louis, Jr. "Zora Neale Hurston and the Speakerly Text." *The Signifying Monkey: A Theory of African-American Literary Criticism*. New York: Oxford UP, 1988. 170–216.

George, Diana, and John Trimbur. *Reading Culture: Contexts for Critical Reading and Writing*. Menlo Park, CA: Longman, 1999.

Greenfield, Eloise. *Honey, I Love*. New York: HarperFestival, 1995.

Hughes, Langston. *The Collected Poems of Langston Hughes*. Ed. Arnold Rampersad. New York: Vintage Books, 1995. 409–10.

Morrison, Toni. *The Bluest Eye*. New York: Washington Square Press, 1970.

————. *The Nobel Lecture in Literature, 1993.* New York: Random House Audio Publishing, 1994. RH/348.

St. Amour, Melissa J. "Connecting Children's Stories to Children's Literature: Meeting Diversity Needs." *Early Childhood Education Journal* 31.1 (2003): 47–51.

SECTION III

Asian American Literature

CHAPTER 10

On Finding a Home

Cynthia Kadohata

I believe most writers have a home. For me, the writerly life means finding that home. Maybe your home is the sea, maybe your home is your
fears, maybe your home is wizardry, and maybe your home is something
as seemingly small as a single incident or a single year of your life. Many
writers have more than one home. For me, some of my homes as a writer
have been my childhood, my family, and the American landscape.

Perhaps because I majored in journalism in college, my writing style has
sometimes possessed a particularly journalistic flavor. People sometimes tell
me that in places it sounds nonfictional rather than fictional. Though virtually none of the stories I tell are from real life, many of the details within
the stories are. In this way, my life and my fiction become so deeply intertwined it is sometimes difficult to separate one from the other.

I was born in Chicago in 1956, not far from where the Cubs play baseball.
But because I can't really remember my early life in Chicago, I think of my life
as starting where my earliest memories start: in Georgia and Arkansas, and also
on the highway, because we moved a number of times when I was still very
young. On the highway, I remember the cheap motels where we stayed, and
the wind blowing on my face as we drove through endless wheat fields.

We moved to Georgia in 1957. My father worked as a chicken sexer,
a profession that at the time was almost all Japanese. I learned to talk in
Georgia and had a very heavy Southern accent. I believe the only other
people of Japanese ancestry in our towns were in the hatchery business.

In 1958 we moved to Arkansas, where my father continued to work in
hatcheries. Over the next few years, I remember spending humid summer days
stringing thread through dandelion necklaces, and I remember catching
bumblebees in a fancy gold change purse left over from the days when my

parents were courting. Where we lived, there were no fences or bushes between homes. You didn't know where one property ended and another began. Dogs ran freely through the fields, and a six-year-old could walk to school by herself. Just like the protagonist in my novel *Kira-Kira*, I had a little brother and a big sister. We played together all day. Back then your parents could let you run off and play by yourself all day and nobody thought it was dangerous. Another true fact that I used in *Kira-Kira* is that the whole hospital staff really did come by to see my brother when he was born, because they had never seen a Japanese baby before.

Just like the sisters in *Kira-Kira*, my mother made us curl our hair. We had to sleep with bobby pins poking into our heads all night. When I was 15 and visiting my father, I talked with a girl I'd known back when I was in elementary school. She told me that she remembered me as the girl with curly black hair.

Just like the father in *Kira-Kira*, my father sometimes worked 100 hours a week, and sometimes we didn't see him except when he was sleeping. In the hatcheries where he worked, there were no windows because the hatchery owners didn't want the chicken sexers to be distracted. I describe real hatcheries in both *Kira-Kira* and my first novel, *The Floating World*.

My mother was a cheerleader in high school and liked to go to dances. She met my father in Chicago at a special dance for Japanese Americans. She got married at 18 and became a stay-at-home mom.

My mother was a voracious reader. She took us to the library every week, and also made us read *Scientific American* articles that I couldn't understand then, and can barely understand today. I still have a stack of the articles that she made us read over the years.

Meanwhile my father didn't have the time or inclination to read. Someone once said to me, "The problems between your parents began when your mother started reading."

My parents got divorced in 1965. It was heartbreaking for me because I was a daddy's girl. After the divorce, my sister, my brother, my mother, and I lived briefly in Michigan before returning to Chicago. The details from *Kira-Kira* are based heavily on my life before we returned to Chicago. Of course, I had no aspirations at the time of becoming a writer.

Much, much later, I attended the University of Southern California, where I majored in journalism and wanted to write nonfiction. During college I worked as a sales clerk at Sears Hollywood. One day I proudly told the other sales clerks that I wanted to be a writer. I wasn't prepared for their reaction. They laughed and laughed at me and said, "What are you going to write about, working at Sears?"

In 1977 I was walking on the sidewalk when a car jumped over the curb and hit me. I was hospitalized for six weeks and had several operations.

The man who hit me with his car had some insurance, but not a whole lot. But I got some money and moved to Boston, where my sister lived, and I tried to become a writer. I started reading contemporary fiction and decided I wanted to write fiction instead of nonfiction. I also worked as a typist to make some money. I lived in a tiny, dark apartment with a lot of cockroaches. I sent out my first story to a magazine in about 1981 and got my first of probably hundreds of rejections. Some relatives told me, "Nobody wants to read about Japanese." I started to think I would never sell a story.

I wanted to sell a story so badly. I felt like a starving animal who was determined not to starve. Basically, I lived in the darkest, dankest apartment in a lovely neighborhood. Everything around me seemed to be shining and full of promise except me and my roaches. I wrote in loneliness and isolation, and I didn't know if I would ever get published. Just thinking of those days gives me the willies.

I didn't sell my first story until 1986, and my first novel—about a Japanese American family—was published in 1989 when I was 33. I published two more novels in 1992 and 1995. Both were for adults.

During the nineties my career was floundering, and I didn't know what to write about anymore. I didn't want to write stories of childhood because one editor had criticized me for continuing to write stories with young Asian American narrators. I had no money. So I went to work as a secretary and also did some freelance publicity work for a Japanese film distribution company.

An old friend of mine worked as a children's book editor. She'd been trying to get me to write a children's novel for many years, and I decided to try it. She helped me decide what to write about. She helped me realize that it was a *good* idea to draw on my childhood, and that it was a *good* idea to find my home as a writer, and not listen to those who thought I should move to a new home.

But though some of the details in *Kira-Kira* are true, the story is not true. The novel is about a young Japanese American girl whose sister dies of lymphoma in Georgia. My real-life sister is alive and well. In fact, when I told her what I was writing about, she got annoyed and accused me of being secretly hostile toward her.

I had to do some research for *Kira-Kira*, as I do for every novel. For instance, the mother in the novel works in a poultry plant; so I found several blueprints of such plants as well as articles about them that helped me imagine what it would be like to work there.

I did some research on swamps, since there are a lot of swamps in Georgia and I had originally planned to write a lot about them in the novel. I even e-mailed an expert on crickets to ask him some questions, since crickets are mentioned in the book.

This combination of real life, research, and imagination all came about because I found a wonderful editor who encouraged me to return home. I don't know how we choose our homes as writers. I don't know why, for instance, all some people want to write about is romantic relationships, or spaceships, or whatever. All I know is that we must be true to our homes when we write.

Immediately after finishing the first draft of *Kira-Kira*, I began work on *Weedflower*, a novel about the Poston internment camp, the camp where my father lived during World War II. I chose Poston to write about because of my father. If he had lived in a different camp, I would have written about that one instead. I began researching the camp while galleys of *Kira-Kira* were being prepared in late 2002.

As you may know, Poston was located on an Indian reservation. The novel is about a friendship between a Japanese American girl and a Mohave Indian boy. About 70 percent of the residents of Poston were from farm families, and part of what *Weedflower* is about is how they changed the landscape of the reservation.

My father was drafted out of Poston and joined the army while his family remained imprisoned.

To help me picture some of the characters for *Weedflower*, I used my boyfriend's uncle and father. Their names were Ichiro and Bull. I tried to use the personalities of what I knew about Ichiro and Bull for two of the characters in my book about Poston, and I even call the characters Ichiro and Bull. I also interviewed many people and read books and articles. I had no trouble developing the characters of Ichiro and Bull.

When I turned in the first draft of my manuscript, my editor hated it. I believe that was back in the fall of 2003. She made me rewrite the manuscript several times. But I couldn't get it right. The reason I couldn't get it right was that I couldn't imagine what it felt like for the main character, Sumiko, to be in a camp. Also, I was worried that nobody would want to read about the camps, because an editor had once told me so.

In the middle of all these rewrites, I was adopting a son from Kazakhstan.

So I took the manuscript with me to rewrite by hand when I went to Kazakhstan to adopt my son. Kazakhstan is part of the former Soviet Union. It's bordered by Russia, China, and several other countries. I was very nervous to be going alone. Since all business is conducted in cash, when I went I had $12,600 strapped to my waist. And there were beggars everywhere, and gypsies who would pat you down if you looked American. One day an old beggar woman knocked on my door, and when I answered she pushed her way in. I pushed her out, and she started pounding on my door and screaming. My heart was beating really hard, but finally she went away.

Nearly every night, I would think about my home in Los Angeles, and I would cry and cry with loneliness.

Then the next day I would go outside to shop for groceries or visit the orphanage. Hardly anybody spoke English, and the adoption agency facilitator was stealing money from the clients of the agency. As a result, the money that was supposed to be going to a translator for us went to her pocket. So most days, we didn't even have a translator, and either we didn't know what was going on, or else another agency's translator helped us.

Every day I tried to work on my manuscript. But I still didn't feel the story was working. Then all of a sudden one day I realized that the way I felt—that my whole life was turned upside down and I was in a place where nothing made sense to me—was probably a lot like the way my character Sumiko felt. And I was so bored some days I thought I would lose my mind. I'd read about the boredom some people felt in the camps, but until that moment I hadn't really understood true, complete boredom.

Suddenly I was able to do the rewrite. And it was all because I understood the main character now. The writing went more easily after this.

After several weeks in Kazakhstan, I went to court, and the adoption was granted. But I had to stay for almost a month more to complete paperwork and other requirements. I got physical custody of my son about a week-and-a-half before I left Kazakhstan. We slept in a hard bed that was about 30 inches wide. This, too, helped me understand how Sumiko might have felt in Poston.

Finally, on June 9, I got to come home. I had piles and piles of paper. But now that I understood the main character, I was moving forward instead of sideways. The novel was published in March 2006.

So my family, the people I worked with at Sears, the magazines who turned me down—basically, the whole world seemed to be telling me not to be a writer, or if I wanted to be a writer, not to write about Japanese, and not to keep writing child narrators.

And years ago I brought a story in one evening for a class workshop. The teacher went around the table and asked the other students to evaluate the story. One by one the others said they didn't understand the story, or they didn't really like the story, or they didn't think the story worked. Almost the whole interminable two hours elapsed in this manner. Not one person spoke well of my story. And yet in a few years, that story became a part of my first published novel.

You or even your parents or everybody you know might feel that nobody cares or wants to read about what you want to write about, but if it's in your heart, then it's what you should write about. So the question that always looms large for me is, "Where do I go from here?" For me, being a writer is a lot like my early years with my family: I'm searching for a home, and when life is good, I find one.

CHAPTER 11

Foreigners Within: An Introduction to Asian American Literature

Traise Yamamoto

Who Are Asian Americans?

"Asian American literature" is actually something of a misnomer, as well as an inadvertently appropriative appellation. Referring to works as varied as Kim Ronyoung's *Clay Walls* (1987), Le Thi Diem Thuy's *The Gangster We Are All Looking For* (2002), Larissa Lai's *When Fox Is a Thousand* (1995) and Joy Kogawa's *Obasan* (1981), the term "Asian American" obscures and elides the identity of Asian Canadian authors (Lai and Kogawa, in this particular case). Thus, some scholars prefer the term Asian North American literature, as it does not assume "American" to be synonymous with "U.S.-based."[1]

Far from a minor matter of semantics, the issues of naming, inclusion and exclusion are central to the field and to the communities gathered under the umbrella term "Asian American." For many years, East Asian ethnic groups— Japanese, Chinese, and Korean—were generally assumed to comprise the totality of "Asian America." However, even prior to the historic changes to immigration law in 1965, which discontinued the use of the national origins quota system and greatly increased the numbers and diversity of Asian ethnic groups in the United States, Asian Indians (South Asians) and Filipinos were conceptually marginalized and therefore often not recognized as being Asian American.[2] After 1965, Asian immigration dramatically increased, particularly in the numbers of immigrants from Thailand, Vietnam, India, the Philippines, Korea, and China. In addition, there were also increases in the immigrant population from Cambodia, Laos, Indonesia, and Pakistan, among other countries. As a result, "Asian American" is more commonly understood to refer to a very large panoply of ethnic groups, though it should be noted that the persistence of East Asian identification remains.

Nowhere is the importance of naming more apparent than in the disagreement over whether even the term "Asian North American" enacts an exclusion of Pacific Islanders, which would include persons who identify as Native Hawaiian, Samoan, Tongan, Guamanian, and Fijian, just to name a few of the groups originating in the region of Oceania. Thus, it is common to see the term Asian Pacific Islander American (APIA) or Asian Pacific American (APA) used with some regularity. However, even these terms are potentially problematic—as an appropriative rather than inclusive impulse—since many who identify as Pacific Islander/Americans consider themselves to be more allied politically and culturally with Indigenous peoples, rather than with Asian Americans who, in this context, would be identified more with colonizing "settlers" than with the marginalized.

Part of the difficulty of naming stems from the very large and flexible range of ethnic groups covered by the umbrella term "Asian American" (which, notwithstanding the above, will be the term used throughout this introduction), as well as the very large percentage—by some estimates 65 percent—of Asian Americans who were born in countries other than the United States. Often, this means that cultural alliances and ethnic identity are specific rather than Asian panethnic, to modify Yen-Le Espiritu's phrase. When an aggregate identity is taken on, it is often as "American," understood as a national identity that underscores citizenship.

"Asian America" is, therefore, a heterogeneous and dynamic grouping of several ethnic groups whose transnational relationship to various countries and cultures in Asia means that any invocation of a "community," with its underpinning assumptions of homogeneity, must rigorously foreground the fact that this appellation is a political grouping. That is, while the term Asian American may be useful for political purposes, it can also obscure the many differences that mark this group: duration of history in the United States, ethnic distinctions, cultural practices, language, and intensity of connection to so-called home countries. While many Asian Americans can claim multigenerational histories within the geographic space of the United States, others have immigrated from countries whose relationship to the United States may range from protectorate states (Guam, the Philippines), to those who have been politically and culturally occupied (Japan, Korea), to those whose statehood is intrinsically tied to narratives of U.S. expansionism (Hawai'i). Still other Asian countries have deep and problematic ties to U.S. military policies (Laos, Cambodia), or to the notion of "Asian Americanness" itself (South Asia, the Pacific Islands of Micronesia).

Whatever the ethnic and national histories they are assumed to represent, it remains the case that Asian Americans continue to be regarded as "perpetual foreigners" whose citizenship—either formal or cultural—is in question. Moreover, they are frequently subject to the concept of "the model minority," and ideologically positioned as either exemplary (in relation to African Americans and Latinos, in particular) or as threat (in relation to white Americans). Whether positioned as paradigmatic "others" or as "model minorities," however, both discourses position Asian Americans as either in deficit or excess of "humanness."

Despite the number of ethnic groups that make up Asian America, the very different cultural backgrounds, and the varying details of each communities' history in the United States, however, there are several thematics that run through and may be said to characterize a body of literature with an over 120-year history. The critic Shirley Geok-lin Lim has said that one "marked feature of Asian American literature and criticism" is its "insistence on past narratives, whether as Old World culture and values, immigrant history, race suffering, communal traditions, or earlier other language traces" (809). That is, much of Asian American literature seeks to recover and represent a past or an experience that has heretofore been unarticulated and unexplored.

Lim's assessment provides a productive place from which to articulate the interlocking and complex thematics of Asian American literature. This introduction begins with a focus on issues of citizenship and inclusion and moves through the major thematics of generational differences and the underpinning issues of memory and the recovery of the past. I end with a consideration of more recent developments in Asian American literature as they are affected by an increasingly mobile group of transnational subjects and by the growing literary presence of heretofore invisible or marginalized groups within Asian America.

Immigration, Citizenship, Foreignness

Cultural belonging and citizenship are extremely important concepts through which to understand Asian American literature because they encapsulate so many of the issues faced by Asian Americans in the United States. Because Asians are physically identifiable as racially other, suspicions about their perpetual foreignness repeatedly recapitulates the hardships and lack of acceptance faced by their immigrant forebears. In novels that deal with the internment of Japanese Americans, for instance, authors thematize the dominant culture's fear that even those who were native-born (second generation, or Nisei) would feel loyalty to Japan. This fear was based on the incorrect supposition that the Nisei would follow their Japanese-born parents, who were themselves incorrectly assumed to be suspect because they were not citizens. Of course, Asian immigrants were barred from becoming American citizens until 1954, but the fact of being noncitizens nevertheless was tautologically used as a rationale for exclusion. John Okada's 1957 novel *No-No Boy*, for instance, can in many ways be read as a narrative that asks at what point racial difference is no longer read as threatening foreignness and how far one must go to disavow cultural identifications and the immigrant parents who represent otherness.

Even following the period after which Asians could become citizens, however, literary texts continue to explore the issue of belongingness. Chang-rae Lee's novel *Native Speaker* (1995) centers around questions of cultural belonging and feelings of inclusion through the figure of protagonist Henry Park, a Korean American who works as a spy—clearly a metaphor for the cultural condition of and lingering suspicion about Asian Americans. Despite the fact that Park is American-born, married to a white American, and father to an American-born child, he nevertheless retains a feeling of separateness and difference that is only heightened as the narrative develops.

Thematics of cultural/national belonging are represented in highly complex ways in Lois-Ann Yamanaka's *Blu's Hanging* (1998), in which belonging and disenfranchisement are metaphorized through the particular status of Hawaii as a former U.S. territory and as a locale distinct from the mainland. The main character's family has been recently left motherless and, though their grieving father works, they are in economic distress. Yamanaka complicates issues of marginality considerably, since her protagonists are Japanese American—a group that enjoys a high level of privilege and status relative to other Asian ethnic groups, Native Hawaiians and non-Asians (with the exception of whites)—but who, because of class and family status, are denied access and inclusion as represented by popular culture and brand-name foods.

Issues of belonging, it should be noted, extend beyond simple inclusion, representation or "tolerance." Rather, belonging involves an acceptance that is not predicated on sundering one's ethnic past, disidentifying from one's cultural inheritance, or disavowing (or feeling the need to play up) one's physical difference. The pressure to assimilate into the "melting pot" is often experienced as the demand to conform to the majoritarian culture, retaining only enough ethnic identity to uphold the liberal ideology of tolerant plurality. That such a veneer is just that is evidenced by the frequency with which an extraneous event will touch off the toggle that switches exotic difference to threatening difference, illustrating the extent to which Asian

Americans, even after several generations and over 150 years in the United States, are considered to be perpetually foreign.

Exclusion, Displacement, and Forced Mobility

The thematic of not fitting in or belonging is frequently twinned with that of displacement and forced mobility. If movement and mobility have been prime tropes for freedom and the reinvention of self in mainstream American literature (consider *Adventures of Huckleberry Finn*, for instance), their less positive iterations have been equally important in Asian American literature. Two primary types of narratives may be identified here: those that chronicle the displacement of Asian Americans within the United States and those that recount uprooting from Asian countries of origin, often as a result of U.S. foreign policy. In novels and autobiographical narratives that feature domestic displacement, Japanese American internment is a frequent topic; in fact, the overwhelming majority of—if not all—Japanese American novels deal with the forced removal and relocation during World War II, either directly or indirectly.[3] While the internment obviously involved literal, physical displacement, it also functions as a metaphor for the psychological and social exile experienced by those who had formerly assumed themselves to be a part of America.

Chinese American texts similarly reflect the exclusion or forced mobility of Chinese immigrants over a long history of discrimination, from mid-nineteenth century purges in California, Oregon, and Washington, to numerous exclusion acts that severely restricted immigration, to the semi-forced concentration of Chinese in the ethnic ghettos of Chinatown. Louis Chu's 1961 novel *Eat a Bowl of Tea* takes place in New York's Chinatown, which, through the 1950s was still feeling the effects of the immigration laws that severely limited the immigration of Chinese women, resulting in the so-called bachelor society that characterized much of Chinese America through the 1950s. Chu's novel examines what is at stake for the community when one of the few sons of a Chinatown resident takes a Chinese wife and brings her back to the United States. The enormous pressure on the couple to have children and thus guarantee the perpetuation of the Chinese in America—as well as to enliven the old denizens of Chinatown—results in the main character's impotence, a highly symbolic consequence of a history of exclusion.

Chinese American playwright and polemicist Frank Chin is even more explicit about the effects of forced mobility on contemporary Chinese Americans. For him, Chinatown is nothing more than a bounded ghetto for the Chinese who are then turned into tourist spectacles. Chin is particularly concerned with the ways in which a history of violent erasure through displacement has emasculated Asian American men. For Chin, as well as for other writers like Shawn Wong (*Homebase* 1979), this erasure calls for a claiming of America as homeland and, as the title of Wong's novel suggests, homebase. Chin's strategy for claiming America is to stand squarely in the landscape of an erased history, claiming a space for those who helped found the United States (such as the Chinese men who helped build the Transcontinental Railroad, but who were excluded from the celebratory photograph at Promontory, Utah in 1869). On the other hand, Wong's protagonist, Rainsford Chan, reverses the trope of forced mobility through the motif of a journey that takes him through a series of places that have been significant to the history of Chinese immigrants and, by extension, the United States. Thus, Wong claims America through the very means by which Asian Americans have been excluded from the realm of juridical and cultural citizenship.

In contrast to narratives that concentrate on the history of Asians within the geographic borders of the United States, other Asian American novelists and poets focus on the upheaval of communities and families in Asia as the result of political processes generated by or involving the United States. Some, like Heinz Insu Fenkl's *Memories of My Ghost Brother* (1996) directly invoke the U.S. military presence. Fenkle's autobiographical novel takes place on an army base in Korea, where the mixed-race main character's white American father is based while preparing for operations in Vietnam, and it explores the tensions and intersections between national, racial and cultural identities as they are made legible through the history of the United States' wars in Asia.

The war in Vietnam provides the background for Le Thi Diem Thuy's lyrical exploration of the relationship between memory and trauma. Throughout the fractured narrative, the main character tries to piece together her memories of her and her father's flight from Vietnam, her mother's arrival, and the death that defines both the American present and the Vietnamese past. Through the figure of the narrator's brother and the atemporizing aspects of memory, Le complicates assumptions about linear time, remembrance, and the association of Asia with the ruptured past.

Generational Differences

Often, themes of not belonging are articulated through the framework of generational conflict, specifically between immigrant parents and their American-born children. Asian American literary critics have rightly argued that a strictly generational reading of Asian American literature is reductive because it most often pits a seemingly static Asian past against a supposedly dynamic American present, portrays cultural transmission as unidirectional rather than reciprocal, and implies a teleology that privileges American identity as the endpoint of identificatory progress and proper assimilation.[4]

Even as one recognizes that such conflicts do not fully account for the dynamics represented between characters or completely structure the narrative, however, the thematic of conflict stemming from generational differences is found in many Asian American literary texts. Most often, these differences revolve around language barriers, differing degrees of identification with ethnic cultural practices, and disagreements over behaviors determined to be too Americanized. That is, first-generation immigrant parents may be portrayed as more likely to fraternize with others in their own ethnic group—often due to language and cultural similarities—while their often English-fluent children are portrayed as more welcoming of friendships across ethnic lines, both Asian and non-Asian. Some narratives, such as Monica Sone's *Nisei Daughter* (1953) tend to deploy these differences to comic effect (though this also offsets Sone's account of the hardships of internment).

But here it is important to recognize that generational differences may only provide a site at which the unequal effects of racism become visible. *The Interpreter* (2004) by Suki Kim shows how the main character's Korean immigrant parents must rely on their oldest daughter to act as a translator who mediates between themselves and the dominant culture, thus upsetting the family hierarchy. Additionally, the racism and exclusion the parents face further work to erode their sense of authority and personhood. In an attempt to reestablish authority within the family sphere, the father attempts to exert control over the daughter, who resists what she sees as excessive restrictiveness. To read this as a purely generational conflict narrative, then, would force us to also read this as a standoff between "Korean tradition" and "American assimilation," which is both reductive and inattentive to the subtleties of Kim's novel. What would be missing, among other things, is a recognition of the ways that racism in the public realm structures relations in the private sphere.

A second consequence of a generational reading is that it tends to essentialize "Asian culture" as an inert artifact. Analyses of Maxine Hong Kingston's *The Woman Warrior* (1975) for example, that read the mother-daughter conflict primarily or only through the framework of generational/cultural difference miss the extent to which the Chinese immigrant mother does *not* represent the source for the transmission of a static shrouded-in-the-past Chinese culture to her American daughter. Rather, the mother herself becomes a figure for how Asian Americans might dynamically negotiate the tensions and contradictions both between and within Chinese and American cultures.

Recovering the Past

Generational conflicts often arise around misunderstandings that result from children not understanding or not knowing about their parents' pasts, particularly in their country of origin or during immigration. Thus, many Asian American fictional narratives involve the discovery of a parent's past. While some of these narratives imaginatively reconstruct the parent's past as simply a time prior to immigration, as in the aforementioned *The Woman Warrior*, a great number of others connect the past to the exigencies and circumstances of war: World War II, the Korean War, and the Vietnam War (what many Vietnamese refer to as the American War in Vietnam). In fact, one might say that the United States' various wars with and in Asia are the ground upon which the past is sundered from the present. But it is also through the recapitulation of the local and private effects of war that Asian American children are able to connect with their immigrant parents.

One of the earliest texts of this kind is Japanese Canadian writer Joy Kogawa's novel *Obasan*, which traces the emotional journey of the main character as she goes through the process of learning what happened to her mother. In learning that her mother died as a result of the atomic bomb dropped on Nagasaki, Naomi is able to join the past she has disavowed with the present from which she is emotionally distant. This bridging of past and present is mirrored by the temporal and geographic bridge that joins Hiroshima and the mass relocation/imprisonment of Japanese Canadians. More importantly, Naomi is able to reclaim the lost mother through her understanding that her mother did not abandon her, but rather tried to protect her daughter through a silence that was misread.

Nora Okja Keller's *Comfort Woman* (1997) locates the daughter's subjectivity at the intersection of the mother's past and her desire to leave it behind, and the child's desire to know what is unknown. Because the mother was forced into sexual slavery in the Japanese Imperial Army's comfort stations in Korea—a past she wishes to keep hidden from her daughter—the maternal body functions as the metaphor for shame and its recuperation. Thus, coming into knowledge of the mother's past is inevitably synonymous with learning about an ethnic past that is located in the mother's country of origin.

However, the very possibility of recovering the past and the connection to the parent that is associated with it are problematized in Lan Cao's *Monkey*

Bridge (1997). In that novel, the daughter's ignorance of her mother's past in Vietnam is paired with the daughter's inability to remember a childhood that was marked by displacement, immigration, and resettlement. In surreptitiously trying to find out about the details of her childhood and her mother's past, the daughter inadvertently enacts her mother's desires. That is, Cao reverses the trope whereby the recovery of the past signals the agency of the child who discovers or finds the truth of the past and of the parent. Rather, Cao presents us with a mother who is fully aware of her daughter's search for the past and maneuvers her daughter to find what she wants her to find.

In these, as in many other Asian American novels, the figure of the mother represents the country of origin, the historic or unknown past, and the force of cultural tradition. It is through the connection to the mother that the first-generation children connect to and/or refuse an ethnicized identification with Asia.

Diaspora and Transnationalism

In recent years, issues of global cultural flows, diaspora and transnationalism have become more prominent thematics in Asian American literary production. Although such issues have always been implicit in the literature from its beginnings, contemporary work tends to self-consciously foreground the continuances and overlapping relationships between Asia and the United States. Some texts, such as Jessica Haggedorn's *Dogeaters* (1990) or Teresa Hak-kyung Cha's *Dictee* (1981) explore the transnational through the lens of colonialism and U.S. imperialism. In these texts, global culture is really less a question of cultural hybridity and more one of imposed political conditions and/or cultural commodities.

While diasporic dispersal due to U.S. militarism constitutes a major thematic, as discussed earlier, writers increasingly look to the mobile nature of Asian American experience as a site of both contestation and creativity. Transnational mobility, rather than suggesting immigration's unidirectional crossing of national borders, describes an ongoing relationship with both the United States and the Asian country of origin, a fluid sense of self that is defined by and through mobility rather than through a spatially static identification with a nation-state and culture. Transnational identification also bespeaks a certain refusal to accept an American nationalism that defines itself in relation to literal or conceptual exclusion, or to temporalized narratives that would seal off the Asian past as inert. Rather, such a model assumes a fluid "crossover between Asia and Asian America" that posits a continuance between the two, rather than a bifurcation that leads to a split self in perpetual conflict (Cheung 9).

Contemporary Directions

It is important to stress that inasmuch as the body of Asian American and Asian Canadian literatures includes the representation of hardships and difficulties, also represented are communities' ways of being, strategies of negotiation, and ability to thrive in ways that show how Asian Americans are subjects in their own lives, not simply objects of external circumstance or legislation. One of the primary avenues through which communities assert their sense of selfhood is through cultural practice. Thus, if one theme in Asian American literature is cultural conflict, its companion theme is cultural hybridity and improvisation. Often, in poetry and novels, autobiographies and plays, one will find examples of linguistic blending, culinary improvisation that puts non-Asian foods to Asian uses (or vice versa), celebrations of holidays that combine Asian tradition with the American context, and so on. In fiction written for younger audiences, it is often the case that an object, practice or belief emerges as centrally important to the main character's sense of self or becomes the means through which some situation is resolved. In such cases, we see adaptation and the recontextualizing of mobile and dynamic cultural practices, rather than inert and static "ethnic habits" marking an orientalized past.

This open and fluid sense of Asian American identity creates new spaces for creativity and cultural hybridities: young Japanese Americans have adapted traditional forms of taiko drumming to the American rhythms of jazz and other musical forms of the Americas, Korean American poets interrupt and fragment lyric forms to reflect the displacement and rupture of colonialism and immigration, South Asians rap to the rhythms of hip-hop laced through with bhangra beats. These new forms and formations are analogues for new models of Asian American identities as Asian America continues to shift and change in response to globalization and transnationalization, and to its various histories and heterogeneous communities.

Over the past decade, Asian American literature has become increasingly complex in its thematics and more formally experimental, and much of this is the result of the greater diversity of writers bringing their voices, aesthetics, and experiences into the literary realm: Southeast Asians and Pacific Islanders, gays and lesbians, Korean and Chinese adoptees, multiracial Asian Americans, those born after 1970 or outside the United States, and those whose primary art lies in other fields. These writers, however, do not simply enrich the field through more inclusive representation; rather, they expand and layer our understanding of what Asian American—and, more generally, American—literature is and can be.

Notes

1. See, for instance, *Asian North American Identities: Beyond the Hyphen*, Eleanor Rose Ty and Donald C. Goellnicht, eds. and *Premonitions: The Kaya Anthology of New Asian North American Poetry*, edited by Walter K. Lew.
2. The Immigration Act of 1924, which included the National Origins Act and the Asian Exclusion Act, limited immigration to 2% of the number of those from a given country who were already living in the United States in the year 1890.
3. In addition to Kogawa's *Obasan*, see for example also John Okada's *No-No Boy*, Jeanne Wakatsuki Houston's *Farewell to Manzanar*, and Julie Otsuka's *When the Emperor Was Divine*.
4. See Lisa Lowe.

Works Cited

Cao, Lan. *Monkey Bridge*. New York: Viking Press, 1997.

Cha, Teresa Hak-kyung. *Dictee*. 1981. Berkeley: Third Woman Press, 1995.

Cheung, King-kok. "Re-Viewing Asian American Literary Studies," editor's introduction. In *An Interethnic Companion to Asian American Literature*. Cambridge: Cambridge UP, 1997.

Chu, Louis. *Eat a Bowl of Tea*. 1961. New York: Lyle Stuart, 1990.

Espiritu, Yen-Le. *Asian American Panethnicity: Bridging Institutions and Identities*. Philadelphia: Temple UP, 1992.

Fenkl, Heinz Insu. *Memories of My Ghost Brother*. New York: Dutton, 1996.

Haggedorn, Jessica. *Dogeaters*. New York: Pantheon Books, 1990.

Houston, Jeanne Wakatsuki. *Farewell to Manzanar*. New York: Bantam Books, 1973.

Keller, Nora Okja. *Comfort Woman*. New York: Viking Press, 1997.

Kim, Ronyoung. *Clay Walls*. Seattle: University of Washington Press, 1987.

Kim, Suki. *The Interpreter*. New York: Farrar, Straus and Giroux, 2003.

Kingston, Maxine Hong. *The Woman Warrior: Memoirs of a Girlhood among Ghosts*. 1975. New York: Vintage, 1989.

Kogawa, Joy. *Obasan*. 1981. New York: Anchor, 1993.

Lai, Larissa. *When Fox Is a Thousand*. 1995. Vancouver: Arsenal Pulp Press, 2004.

Lê, Thúy Diem Thi. *The Gangster We Are All Looking For*. New York: Knopf, 2003.

Lee, Chang-rae. *Native Speaker*. New York: Riverhead Books, 1995.

Lew, Walter K. *Premonitions: The Kaya Anthology of New Asian North American Poetry*. New York: Kaya Production, 1995.

Lim, Shirley Geok-lin. "Feminist and Ethnic Literary Theories in Asian American Literature." *Feminisms: An Anthology of Literary History and Criticism*, 2nd edition. Eds. Robyn R. Warhol and Diane Price Herndl. New Brunswick: Rutgers UP, 1997. 807–26.

Lowe, Lisa. *Immigrant Acts: On Asian American Culture Politics*. Durham: Duke UP, 1996.

Okada, John. *No-No Boy*. 1957. Seattle: U of Washington P, 1976.

Otsuka, Julie. *When the Emperor was Divine*. New York: Viking Press, 2003.

Sone, Monica. *Nisei Daughter*. 1953. Seattle: U of Washington P, 1979.

Ty, Eleanor Rose, and Donald C. Goellnicht, eds. *Asian North American Identities: Beyond the Hyphen*. Bloomington: Indiana UP, 2004.

Wong, Shawn. *Homebase*. 1979. New York: Plume, 1991.

Yamanaka, Lois-Ann. *Blu's Hanging*. New York: Farrar, Straus and Giroux, 1997.

CHAPTER 12

Acts of "Desicreation": Urban Space and South Asian American Identity in Tanuja Desai Hidier's *Born Confused*

Melinda L. de Jesús

Saris, *mendhi*, and *bindi*[1]—pop-culture icons Madonna and Gwen Stefani transformed these aspects of traditional Indian women's culture into edgy, mainstream fashions available to all in trendy stores like Urban Outfitters and Target.[2] But does mainstream America know any more about South Asian Americans beyond the character "Apu," the convenience store owner on "The Simpsons"? According to the U.S. Census, South Asian Americans comprise 1.9 million of the 13.1 million Asian Americans in the United States today.[3] South Asian communities have existed in the United States since the nineteenth century,[4] yet despite being the third largest Asian ethnic group in the United States (behind Chinese and Filipino Americans, respectively),[5] South Asian Americans are largely invisible to mainstream America and are marginalized within current constructions of contemporary Asian America itself. Indeed, the rash of hate crimes that this community experienced—particularly Sikh Americans—post-9/11 clearly demonstrate how little the United States knows about the South Asian American.[6] Stereotyped as "model minorities," "unassimilable aliens," and now terrorist threats, South Asian Americans remain simultaneously invisible yet hypervisible.[7] Not surprisingly, South Asian American representation in contemporary children's literature reflects these same realities.

The State of South Asian American Children's Literature

While there are many children's books available that retell Indian folktales, there are very few books about the contemporary experiences of *desi* (second-generation

South Asian American) children and youth: Uma Krishnaswami's *Chachaji's Cup* (2003) is the first picture book, and *Born Confused* (2003) is the first young adult novel. This is ironic when we consider the fact that the 1928 Newbery Medal was awarded to South Asian author Dhan Gopal Mukerji for *Gay-Neck, Story of a Pigeon* (Krishnaswami 24). Given this reality, Dolores de Manuel and Rocio G. Davis' recent overview of Asian American children's literature criticism is imbued with an even greater sense of urgency: "Asian American children's literature, far more than a 'lite,' miniaturized version of the larger issues in ethnic literature, must be read as a multilayered and nuanced attempt to establish the place of Asian American writers for children in American culture, and to creatively engage their marginal positioning" (vi). Indeed, as I have written elsewhere, we have yet to see a significant body of young adult fiction and critical theory by and about Asian Americans.[8] Some young adult books purport to be about Asian American youths yet merely employ shallow, stereotypical renderings of Asians, thus serving to promulgate or maintain racist ideology, ironically, in the name of multiculturalism (Kate Emberg's *The Language of Love* is a particularly heinous example). Certainly established writers like Laurence Yep, Yoshiko Uchida, and Marie G. Lee, along with recent standouts An Na (*A Step from Heaven*) and Cynthia Kadohata (*Kira-Kira*), have done much to put Asian American young adult fiction on the map, yet these same writers represent the continuing hegemony of the "big three" of Asian American ethnic groups—Chinese, Japanese, and Korean American—which continue to dominate conceptions of both Asian America itself and its cultural representations. Like Filipino Americans and Southeast Asian Americans, South Asian Americans are underrepresented in mainstream children's literature and marginalized within constructions of Asian American writing. This reality is further compounded by the fact that very few children's books marketed each year (contrary to assumptions about the pervasive presence of multicultural literature today) reflect the cultures and realities of contemporary Asian Americans. For example, in a telling recent study, J. Marin Younker and Sarah M. Webb found that of the 241 young adult titles listed as the Young Adult Library Services Association's "Quick Picks for Reluctant Young Adult Readers" and "Best Books for Young Adults" in 2000–2005, only 57 included "teen minority characters." Thirty of these books had a minority main character, yet only 5 (or 17 percent) were Asian Americans (198). The authors also critiqued the stereotyping of Latino and Asian characters as immigrants or children of immigrants, and the description of all teens of color as overly involved in poverty, crime, drugs, or teen pregnancy (197).[9]

Tanuja Desai Hidier's stunning first young adult novel, *Born Confused* (Scholastic/Push 2002), selected as one of the 2003 American Library Association's "Best Books for Young Adults," is a terrific antidote to this marginalization and stereotyping. Offering readers a well-written, humorous, and compelling story of a South Asian American young woman's coming of age, the novel chronicles protagonist Dimple Lala's tumultuous summer between junior and senior year. A suburban New Jersey "ABCD" (American Born Confused Desi), Dimple begins the novel wholly uncomfortable in her "Indian-ness," always in the shadow of her childhood best friend and confidante, blond-haired, blue-eyed beauty queen Gwyn Sexton. Desai Hidier's novel chronicles how these two very opposite characters evolve as young women, and how their friendship must change to meet the new challenges presented by identity, family, and boyfriend issues.

Born Confused is characterized by its distinctive narrative voice and humor. Narrator Dimple's aspirations as a photographer are clearly signaled through the novel's vivid imagery replete with evocative descriptions rich in sensory detail. And unlike more sanitized Asian American young adult fiction by Marie Lee and Lensey Namioka, for example, *Born Confused* includes some very funny and achingly accurate, striking scenes of adolescent drama/angst, all told in protagonist Dimple's formidably witty and sometimes sarcastic, perceptive voice. Singlehandedly shattering stereotypes of Asians as straightedge nerds, for example, Desai Hidier shows Dimple getting drunk and puking on her first date, and later has Dimple hallucinating while smoking pot for the first time, then coming home high and devouring Indian food in a fit of munchies. Other surprisingly funny scenes include Dimple's mother's ranting after Dimple's cousin Kavita's heart is broken by her girlfriend: "The story of love between women in India is nothing new, she added shrugging. It is an age old saga. But love between women in New Jersey? That is taking a little getting used to" (376–77); as well as the hilarious send-up of impenetrable postcolonial academic discourse in the scene where Dimple and Gwyn attend the NYU South Asian identity conference (293).

Moreover, as I've argued elsewhere, the Asian American young adult novel is most often characterized by a specific interracial love triangle where an Asian American girl must choose between a white boyfriend or an Asian American one; she usually goes for the white boy.[10] In *Born Confused*, the triangle is reversed: here Dimple and Gwyn fight for the affections of "suitable boy" Karsh Kapoor, a New York University student and famous bhangra remix[11] deejay, "Gulab Jammin."[12] Yet beyond this somewhat formulaic plot (coming of age, heterosexual romance) *Born Confused* is an anomaly: its writing is engaging and witty, its characterizations are complex and believable, and its introduction to contemporary South Asian American culture—especially desi youth culture—is an important representation in multicultural young adult fiction.[13] As one of the first examples of children's literature to focus on South Asian American contemporary life,[14] *Born Confused* refutes the invisibility and marginalization of South Asians in both mainstream American and Asian American discourse while it celebrates and also models for us the possibilities inherent in contemporary South Asian American cultural production. Below I explore the complex relationship between urban space and South Asian American identity presented in the novel and discuss the contribution of *Born Confused* to the genres of Asian American and multicultural young adult fiction.

Acts of Desicreation, or South Asian American Identity and Urban Space

> The question of hybridity is doubly complicated for desi youth in New York, for they are reworking hip-hop not only into their own youth culture but into a *remix* youth culture, one that expresses the cultural imaginaries of second-generation youth from an immigrant community of color. Fundamentally desi youth turn to hip-hop because it is key to marking their belonging in the multiethnic urban landscape of New York City. (Maira 58)

Ethnic young adult novels, like most coming of age stories, explore the protagonist's identity development; in *Born Confused*, the author makes a unique choice in presenting Dimple's struggles with her racial and gender identity issues: Desai Hidier continually juxtaposes urban and suburban settings as polarized spaces of possibility and limitation. In this way the author integrally links urban space to South Asian American identity and to "desicreation"—the creation of hybrid identities and cultures—and thus advances the concept of Asian American art as "cultural fusion" through its invocation of different forms of desicreation.[15] Beyond the author's use of the term initially as the name of the social event where Dimple is first exposed to New York City's burgeoning desi community and youth culture, desicreation refers to the creation of hybrid desi identities (for example, the characters of Dimple, Karsh, Kavita, and Zara) as well as desi cultural production: Karsh's deejaying bhangra remix, Dimple's photography, Trilok "Jimmy" Singh's break dancing (and *Born Confused* itself). Moreover, desicreation should be understood as a state of mind: it enables Dimple to break out of her own self-loathing and self-limitations and embrace her hybrid identity as an ABCD, and to trust her instincts as an artist.

For example, Dimple's *acts of desicreation* are shown through Tanuja Desai Hidier's specific juxtaposition of urban and suburban spaces in this novel. Broadly, for Dimple suburban New Jersey represents "Generica"—Generic

America—the space of limitation, anxiety, and whitewashing, while New York City represents a vibrant space for Dimple's growth as an artist and a woman coming to terms with being an ABCD. When the novel begins, Dimple is only comfortable behind her camera nicknamed "Chica Tikka," working her darkroom, alone, or hiding in the shadow of Gwyn. She is not sure where she belongs or who she is: "So not quite Indian, and not quite American. Usually I felt more along the lines of Alien (however legal, as my Jersey birth certificate attests to) . . . Sometimes I was too Indian in America, but in India I was definitely not Indian enough" (13). In these early scenes Desai Hidier specifically uses the suburban New Jersey mall as the location for scenes of Dimple's identity angst and humiliation. The mall represents American consumerism at its whitest, and it is in this location that Dimple has her breakdown in the dressing room of the store named "Style Child" because she cannot fit her brown body into any of the tiny clothes that she desires (those that Gwyn wears). Beyond the typical coming of age novel's depiction of the female adolescent's trauma in dealing with her developing body, this scene searingly encapsulates Dimple's intense self-loathing and anger at her bodily difference from her white New Jersey peers—she wants to fit into white America, be like Gwyn. Indeed this same mall is the site of Dimple's disastrous first and only date with Julian, where she, dressed exactly like Gwyn in an ill-fitting "Style Child" outfit, and flashing a new fake ID, drinks too much in an effort to fit in and ends up barfing, humiliated, in the movie theater bathroom. Finally, the mall is the setting for Dimple's show down with Gwyn over Karsh and what appears to be the ending of the girls' long friendship.

In contrast, Desai Hidier employs the urban landscape of New York City to signify the space of possibility that enables Dimple to break free of her own internal colonization, alienation, and isolation: New York City itself becomes the site of possibility, of hybridity, the catalyst for new identities and ways of seeing. For example, when Dimple first goes to Manhattan to attend the "Desicreation" dance at the Hotpot at the insistence of her cousin Kavita, she suddenly realizes that there are many other South Asians, and a new South Asian culture and scene she had no idea existed:

> But upon a closer sidelong glance I realized this was a breed of Indian I had never seen before in my life . . . these other girls. . . . were studded and salvar'd and pleathered and nose-ringed to the max themselves . . . These were definitely not the aunties. Where had they been hiding all this time? These Indians who looked somewhat present in the twenty-first century? Why hadn't I seen them at Garbha and Diwali parties and the occasional wedding? Or had I—and they'd been disguised in those contexts as I'd been? (187–88)

Here Dimple finds comfort in being among others like herself—she finally fits in:

> It was a strange revelation to be brown among the brown. Sure, it had happened in social situations with relatives and family friends, but on those occasions it still seemed we were a tiny ghee-burning coconut-breaking minority tucked away in someone's kitchen while the whole white world went on outside. And even in those instances I had never felt like my world was necessarily the one inside . . . But here it could be different. This was New York City and the new century; these people were not my relatives and the chicas wore cool shoes . . . (195)

Moreover, during this dance Dimple first encounters her artistic muse, the transgendered Zara Thrustra, and also learns that Karsh, whom she initially dismissed as a nerdy son of her parents' old friends, happens to be the hot deejay, Gulab Jammin, whose music defined "Desicreation" and inspired her own photography during the event. Following these encounters, Dimple questions her assumptions about her culture and identity and begins to understand what it really means to be ABCD.

Indeed, later in the novel, while attending the NYU conference on South Asian identities, Dimple, who had been preparing for the event through a crash course in Indian history and mythology in order to impress Karsh, begins to understand how South Asian identity is forever changing, and is created in the moment: "a history of a people in transit—what could that be card catalogued under? And the history of the ABCD. . . . [T]he way these people were talking . . . was hummingly sculpting the air, as if they were making history as they spoke. Making it, messily but surely, even simply by speaking. I was feeling it too—a sense of history in the making" (297). It is no accident that soon after this realization, Dimple finally understands that Zara is male and that her cousin Kavita is a lesbian. Desai Hidier offers these characters as important foils for Dimple—models of ABCDs who push past racial, gendered, and sexual stereotypes and create their own realities.

The most important scene happens near the novel's end when Dimple, usually so shy, summons her courage and vision and walks out into the evening, capturing with Chica Tikka the city's transformation from dusk to night to daybreak. Thus New York City itself becomes the backdrop for and the subject of Dimple's moment of self-actualization as a young woman of color and a budding artist: her process of "becoming" is signified in her solo trip through the city to photograph its turning from day into night. The pictures become her chronicle of her own transformation into an adult and an artist—alone with her camera, following her heart and her artistic impulses, unafraid, she performs multiple acts of desicreation and transforms herself into one who defines the image and the representation. These sections of *Born Confused* read like a love letter to the city itself:

> When I left Kavita's the sun was running down and I followed it only to lose it, then come upon it again on Spring Street, a block from the river. Buildings flushed like blood just before it breaks through the skin; the cobblestones distinguished themselves, thinly iced cupcake flowers tinkering together with an almost audible echo. In the near distance the water went steely pink with the great fire nesting over it, the burning ball of flame that always seemed so much nearer when it fell in New York's choppy sky than from the uncharted heights of New Jersey, as if there weren't really that much distance between us, as if there really wasn't that far to fall. (435)

As the evening ends, Dimple finds Zara waiting tables at the restaurant BNBB, and then photographs her transformation from waiter, to Indian goddess and back again. Initially, the naive Dimple aspired to be Zara: "The woman was the image of all the grace and femininity I longed for—but with the silver lining of being, in a way, within reach" (202). This early scene is ironic and humorous, for the savvy reader understood immediately that Zara, Dimple's ideal of womanhood, was biologically male. But what Dimple finally learns from Zara in this powerful scene is that one controls her own image/identity instead of letting others define it for her: "Believe it or not, Dimple, I am just a regular person who has decided to be who I am in life. That's all. That's how you make your life magical—you take yourself into your own hands and rub a little. You activate your identity. And that's the only way to make, as they say, the world a better place; after all what good are you to anyone without yourself?" (442). In sum, *Born Confused* may be read as a homage to desi culture and identity, and to New York City itself. Here the city represents a locus of possibility, of new identities, and change—it enables new ways of seeing and being. Indeed the novel's narrative itself is very visual because it seeks to represent in language what Dimple's eyes see through her camera. Likewise, the novel is replete with sections on ways of seeing and reseeing, ways of being: Kavita, Karsh, Gwyn, and even her parents help Dimple to embrace her ABCD self and her art; and Dimple learns to "resee" her relationships with and understandings of them in turn.

Conclusion

Critics Dolores De Manuel and Rocio G. Davis assert that "The mission of establishing Asian American children's literature as a central part of the American literary consciousness is still far from complete" and note the need for further study on the literature of "ethnic groups like South Asians" (xii); *Born Confused* provides a terrific starting point for both of these endeavors. At first glance, the novel reads as an ABCD Cinderella story: unbeknownst to Dimple, Gwyn, from whom she is estranged, and Karsh arrange for Dimple's photos of Zara to be the centerpiece of the *FUSE* magazine launch—and an artist is born. Dimple "gets" Karsh, regains Gwyn's friendship, and Gwyn "gets" Trilok "Jimmy" Singh. In the simplistic world of the young adult heterosexual romance, Dimple has attained the prize—a boyfriend. But *Born Confused* goes much further than this conventional, heterosexist plot. Dimple's hard-won appreciation for herself, her friends, her family, and her culture, not just her winning Karsh, signal her growth into adulthood: rather than rejecting her Indianness, she uses her ABCD realities to create a new way of being. In this way, *Born Confused* signifies a reaffirmation of the Asian American vision of cultural fusion—creating your own way to be both Asian and American—as well as an important contribution to the field of Asian American feminist studies.[16]

Moreover, *Born Confused* is an important contribution to ethnic young adult fiction for the following reasons: (1) its vibrant evocation of desi culture piques readers' interest about contemporary South Asian American culture (like bhangra remix), while providing a glimpse into the struggles and aspirations of young South Asian Americans today; (2) it presents a uniquely drawn portrait of a strong female protagonist and a detailed rendering of contemporary Asian American young womanhood from a marginalized Asian ethnic group; and (3) its unique narrative voice and themes render it a strong contribution to the field of Asian American literature itself.

In "The Power of Culture" Lisa Lowe writes: "Alternative cultural forms and practices do not offer havens of resolution but are rather often eloquent descriptions of the ways in which the law, labor exploitation, racialization, and gendering work to prohibit alternatives. Some cultural forms succeed in making it possible to live and inhabit alternatives in the encounter with those prohibitions; some permit us to imagine what we have still yet to live" (19). Clearly *Born Confused* fulfills both of Lowe's criteria for "alternative cultural forms": as a portrait of the artist as an ABCD teen from the Jersey suburbs, this artist novel and coming of age story is an important celebration of the struggle for Asian American cultural fusion while simultaneously signifying, beyond mass marketed *mendhi* and *bindhi* kits, the complexity and vibrancy of desi youth culture unfolding in the twenty-first century.

Notes

1. *Mendhi* is a temporary skin decoration made with henna; *bindi* is a forehead decoration.

2. See Sunaina Maira's "Henna and Hip Hop: The Politics of Cultural Production and the Work of Cultural Studies" for a savvy critique of this phenomenon.
3. Facts for Features: Asian Pacific American Heritage Month, May 2004 http://www.census.gov/Press-Release/www/releases/archives/facts_for_features_special_editions/001738.html.
4. Ronald Takaki discusses this history in "'The Tide of Turbans': Asian Indians in America," Chapter 8 in his *Strangers from a Different Shore: A History of Asian Americans* (1998).
5. See the following for current demographic statistics for Asian Americans today: Table 4, The Asian Population, Census 2000 Brief (February 2002), U.S. Census Bureau, http://www.census.gov/prod/2002pubs/c2kbr01-16.pdf.
6. Nazli Kibria writes: "The contemporary racialization of South Asian Americans is . . . being shaped by the rise, as the twenty-first century begins, in hate crimes and other expressions of hostility against South Asian Americans. Against the backdrop of a more general surge of anti-immigrant sentiment and legislation . . . job losses in the U.S. economy have been blamed on the out-sourcing of jobs to India as well as the influx of technically skilled H-1B workers from India. Hostility toward South Asian Americans has also risen in the aftermath of the 9/11 terrorist attacks on the United States. The National Asian Pacific American Legal Consortium (2001) reports that in the 3-month period following the September 11 attacks, there were nearly 250 bias-motivated incidents and two murders targeting Asian Pacific Americans. South Asian Americans, regardless of national origin or religion, have been specifically targeted on the basis of their perceived physical resemblance to and affinity with the terrorists. This has been especially the case for Sikh Americans" (216).
7. See Nazli Kibria's discussion of South Asian Americans and "racial marginalization" (215).
8. See "Two's Company, Three's a Crowd? Reading Interracial (Heterosexual) Romance in Contemporary Asian American Young Adult Fiction" and "Mixed Blessings: Korean American Identity and Interracial Interactions in the Young Adult Novels of Marie G. Lee."
9. Younker and Webb write: "Why is it that teen fiction featuring white characters portrays a range of experiences, but multicultural teen fiction doesn't? . . . we have noticed that many tend to focus on crime, teen pregnancy, drugs, immigration, and/or poverty, reinforcing stereotypes for both minority and non-minority teen readers" (197).
10. de Jesús, Melinda L. "Two's Company, Three's a Crowd? Reading Interracial (Heterosexual) Romance in Contemporary Asian American Young Adult Fiction."
11. Sunaina Marr Maira in the seminal *Desis in the House: Indian American Youth Culture in New York City* defines bhangra remix music as "Indian folk music mixed with American dance music and produced by Indian American deejays for dance parties held at clubs, restaurants, or college campuses" (12).

12. "Gulab Jammin" is pun on the sweet Indian dessert, *gulab jamun.*

13. Maira writes: "These second generation youth have collectively created a new culture, based on dance parties and music mixes, that is as much a part of New York—and also global—club culture as it is of a transnational South Asian public culture. They have crossed national boundaries to identify collectively as "desi," a colloquial term for someone "native" to South Asia, and one that has taken hold among many second-generation youth in the diaspora of Indian, Pakistani, Bangladeshi, Sri Lankan, or even Indo-Caribbean, descent" (2). See Maira's book for an exploration of desi youth culture and the bhangra remix phenomenon.

14. Uma Krishnaswami's *Chachaji's Cup* (2003) is the first picture book about contemporary Indian American life. See her article, "On the Seashore of Worlds: Selected South Asian Voices from North America and the United Kingdom," for a discussion of the state of South Asian children's literature in English.

15. "Cultural fusion" refers to art that is specifically *both* Asian and American. Yen Le Espiritu characterizes Asian American art as "cultural resistance," productions which "perform the important tasks of correcting histories, shaping legacies, creating new cultures, constructing a politics of resistance and opening spaces for the forcibly excluded" (98).

16. The field of Asian American women's studies has developed greatly in the last 20 years, and is marked by its commitment to represent the diversity inherent within Asian American feminist thought. South Asian American feminist writers contributed to the landmark anthologies about Asian American women, *Making Waves* (1989) and *Making More Waves* (1997), as well as the seminal *Our Feet Walk the Sky: Women of the South Asia Diaspora* (1993) and *Dragon Ladies: Asian American Feminists Breathe Fire* (1999), the third wave feminist volume *Colonize This: Young Women of Color on Today's Feminism* (2002), and the important girls' studies anthology, "YELL-Oh Girls! Emerging Voices Explore Culture, Identity, and Growing Up Asian American."

Works Cited

de Jesús, Melinda L. "Mixed Blessings: Korean American Identity and Interracial Interactions in the Young Adult Novels of Marie G. Lee." *Children's Literature Association Quarterly* 28.2 (2003): 98–109.

———. "Two's Company, Three's a Crowd? Reading Interracial (Heterosexual) Romance in Contemporary Asian American Young Adult Fiction." *LIT: Literature, Interpretation, Theory* 12 (2001): 313–34.

De Manuel, Dolores, and Davis, Rocio G. "Editor's Introduction: Critical Perspectives on Asian American Children's Literature." *Lion and the Unicorn* 30.2 (2006): v–xv.

Desai Hidier, Tanuja. *Born Confused.* New York: Push/Scholastic, 2003.

Emberg, Katherine. *The Language of Love.* New York: Bantam, 1996.

Espiritu, Yen Le. *Asian American Women and Men: Labor, Laws,and Love*. Thousand Oaks: Sage, 1997.

Hernandez, Daisy, and Bushra Rehman, eds. *Colonize This! Young Women of Color on Today's Feminism*. New York: Seal Press, 2002.

Kadohata, Cynthia. *Kira-kira*. New York: Atheneum, 2004.

Kibria, Nazli. "South Asian Americans." *Asian Americans: Contemporary Trends and Issues*. Ed. Pyong Gap Min. 2nd ed. Thousand Oaks: Pine Forge/Sage, 2006. 206-27.

Kim, Elaine H., Lilia V. Villanueva, and Asian Women United of California, eds. *Making Waves: An Anthology by and about Asian American Women*. Boston: Beacon Press, 1989.

———. *Making More Waves: New Writing by Asian American Women*. Boston: Beacon Press, 1997.

Krishnaswami, Uma. *Chachaji's Cup*. San Francisco: Children's Book Press, 2003.

———. "On the Seashore of Worlds: Selected South Asian Voices from North America and the United Kingdom." *Bookbird* 42.2 (2004): 24–30.

Lowe, Lisa. "The Power of Culture." *Journal of Asian American Studies* 1.1 (1998): 5–29.

Maira, Sunaina Marr. *Desis in the House: Indian American Youth Culture in New York City*. Philadelphia: Temple UP, 2002.

———. "Henna and Hip Hop: The Politics of Cultural Production and the Work of Cultural Studies." *Journal of Asian American Studies* 3.3 (2000): 329–69.

Na, An. *A Step from Heaven*. New York: Puffin, 2003.

Nam, Vickie, ed. *YELL-Oh Girls! Emerging Voices Explore Culture, Identity, and Growing Up Asian American*. New York: Harper, 2001.

Takaki, Ronald. *Strangers from A Different Shore: A History of Asian Americans*. 2nd ed. Boston: Back Bay Books, 1998.

Women of South Asian Descent Collective, eds. *Our Feet Walk the Sky: Women of the South Asian Diaspora*. San Francisco: Aunt Lute, 1993.

Younker, J. Marin, and Sarah M. Webb. "Mind the Gap: What's Missing in Realistic Teen Fiction about Minorities." *Voice Youth Advocates* 28.3 (2005): 197–201.

CHAPTER 13

Examining History: Representing War in Asian American Autobiographies for Children

Rocío G. Davis

In the context of perspectives that acknowledge how children's literature creates and develops cultural memory, autobiographical writing for children arguably plays a crucial role in promoting critical views on history and society. As a cultural product, autobiographical writing for children is an independent but interdependent literary artifact, and an analysis of Asian American life writing for children expands the paradigms of research in Asian American autobiography. Children's literature, more-over, is evaluated by a multiple audience, which includes adults involved in education—teachers and librarians—as well as parents who supervise their children's reading. As such, this literature "becomes a particularly intense site of ideological and political contest, for various groups of adults struggle over which versions of ethnic identity will become institutionalized in school, home, and library settings" (Smith 3). An Asian American author who writes autobiography for children gestures toward a necessary nuancing of the implications of life writing within the context of identity formation, and reconfigures the genre of autobiography with insurgent possibilities.

Asian American children's literature highlights the meaning or value that society attributes to history, national and ethnic affiliation, intercultural relationships, and how groups occupy or influence the places they are in and the communities they form. The target audiences of these texts— "mainstream" and "ethnic" children—are addressed in doubled ways. Children from dominant groups would learn about other histories and cultures while Asian American children would be encouraged by the authors to resist "pejorative categorizations by asking the reader to reimagine herself, to identify herself with the text's cultural models"; readers from other ethnic groups would be encouraged to overcome prejudice and stereotypes through cross-cultural understanding (Smith 4). For writers today, issues of history, heritage, peer communities—cultural and scholastic—and strategies of self-formation are harnessed as impetus for their child readers' processes of empowerment and agency. As Carole Carpenter argues, the most successful children's books reject the assumption that children are merely receivers of culture, presenting them as "creative manipulators of a dynamic network of concepts, actions, feelings, and products that mirror and mould their experience as children" (57).

Nonetheless, when the network of concepts involves ethnic appreciation and understanding, autobiographical texts play an operative role in articulating the context within which children can engage in significant processes of self-awareness and self-formation. The evolution of recent ethnic autobiography for children has been toward historical realism and intercultural narratives that emphasize the varied cultural influences a child growing up in the United States experiences. This new historicism in children's literature, according to Mitzi Myers, helps "integrate text and sociohistoric context, demonstrating on the one hand how extraliterary cultural formations shape literary discourse and on the other how literary practices are actions that make things happen—by shaping the psychic and moral consciousness of young readers but also by performing many more diverse kinds of cultural work, from satisfying authorial fantasies to legitimating or subverting dominant class and gender ideologies" (42). Many of these texts, for example, focus on historical events that are not taught or transmitted in American school curricula and are therefore in danger of being lost to these children. By incorporating historical information into autobiographies of childhood, writers not only present the facts of history in ways that encourage identification and understanding, but offer all American children a way of looking at the past. The potent issue of authenticity in life writing therefore endorses "the didactic imperatives both embedded in the texts and imposed contextually by adult arbiters" (Smith 6). Discursively, the increasing number of texts about Asian or Asian American children entitles them to claim a space for themselves in America's own history and in its stories about its children. In this paper, I will contextualize autobiographies for children about war and upheavals in Asia, specifically Huynh Quang Nhuong's *Land I Lost*, Jiang Ji-Li's *Red Scarf Girl*, Da Chen's *China's Son*, Yoko Kawashima Watkins's two-volume account of her childhood in Korea and Japan, and Sook Nyul Choi's autobiographical/historical trilogy *Year of Impossible Goodbyes*, *Echoes of the White Giraffe*, and *Gathering of Pearls*, as texts that present a revisionary range of possibilities for child readers, as they become more intelligently aware of what it means to be Asian or of Asian descent in the United States.[1] Specifically, these autobiographical texts center on the experience of war or civil upheavals in the twentieth century from the Asian perspective, which interrogates uncritical versions of Asian history and immigrant histories.

In autobiographical accounts of Asian countries destroyed by war, writers offer their child readers views that generally contrast with uncritical American opinions about those countries. Though war stories in the adventure mold have shifted to focus on a more realistic and personalized treatment of war, "the domestic repercussions of evacuation, family separation, persecution, and the dangers and readjustments of a refugee existence have dominated children's literature on the subject" (Lathey 65).[2] In all the books considered, the authors foreground family events against the background of bellicose conflict. The drama of war leads to family loss and separation, which ultimately provokes crises in the protagonists. As Gillian Lathey points out, "The potential or actual fragmentation of the family is central to an interpretation of war from the child's point of view. Political information reaches children in piecemeal fashion in many Second World War texts, but overheard snatches of radio broadcasts or worried conversations between adults are brought into sharp focus by the impending departure of the father, or plans for evacuation of a journey into exile" (66). This doubled representation allows writers to reflect simultaneously on personal experience and evolving perspectives on national affiliations and/or configurations. The subjects represented are therefore individuals who are also members of communities and citizens of countries.

The texts I will discuss illustrate these points in diverse ways. Huynh Quang Nhoung's idyllic account of his childhood in Vietnam, *The Land I Lost*, is marked by nostalgia for a lost time and place. The separate but interrelated stories about growing up in a hamlet in the central highlands of Vietnam focus on discrete memories of his childhood adventures with animals—particularly his water buffalo, Tank—his family, and friends. The stories are often idealized, in compliance with the nature of memories of a lost time and place, even when recounting episodes of real danger from menacing animals. Aimed at an audience of young children, Huynh's book blends pathos and humor, as in the story about his opera-loving, karate-expert grandmother who saved her family from bandits. He also recounts the danger in the fauna of the region—monkeys, snakes, crocodiles—his Huckleberry Finn-type escapades with his cousin, as he blends local legend and folktales in with his remembrance of their life. By setting his stories in approximately an entire year's cycle—the summer, the rainy season—Huynh offers an engaging portrait of a childhood in rural Vietnam as well as explains the way the seasons evolve in that country.

This portrayal locates the protagonist in a setting that validates a peaceful Vietnam for the American child readers whose only idea of that country might arise from stories about the Vietnam War. By focusing on the landscape, the myths, the customs, and traditions, and recounting them with humor, Huynh offers readers a vision of a prewar country, where peace prevailed and children played. At the end of the narrative, by introducing the terrible consequences of the war, the author alludes to the historical circumstances that led to the massive immigration out of the country. In the introduction, the author says that he "planned to return to my hamlet to live the rest of my life there. But war disrupted my dreams. The land I love was lost to me forever" (xi). Huynh's perspective on his country radically differs from that of most American readers whose only image of Vietnam might be that of a country riddled with strife and from where one must escape. His nostalgia serves an important didactic purpose: as the author captures a lost past, it offers child readers another perspective on Vietnamese refugees and immigrants, victims of war, who continue to long for the country they were forced to leave behind.

Two other autobiographies that center on life in Asia are Ji-Li Jiang and Da Chen's accounts of China's Cultural Revolution. Both Jiang and Chen are children of landowning families, which condemns them to being despised by their neighbors, schoolmates, teachers, and community leaders. Jiang's *Red Scarf Girl: A Memoir of the Cultural Revolution* traces her trajectory of self-awareness as she learns the real meaning and consequences of the Cultural Revolution. Her narrative opens with her description of life before the Cultural Revolution: "I was happy because I was always loved and respected. I was proud because I was able to excel and always expected to succeed. I was trusting, too. I never doubted what I was told: 'Heaven and earth are great, but greater still is the kindness of the Communist Party; father and mother are dear, but dearer still is Chairman Mao'" (1). The Cultural Revolution begins when she is 12. She describes her evolution from an enthusiastic follower of Mao's dictum to abolish the "Four Olds"— old ideas, old culture, old customs, and old habits—to a thoughtful teenager who, having witnessed numerous indignities forced on family members and neighbors, elects loyalty to her family over the "Proletarian Dictatorship."

Jiang reveals the confusion and fanaticism that resulted from the cult Mao encouraged in the late 1960s. To make this political story more effective, Jiang centers on the radical choice that she has to make between dedication to the Revolution and love for her family. At a time when children who betrayed their parents were praised as heroes, she comes close to changing her name to dissociate herself from her landowning family. But in a dramatic episode when members of the Dictatorship Group come to the house in search of a letter that "proves" that the family is landowning, Ji-Li deliberately lies to protect her family. At this point, she realizes: "I would never do anything to hurt my family, and I would do everything I could to take care of them. My family was too precious to forget, too rare to replace" (262–63). In the end, she concludes:

> Once my life had been defined by my goals: to be a *da-dui-zang* [Student Council President], to participate in the exhibition, to be a Red Guard. They seemed unimportant to me now. Now my life was defined by my responsibilities. I had promised to take care of my family, and I would renew that promise every day. I would not give up or withdraw, no matter how hard life became. (263)

Looking back at her childhood, the author notes with pain how the Chinese people were victims of a power struggle. Jiang explains how memories of her childhood never left her, even after she moved to the United States. She decided to write her autobiography because, as she explains: "I wanted to do something for the little girl I had been, and for all the children who lost their childhoods as I did" (266). This strategy for empowerment communicates to child readers the healing power that literature can play in each person's life, particularly when burdened with a traumatic history. Though Jiang makes positive choices she is still burdened by the historical context that oppresses those who wish to think freely.

David Henry Hwang, in his foreword to Jiang's autobiography, presents a brief historical contextualization for the story, stressing how Mao's strategy brought "untold suffering to those very masses in whose name the battle was waged, as well as disabling an entire group of young people who are now known as the 'lost generation'" (xvii). Another member of this lost generation is Da Chen, also a grandson of landowners, whose family was systematically persecuted. Chen's *China's Son* is set in a remote rural village, Yellow Stone, also subject to the consequences of Mao's revolution. Chen's father is repeatedly interred in labor camps, and Da's siblings leave school to become farmers. Da understands that excelling in school is the only way he can climb out of the hole in which they have placed him: "I shone, despite their efforts to snuff me out" (37). But he eventually also has to leave school in the face of constant humiliation. Chen's narrative includes humor, particularly in his account of his relationship with a gang of older boys—a kind of extended family who ignores his privileged background and teaches him to smoke and gamble. After Mao's death, Da realizes that an education is the only way to overcome the stigma his family suffers, and he prepares for college exams, eventually getting accepted into the Beijing First Foreign Language Institute. In this account that emphasizes his family relationships and school, the author does not present himself as an ideal child—compared to Jiang, for example, who seems much more mature at an early age—Chen is oftentimes childish and irresponsible, frustrated at the dead-ends that the government imposes, and almost gives in to desperation. Fortunately, he manages to find a place for himself when he decides to take schooling seriously, paving the way for his version of the success story.

Read together, these two autobiographies paint a multilayered picture of China's recent history though a representation of lives of the country's children. Several threads link these different accounts: both protagonists are fiercely loyal to China and mourn the destruction wrought by the abuse of power. Chen chooses to retitle his adapted memoir "China's Son," which symbolically foregrounds his perception of himself. Similarly, Jiang's title highlights the emblem of the Youth Pioneers that she proudly wears, until she becomes aware of the ultimate conditions of the regime. Further, neither of the protagonists wants to leave his or her homeland but both understand that immigration becomes the only option. As Jiang explains: "I was willing to take on the struggle to establish myself in a new country because I knew that was the price I would have to pay for the freedom to think, speak, and write whatever I pleased" (271). Jiang and Chen acknowledge the need to write their autobiographies as manifestations of their survival and to humanize the story of China's Cultural Revolution. Chen describes his work as "a book about love in the face of hate, a book of hope for the hopeless" (prologue); Jiang also hopes that her book will contribute to her mission "to promote cultural exchanges between the United States and China" (271). For child readers, these narratives provide access to the experiences of other children who have to make difficult choices and overcome harrowing odds to survive, as well as to individual stories behind immigration. Importantly, these stories stress the love for the mother country that the protagonists feel because it is their home, even though political circumstances necessitated leaving it. They emphasize that immigration was not a sign of a lack of loyalty but is a strategy for survival. The China represented in these texts is, and always will be, *home* for the protagonists—a home they look back to with longing and sorrow. This notion offers an important cultural perspective to American readers, who can then understand, through autobiographical texts, how and why the mother country continues to live in the consciousness of immigrants.

The autobiographies by Watkins and Choi explain the wars in Japan and Korea, as well as open up a new perspective to the war in Asia for American readers who have been taught that the United States "won" World War II. Here, the story is told from the point of view of the "losers," and recounts what happened to the Japanese and Koreans after the war, a strategy that aims to teach children lessons about the real victims of war and its aftermath. And, finally, these texts posit Americanization as an individual process, rather than an inherited patrimony. These narratives therefore suggest to Asian American children that itineraries of affiliation are highly personal and unique, and attest to a multiplicity of historical and cultural experiences as constitutive of citizen's lives, including the experience of a childhood in an Asian country. By discussing how these texts function culturally and how they may be used didactically, we understand how they help American children negotiate their daily cultural realities.

Yoko Kawashima Watkins's two-volume account of her childhood in Korea and Japan tells the story of a Japanese colonial family living in Korea that had to return to Japan and adapt to life in their "homeland."[3] *So Far from the Bamboo Grove* is the first account of the Japanese experience in Korea during World War II written for children, an important contribution to the canon of juvenile literature. It narrates the story of the Kawashima family, happily settled in Korea, from the point of view of 11-year-old Yoko, whose father was a Japanese government official working in Manchuria. The portrayal of their life in Nanam, in the north of Korea close to the Chinese border, in the early 1940s is happy—they live as Japanese and admit that they consider themselves separate from the Koreans. Comfortable in their colonial existence, symbolized by the eponymous bamboo grove, they do not consider that the Koreans might desire their independence.[4] The narrative opens in 1945, shortly before the end of World War II, when the Koreans want to regain control over their homeland and as Russian communist troops enter North Korea to overturn the Japanese occupation. When violence escalates that summer, Yoko (called "Little One" by her family), her teenaged sister Ko, and their mother make their way back to Japan with difficulty, as their father was fighting in the war. Their eight-month journey, which the narrator recounts in vivid detail, involves fighting to get on trains, a 45-mile trek to noncommunist Seoul in the South, being threatened by bands of soldiers and bombing raids, and the sea voyage back to Japan. In the process, they lose everything they own and undergo severe trials: hunger, injury, witnessing violence, and death. Eventually, when they reach Japan, they find their grandparents dead and their family home destroyed by Allied bombers. Yoko's mother dies of weakness and sorrow a few weeks later, leaving both girls alone in crippling poverty. Yoko and her sister survive through the kindness of strangers and their admirable resilience and resourcefulness, and the first book ends with their reunion with their older brother, Hideyo.

Watkins's story of war is told in stark, realistic detail that does not spare the reader any of the pain Yoko experienced. She narrates straightforwardly her memory of witnessing a rape and scavenging through garbage cans for food. The story of their escape is loaded with dramatic details: of a newborn baby on the Red Cross train who must be bathed in urine because there is no water, of the shrapnel in her ear that leads to her hearing loss, of the selfishness and cruelty of some of the struggling refugees. The mother's death is also narrated honestly, free of cheap sentimentalization or sensationalism. Interestingly, the author constructs a doubled account of the family's escape from Korea: she alternates chapters in first person with a third-person narration of Yoko's brother's journey.[5] In the narration of these events, the reader witnesses a profound change in the protagonist. From a spoiled youngest child, she develops into a strong, resilient girl who places family above all and endeavors to rise above the poverty and rejection experienced in Japan. This child, though often on the brink of desperation, manages to sustain her optimism and continue to value the important things—family bonds, the need to stay together, the desire to continue living and making something of herself, small acts of kindness that change people's lives.

Jean Fritz, in the foreword to Watkins's book, notes that it is the story of Yoko's "victory," which includes "her struggle to master English and record the nightmare of her private war story" as a "demonstration of the persistence and will she showed as a little girl, escaping from Korea and learning to survive when—as she says—she was 'in the most bottom of the bottom.'" The family story continues in the award-winning *My Brother, My Sister, and I*, which takes up the story immediately after the first one ends. The teenage siblings struggle to survive, living in an abandoned factory and working at all sorts of odd jobs—including cleaning toilets—for money for food. A fire in the factory leaves Ko wounded and crippled, and the three of them are involved in an investigation for arson and murder. Though the center of the story is the siblings' bonding together to survive, it also highlights typical teenage crises: petty jealousies and sibling rivalries, tensions and insecurities. The story also focuses on Yoko's attempts to succeed in school, despite her classmates' taunting her about her poverty. This story ends with a reunion with their father who had been interned in a Siberian prison camp and made his way to them—a separation of six years. In her afterword, Watkins explains how she later married an American and immigrated to the United States, where her sister eventually joined her.

Both these autobiographies highlight the importance of looking at narratives of war from both perspectives—those of the "winners" and those of the "losers"—in order to, ultimately, understand that everyone becomes a victim when there is a war. Interestingly, Watkins's story focuses on her liminal position in her diverse locations—an issue that resonates with many ethnic readers. As a child of a Japanese colonial family in Korea, she comprehends that she is not welcome there when the war breaks out, shattering her complacent sense of stability. Later, in Japan, her "home," she realizes that the colonizers—called "returnees"—are looked down upon because they did not really have a place in Japanese society because, in subtle ways, they were blamed for causing the tragedy that had befallen the country. Her marriage to an American, though recounted positively as a way to escape her displacement in Japan, also required another relocation and readjustment.

Another narrative that focuses on the Japanese-Korean war but from the opposite perspective is Sook Nyul Choi's award-winning autobiographical/historical trilogy—*Year of Impossible Goodbyes* (1991), *Echoes of the White Giraffe* (1993), and *Gathering of Pearls* (1994)—which narrates events of twentieth-century Korean history from the point of view of a young girl. The first two books provide an interesting contrast with Watkins' texts as they offer the opposite perspective on the same events—this time of a Korean child dealing with the effects of Japanese colonization and war. Choi was born in Pyongyang, Korea and immigrated to the United States to attend Manhattanville College, where she earned a BA in European history. As an educator—she has taught creative writing in high schools—she notes the lack of knowledge about Korea by Americans, and therefore writes to help young Asian Americans learn about their heritage and foster a better understanding of Asia and Asian Americans. As she explains, "I also feel it is important to create literature about Asia and Asian American experiences for young Asian Americans to learn about their heritages and to feel that there is a voice for them to relate to" ("Sook Nyul Choi" 47).[6] This evident didactic purpose locates her autobiographical novels in a dialogue with other writing, notably with Watkins's books. Taken together, these texts provide a rounded perspective on the conflict in the Pacific around the time of World War II. By focusing on the child's experiences, these texts serve to humanize the official stories told about the Japanese colonization and the war and to remind us that war is not a question of siding with one side or another but that suffering is a universal experience.

Year of Impossible Goodbyes narrates the events of Korean history during World War II and its aftermath. Ten-year-old Sookan Bak lives in Pyonyang and struggles to preserve her Korean identity from the intentions of the

Japanese colonizers to eradicate it. She describes the incessant repression of the Japanese who humiliate them and deliberately destroy everything that gives them a sense of self-worth and pride: the Koreans are not permitted any religion apart from Shintoism and are forbidden from speaking their language; things of beauty are confiscated—they are denied the aesthetic pleasure of a pine tree in their garden; young women are forced to serve as "spirit girls" for the Japanese army. The fear they live in makes her even doubt her pride in being Korean: "I thought of the Japanese children who went to the special school and lived in pretty houses that Koreans used to own. The Japanese could have whatever they wanted in Korea" (30). On her first day at school she has to sing the "Kimigayo," pledge loyalty to the Emperor and, most traumatic of all, respond to her Japanese name "Aoki Shizue," which makes her confused and afraid: "I knew I had no choice. My baptismal name and my Korean name would only be used at home from now on. Here I would have to answer to this strange Japanese name; I was someone I did not want to be and I had to pretend" (73). When the Japanese lose the war in 1945, the exhilaration the Koreans feel to be free—flying the Korean flag, speaking openly in Korean, dressing in the colorful *hanbok*, and listening to Korean and Western classical music—does not last long. The Russian takeover promises to be even more dangerous, and Sookan's mother—alone, as her older sons are in jail and her husband detained in Manchuria—decides to leave for the American-controlled south Korea with her young children, Sookan and seven-year-old Inchun. The journey is recounted in dramatic detail, including the children's separation from their mother and their desperate flight to cross the border to the South, where their father awaits them.

The text conveys the young girl's thoughts—her fears and anxieties, her little victories and dreams—as well as the details of daily life in the midst of colonial occupation and war. Choi knows how to convey with small details the characters' deepest emotions: the children bathing their grandfather's feet and discovering that his toenails had been pulled out under torture by the Japanese; the shame of Korean schoolchildren who urinate at their desks because they are not allowed a break from reciting Japanese propaganda; the desperation of the girls dragged out to be raped by Japanese soldiers. The Korean protagonist's pride in her heritage, cultural identity, and family are at the center of the novel. In the context of narratives of war, this text illustrates how civilians become the helpless victims of political struggles but how family bonds continue to be essential for survival. The "goodbyes" of the title refer to the family's exile and the end of Sookan's childhood as the story ends with the family reunited in Seoul, trying to begin a new life.

The family's story continues in *Echoes of the White Giraffe*, where Sookan, now 15, her younger brother, and mother leave everything behind in war-ravaged Seoul to live in a mountaintop refugee hut in Pusan. Once again, Sookan and Inchun are separated from their father and older brothers, this time because of the Korean War. The novel centers on the family's poverty and the sense of alienation typical of refugees. Though she tries to maintain an illusion of normalcy—attending a makeshift school, developing friendships—the separation from the rest of the family also weighs heavily on them. Sookan experiences her first romance, a "forbidden" relationship with Junho, a handsome adolescent. The end of the war does not solve problems, as the family struggles back to Seoul to try and pick up the strands of their lives, made more tragic by the children's father's death.

Less dramatic than the first volume, Choi's second book is more introspective as it examines the consequences of war on those who grow up in its shadow. Sookan also begins to show signs of independence and struggles with her personal feelings in the face of tradition and customs. With Junho, Sookan's love interest, for example, though both characters are deeply pious and want to enter religious life, they establish a relationship based on their love of poetry and music. Junho eventually enters the priesthood, and Sookan applies for admission into a U.S. university. The effect of war on these young people is portrayed, in general, in positive terms: they have to accept the consequences of the events, including the death of close family members and the sense of displacement brought about by constant relocations and loss of a history. Their resilience, determination, and confirmation of their faith in God and their families lie at the core of the autobiography. This is evidenced by the character Baik Rin (White Giraffe), a poet who, though dying of tuberculosis, greets everyone cheerfully each morning from the top of his mountain, reminding the refugees to appreciate each new day. This optimism serves as a symbol of hope to those who hear him. Whereas *Year of Impossible Goodbyes* centers on the child's narrative of rapid and dramatic historical events, *Echoes of the White Giraffe* engages the emotional struggle of coping with tragedy, of making history part of each person's configuration of his or her own path in life.

The final book in the trilogy, *Gathering of Pearls*, recounts Sookan's immigration to the United States in 1954 and her experiences as a freshman at Finch College in New York. It expands on some of the themes introduced in the previous book: Sookan's willingness to challenge tradition and live an independent life. At the center is her process of adaptation to her new life and her connection with her family in Korea, dramatizing her evaluation of both cultures and her own position between them. By describing her relationships with new friends, Sookan learns to navigate new possibilities and has to rethink traditional values and forms. Here, Choi presents the typical dilemma of the young immigrant who has to negotiate her responsibilities against individualism and a newfound sense of independence, traditional values against freer perspectives. This story ends with the death of Sookan's mother at the end of the daughter's freshman year. The family fails to tell her of her mother's death until after the funeral, and Sookan cannot travel back to Korea. The text concludes with Sookan's "gathering of pearls," remembering and treasuring her mother's teachings, realizing that she has been given the strength to forge a new life. Though the third volume is less engaging than the earlier two, the trilogy effectively describes an important story of the Asian diaspora, through an evolving child/young adult character faced with significant choices.

Choi's writing negotiates history and the consequences of Asian immigration by illustrating the choices and difficulties Korean children in Asia and in the United States face. Her perspective is generally positive, and she notes the difficulties of this situation in ways that suggest possibilities for children and young adults and allow them to attend actively to the realities of Asian Americans. Both Watkins and Choi choose to narrate their autobiographical accounts in third person, unlike the first person used by Huynh, Jiang, and Chen. Yet, the autobiographical pact exists: the girl protagonists have the same names as the author, confirming the authenticity of the narrative through personal testimony. Their voices, then, are presented as a valid perspective on historical situations and provide readers with access to traumatic events of the past through personal accounts. Texts like the ones considered in this essay invite child readers, parents, and educators to give new dimensions to psychological insights into children's responses to memory of wartime trauma. Importantly, the authors are concerned with stressing the humanity of all the sides presented in the conflict: Watkins's account, for example, offers a privileged glimpse of the suffering of the "returnees" to Japan, a group previously criticized for their colonization of Korea.

These texts, which center on preimmigration life and, specifically, the experience of war in Asian countries, function crucially in reimagining the place of Asians in America. Specifically, apart from validating a non-American childhood setting for the Asian American subject, these texts reconfigure America's image of its children, or at least of its citizens' pasts. Importantly, these autobiographies give child readers access to many of their parents' or grandparents' historical or cultural stories, or, if they are immigrants themselves, it repositions their experiences in the American literary context. These autobiographies also illustrate a palimpsestic itinerary of location and affiliation, complicating in effective ways the traditional fixed representation of the American child's awareness of position. Further, these texts might challenge official versions of historical events. Art may be said to transform historical accounts and official versions by the process of trying to reestablish order or come to terms with secrets and disorder. The autobiographical discourses of history, such as the texts by Hyunh, Jiang, Chen, Watkins, and Choi, work retrospectively, making a reinterpretation of the past through the inventiveness of its current representation imperative. The writing of history problematizes the manner in which we view and understand the articulation of personal and communal creation and inscription. Moreover, these texts suggest that "'history' is not 'behind' the text, but *in* the text, in its sinews, textures, syntax, vocabulary, as process of articulation"; the shift in preposition moves us away from the positivist reduction of history to simple source material toward a more active engagement with language and literature as themselves active forms (Pendergast 22). Inscribing the stories of characters who experienced the events of the past allows writers to reexamine the manner in which historical discourse has been received, often stressing the need for reinterpretation. The personal prevails over the official, the private stories over the public versions.

Asian American writers use literary forms like autobiography to creatively interpret or reexamine history as part of a strategy of writing themselves into the imaginative construction of the United States. This way, they stake a claim in the development of the world they feel themselves a part of but which had often erased them in its official version of itself. Importantly, as Leland Jacobs points out, "current concerns for the preservation of a democratic way of life in the world give rise to beliefs that to comprehend the historical growth of the democratic ideal in our country helps to reinforce faith in that ideal" (268). Further, Stephen Slemon has suggested that among the various challenges to inherited concepts of history is the attempted imaginative recovery of "those aspects of culture that have been subject to historical erasure" (165). The problem of the inscription of history becomes particularly crucial for the ethnic writer who has to deal with the inflections of truth and fiction—official and nonofficial versions of events, of time and space, of the danger of obliteration from mainstream memory. Ethnic children's writers often "work consciously to respond to prejudiced narratives of ethnicity through signification, allusion and confrontation. Texts recoup lost heroes, fill the gaps of historical memory, subvert ethnic stereotypes, and advance revisionary versions of cultural identity. Children's texts are often intensely dialogic: they interact with biased versions of the past that have previously been fortified within the classroom setting" (Smith 6). For Asian Americans, autobiographies for children provide more than mere insight into the past; they go beyond historical data to offer new ways of understanding the past. These texts thus perform important emancipatory work for both ethnic communities and the general public, revising uncritical perspectives on history and making the stories of our histories part of the stories of our present experience.

Notes

1. Many of these books have won important children's literature awards: *The Land I Lost* was named an ALA Notable Children's Book of 1982, a 1982 Teacher's Choice Book (NCTE), a Library of Congress Children's Book of 1982, and won a 1982 William Allen White Children's Book Award; Jiang's autobiography was named a Notable Children's Book of 1997 by the ALA, one of the Best Books for Young Adults by the ALA, and a Publisher's Weekly Best Book of 1997; *So Far From the Bamboo Grove* was named an ALA Notable Book; *My Brother, My Sister and I* was named an ALA Best Book for Young Adults and a *New York Times* Notable Book, among others; *The Year of Impossible Goodbyes* was awarded the Judy Lopez Book Award by the National Women's Book Association (1992), Selected for "Best Books for Young Adults" list by the Young Adult Library Services Association (YALSA) and named a Notable Book by the American Library Association, among others; *Echoes of the White Giraffe* was cited in the State Book Award Master Reading List: Tennessee; *A Gathering of Pearls* won the 1995 Books for the Teen Age Award.

2. See Gillian Lathey's "Autobiography and History: Literature of War" for a detailed description of how representations of war in children's literature has evolved. See also Pat Pinsent's "Postmodernism, Hew Historicism and Migration: New Historical Novels" for perspectives on evolving ethnic writing for children.

3. A third book by Watkins, *Tales from the Bamboo Grove* (New York: Simon & Schuster, 1992) may be read as a companion piece to these two autobiographies. This book is a collection of six Japanese folk tales that the author recalls hearing from her parents in her early childhood, when they still lived in Korea. The introduction to this book describes her childhood in Nanam, and she stresses how the memory of the happy and secure existence that time—when she learned these stories—sustained her during the war.

4. Watkins does not engage in detail to promote, justify, or condemn the Japanese colonization of Korea and Manchuria. Perhaps because of the nature of her children's text, she avoids a political discussion of Japan's imperialist policies and its consequences, focusing rather on her personal story of survival. Her position is, in a sense, consistent with that of herself as a child narrator, who would obviously be unaware of the larger political context and unable to criticize what her parents supported, which was the only life she knew.

5. Hideyo is working at an ammunition factory when the women escape, and he has to make his way alone across Korea and to Japan. At one point, injured and starving, he is taken in by a Korean family who, risking their lives, nurses him back to health and offers him a permanent home. Hideyo chooses to try and

find his family and, after a dangerous swim across the Imjon River, which crosses the thirty-eighth parallel, he makes it to safety and to Japan where he is reunited with his sisters.

6. See Choi's essay for a description of her creative position in relation to historical and cultural themes in Asian American literature.

Works Cited

Carpenter, Carole H. "Enlisting Children's Literature in the Goals of Multiculturalism." *Mosaic* 29.3 (1996): 53–73.

Chen, Da. *China's Son: Growing Up in the Cultural Revolution*. New York: Delacorte Press, 2001.

——————. *Colors of the Mountain*. New York: Anchor Books, 2001.

Choi, Sook Nyul. *Echoes of the White Giraffe*. Boston: Houghton Mifflin, 1993.

———. *Gathering of Pearls*. Boston: Houghton Mifflin, 1994.

———. "Sook Nyul Choi, Memoirist and Novelist." *Yellow Light: The Flowering of Asian American Art*. Ed. Amy Ling. Philadelphia: Temple UP, 1999. 46–54.

———. *Year of Impossible Goodbyes*. Boston: Houghton Mifflin, 1991.

Davis, Rocío G. "Reinscribing (Asian) American History in Laurence Yep's *Dragonwings*." *Lion and the Unicorn* 28.1 (2004): 390–407.

Huynh, Quang Nhoung. *The Land I Lost: Adventures of a Boy in Vietnam*. New York: Harper Trophy, 1982.

Jacobs, Leland B. "Some Observations on Children's Historical Fiction." *Signposts to Criticism of Children's Literature*. Ed. Robert Bator. Chicago: American Library Association. 1983. 267–69.

Jiang, Ji-li. *Red Scarf Girl: A Memoir of the Cultural Revolution*. New York: Harper Trophy, 1997.

Kang, Younghill. *The Grass Roof*. New York: Scribner's, 1931.

———. *The Happy Grove*. New York: Scribner's, 1933.

Kogawa, Joy. *Naomi's Road*. Toronto: Stoddart, 1995.

———. *Obasan*. Boston: David R. Godine, 1981.

Lathey, Gillian. "Autobiography and History: Literature of War." *Modern Children's Literature: An Introduction*. Ed. Kimberly Reynolds. London: Palgrave MacMillan, 2004. 58–73.

Mah, Adeline Yeh. *Chinese Cinderella*. New York: Dell Laurel-Leaf, 1999.

———. *Falling Leaves: The True Story of an Unwanted Chinese Daughter*. New York: John Wiley & Sons, 1998.

Myers, Mitzi. "Missed Opportunities and Critical Malpractice: New Historicism and Children's Literature." *Children's Literature Association Quarterly* 13.1 (1988): 41–43.

Pendergast, Christopher. *Paris and the Nineteenth Century*. Oxford: Blackwell Publishers, 1992.

Pinsent, Pat. "Postmodernism, Hew Historicism and Migration: New Historical Novels." *Modern Children's Literature: An Introduction*. Ed. Kimberly Reynolds. London: Palgrave MacMillan, 2004. 173–90.

Slemon, Stephen. "Post-Colonial Allegory and the Transformation of History." *Journal of Commonwealth Literature* 23.1 (1988): 157–68.

Smith, Katherine Capshaw. "Introduction: The Landscape of Ethnic American Children's Literature." *MELUS* 27.2 (2002): 3–8.

Uchida, Yoshiko. *Desert Exile: The Uprooting of a Japanese American Family*. 1982. Seattle: U of Washington P, 1989.

———. *The Invisible Thread*. 1991. New York: Beech Tree Books, 1995.

Watkins, Yoko Kawashima. *My Brother, My Sister, and I*. 1994. New York: Simon Pulse, 2002.

———. *So Far From the Bamboo Grove*. New York: Beech Tree, 1986.

———. *Tales from the Bamboo Grove*. New York: Simon & Schuster, 1992.

SECTION IV

Latina/o Literature

CHAPTER 14

Writing on Violence and Healing for Young Audiences: An Interview with Rigoberto González

Tiffany Ana López

*I*nterviewed Rigoberto González in Riverside, California, on March 20, 2009. In our conversation we discussed his growing up experiences as Chicano, gay, and a child of migrant farmworkers, and the impact this has had on his writing for children. We also explored the range of his writing across genres and the ways his adult works resonate into his writing targeted toward Latina/o children, including his recent three-book juvenile fiction series, The Mariposa Club (Alyson Books, 2009), focused on the lives of queer Latina/ o youth. Our discussion worked from my interest in Gonzalez's ongoing engagement with matters of violence, most especially economic violence, as well as violence of thought, such as racism and homophobia; the publishing of his children's books with Children's Book Press, the nation's most important publisher devoted to multiethnic children's picture books; and his position as a visiting writer in impoverished schools and its impact on his writing Soledad Sigh Sighs (2003) and Antonio's Card (2005), the two children's books discussed within this volume's featured critical essay in on violence and trauma in Latina/o children's literature.

Rigoberto González was born in Bakersfield, California. The son and grandson of migrant farmworkers, he spent much of his childhood traveling between Michoacán, Mexico, and the California central valley. In addition to his two bilingual children's books referenced above, he is the author of two poetry books, *So Often the Pitcher Goes to Water until It Breaks* (University of Illinois, 1999) and *Other Fugitives and Other Strangers* (Tupelo Press, 2006); a novel, *Crossing Vines* (University of Oklahoma Press,

2003), a collection of short stories, *Men without Bliss* (University of Oklahoma Press, 2008), and a memoir, *Butterfly Boy: Memories of a Chicano Mariposa* (University of Wisconsin Press, 2006). For the past seven years, he has authored over 150 book reviews in his bimonthly Latino book column for the Texas *El Paso Times*. He is also a contributing editor for *Poets & Writers*, member of the board of directors of the National Book Critics Circle, and curator of The Quetzal Quill Reading Series, a national venue for showcasing and promoting new voices in American Literature. His current projects include an edited series for the University of Arizona Press on the best of the pivotal journal, *Camino del Sol*, and an edited collection of works by the poet Alurista for Bilingual Press/Editoral Bilingue. The recipient of numerous awards, including an American Book Award from the Before Columbus Foundation (for *Butterfly Boy*), a John Simon Guggenheim Memorial Foundation Fellowship in Creative Writing, a National Endowment for the Arts grant, a University Award from the Academy of University Poets, four Pushcart Prize nominations, and a John Guyon Prize of Literary Nonfiction, González is associate professor of English at Rutgers University.

López: *Soledad Sigh Sighs* focuses on the life of a young girl grappling with the responsibility and loneliness of being a latchkey kid, and *Antonio's Card* concentrates on a young boy with two lesbian mothers who is struggling emotionally with how to present his Mother's Day card for viewing by his entire class. I read these two children's books as extending your ongoing engagements with violence and healing throughout your writing. *Soledad Sigh Sighs* depicts the resonances of economic violence: Soledad's struggles are the result of her entire family having to prioritize economic survival over the preservation of her childhood. In *Antonio's Card*, the young boy is clearly burdened by a sense of representational violence resulting from the unquestioned images of compulsory heterosexuality associated with Mother's Day as a national holiday, which has yet to be revised to include broader conceptualizations of motherhood, be it queer motherhood or what I term public motherhood to describe those of us who choose not to have children biologically or through adoption but nevertheless see ourselves as educators and activists who are deeply involved in the raising of children in the public sphere. How do you situate your children's books as part of a larger dialogue within American as well as Latino literature and culture?

González: I want my contribution to be creating and promoting writing that helps people. I define myself as an activist writer, which means that I see my work serving the communities I write about, and I am unafraid to be political about that. My work stands in conversation with Chicano writers who understand themselves as charged to bear witness to the ways violence defines and shapes our lives, both historically and individually. We write from a shared place of urgency and purpose. In writing the *Mariposa Club*, for example, I was inspired by the story of Lawrence King, a young gay man who was murdered by his schoolmate in Oxnard, California in 2008. This case speaks to how effeminate men are still viewed as a threat, and they remain targets of violence in high school. I was closeted during high school and afraid about being found out. I want the *Mariposa Club* books to help young people to be able to talk about gay identity and to help queer youth feel less afraid. California propositions (like 187, 209, and 8) illustrate that immigrants and queers are continued targets of hate and oppression. As a writer, I feel charged to address those issues, whether that be in an explicit way, as I do in my essays and poetry for adult audiences, or in a subtle way, as I do in *Antonio's Card*. Generally, I write struggle-driven, rather than plot-driven work. I also write about specific communities: the Chicano community, the Queer community, and communities that deal with poverty and oppression.

López: How does your personal history inform your writing for children?

González: I grew up poor, in both Mexico and the United States. Poverty and oppression are never comfortable homes. My mother died when I was 12 years old; she was only 31. I was a melancholy and withdrawn child, especially after her death. All of this contributed to my need for a different view of the world, which I eventually found through reading and the discovery of books in the school library. There were always many of us crowding the small space of an apartment, and books often provided the only sense of space. I remember being left alone when reading. I lost myself in the pages of mysteries and adventure stories. They provided an escape from personal frustrations and economic crisis. Books also came to my rescue when I started seeking answers about my sexuality. I was afraid to tell my family that I was gay, so I consulted books on the matter. Eventually I wanted to use my experiences as a reader to create my own writing. Also, in my work as a visiting writer in classrooms populated with many children from poverty, I am struck by how their stories of struggle mirror my own. I want them to be able to find reflections of their lives in a library book. When I recently read *Antonio's Card* as part of a reading put together for children of queer families, I was truly moved when children came up and happily exclaimed, "I have two moms!" *Soledad Sigh Sighs* is based on my time working with children in New York classrooms. So many children have to absorb their parents' economic struggles. I have been very outspoken about the need to preserve after school programs because they directly impact our communities. Taking them away means seeing a rise in pregnancy, drug use, and illiteracy, all of which are a form of assault on our communities.

López: How does your growing up as the child of migrant farmworkers inform your writing for children? This is something you often write about in your poetry, short stories, novel, and memoir yet do not explicitly address in either of your children's books. Yet, the kinds of hardship experienced by children sent to work in the fields, to me, seems very present in *Soledad Sigh Sighs*.

González: I come from three generations of migrant farmworkers who moved periodically from one side of the border to the other. Economic necessity led to relocation in constant search of employment, something that made me connect with the lives of the working class and poor children I have worked with as a visiting writer to elementary schools. The fact that I received a formal education and don't work in the agricultural fields does not mean that I don't still have a sense of the work ethic fostered throughout my growing up years. I take strength from my cultural history, which is one of labor and survival. Also, mentorship is a Chicano value. I have a formalized education yet continue to migrate as a visiting writer. My writing also migrates across genres as I carry forward particular questions, images, and ideas. For example, my forthcoming book, *Black Blossoms* (2011), is a collection of essays that I describe as "literary retablos"[1] about people who have influenced my life. I also have a long-term project envisioned about Mexicans in New York. I write across genres because I have taken on a duty to populate the shelves with many books and to also address multiple audiences, including children. I wasn't exposed to any kind of ethnic literature at all until college. I feel the need to change that and expand the possibilities for a new generation of readers. Teachers and mentors instilled in me this fire for success, and I want to pass that on to others.

López: What is the role of identity—terminology as well as cultural politics—in your writing for children?

González: Identity gives me history and provides cultural context and trajectory. I identify as Chicano, gay, a Mexican immigrant, and a New Yorker now that I've lived in New York longer than in California or any other U. S. city. I have a problem with the terms Latino and Hispanic because they erase specific memories and peoples. Often used as a catchall term, "Latino" is abstract and faceless, and it ultimately diffuses both our political power and our cultural history. This is why I use the term Chicano, which is specific in the way it designates political consciousness and a culturally specific history. At the University of California at Riverside where I studied, the library there was named after Tomás Rivera, a Chicano writer and a Chancellor of that University. I was curious about him and discovered his novel *And the Earth Did Not Devour Him/ . . . y no se lo tragó la tierra*. This showed me that migrant life was a valid subject for a book. In my two children's books, it was important to me to portray Soledad not as Latina but as Puerto Rican and to show Antonio living in a multicultural urban city. I wanted to reflect the importance of one's cultural history and geography to one's evolving sense of self. For a child to see that reflected not just in one book, but also on the shelves of libraries and bookstores is incredibly important. As I writer, I want to participate in the expanding of this space and in keeping the legacy of Chicano literature alive through my own writing, through the activism of building a coalition of Chicano and Latino writers, and through the mentorship of young Chicano writers.

Notes

1. According to renown Chicano art historian Tomas Ybarra Frausto, *retablo* translates *retro tabula*, which literally means "behind the table." In Chicano art history the term describes small paintings on sheets of tin presented to holy personages as commemorations of a favor received or a miracle granted. The genre arises from the Medieval Catholic church tradition. See page 71, "Santa Barraza: Borderlands Chronicles" in *Santa Barraza: Artist of the Borderlands*, edited by Maria Herrera Sobek, College Station Place: Texas A & M University Press, 2001. pp. 67–75.

Works Consulted

Bennett, Steve. "I Don't Subscribe to the Idea of Art for Art's Sake." *The Fine Print: A Book Blog with a Texas Accent*. 13 March 2009. blogs.mysanantonio.com/weblogs/fine_print/2009/03/-what-did-you-think.html#more (accessed 31 March 2009).

"Bio-Rigoberto Gonzalez." *www.rigobertogonzalez.com*. 31 March 2009. http://www.rigobertogonzalez.com/bio.html.

"Interview with Rigoberto Gonzalez." By Daniel Olivas. *La Bloga* 19 November 2007. 31 March 2009. labloga.blogspot.com/2007/11/interview-with-rigoberto-gonzlez.html.

"Rigoberto Gonzalez Interview." By Gregg Barrios. Gemini Ink Literary Center. San Antonio, TX. *Youtube*. 6 March 2009. 31 March 2009. www.youtube.com/watch?v=NPHZq3-PNqk.

"Rigoberto Gonzalez: Mini Interview." By Eduardo C. Corral. *Lorcaloca* 8 January 2007. 31 March 2009. http://lorcaloca.blogspot.com/2007/01/rigoberto-gonzlez-mini-interview.html.

"Rigoberto Gonzalez Interview." *The Progressive*. 31 March 2009. www.progressive.org/radio_gonzalez07.

CHAPTER 15

Art, Activism and Community: An Introduction to Latina/o Literature

Tanya González

Latinos are the fastest growing "minority" group in the United States.[1] This large and heterogeneous group is comprised of those descended from Latin America—the Spanish-speaking nations in North, Central, and South America—as well as the Caribbean. Because of the diversity in cultural and ethnic experiences, Latina/o is often used as the umbrella term. In literary studies, the term Latina/o includes all of the literature written by those of Caribbean and Latin American descent who are born and/or raised in the United States. Mexican Americans who identify with Civil Rights aims do not often use the term Latina/o, opting instead to identify their community and cultural production as Chicana/o. The term Chicano also emphasizes Mexican American indigenousness to the U.S. Southwest, given that some Mexican Americans have lived in the land that is now the United States for hundreds of years. Throughout this introduction I distinguish the specific ethnic identifications of authors with terms such as Chicana/o, U.S. Puerto Rican or Nuyorican,[2] Cuban American, and Dominican American. Nevertheless, when discussing the overarching themes and common literary histories, I use the general term Latina/o.

The particular national groups subsumed under the term Latina/o consume different foods, speak different dialects (of Spanish and English), practice different customs and traditions, and have different histories in relation to their presence in the United States. A common assumption is that Latina/o food, for instance, consists mainly of corn-based tacos, burritos, enchiladas, tamales, and tortillas, when in fact these dishes are Mexican

American and are not part of Puerto Rican, Cuban, or Dominican cuisine. In Central and South American countries wherein, like Mexico, corn plays a prominent role, there are many distinctions in its usage like sweet corn tamales in several South American countries. These variations in cuisine parallel the linguistic differences between Latina/o cultures. While they may speak Spanish, there are geographic and cultural distinctions that influence the words Latinas/os may use for certain foods. For instance, the beans can have different Spanish names depending on if someone is from Mexico (*frijoles*) or Puerto Rico (*habichuelas*). This example can be multiplied for each cultural/national group classified in the United States as Latina/o. When Spanish speakers hear these dialects or specific vocabulary choices, they can often identify the cultural heritage of the speaker. The speed and accent of Spanish also shifts depending on a speaker's native culture and is also an indicator of distinct national heritages.

Like the unique linguistic and culinary traits, Latina/o customs can also vary from group to group. One date that has become synonymous with U.S. Latina/o culture is the *Cinco de Mayo* (5 of May) celebration. This date is celebrated in honor of the 1862 Battle of Puebla, when "5,000 ill-equipped Mestizo and Zapotec Indians defeated the French army in what came to be known as the 'Batalla de Puebla' on the fifth of May" ("Cinco de Mayo"). Even though the Mexicans were eventually defeated in this war and the date is not universally celebrated in Mexico, this small defeat of a Western power has become quite a large celebration in the United States. The day is a symbol of Mexican pride for the Mexican American and Chicano communities and is filled with parades, mariachis, and other entertainment. While no other Latina/o group celebrates this day, advertisers and retailers have picked up the Cinco de Mayo as a Latina/o holiday and an opportunity to market to the Latina/o community.

Finally, not all Latino groups have had the same historical presence in the United States. Some Mexican Americans have been in what is now the United States since the Spanish Conquistadors and Catholic Missions settled the land. These individuals became Mexican Americans because of a border change after the 1848 Treaty of Guadalupe Hidalgo. Alternately, the United States acquired Puerto Rico from Spain after the Spanish American War in 1898. Puerto Rico was made a commonwealth of the United States, and the island's inhabitants were granted U.S. citizenship in 1917.[3] This is quite different from how the U.S.-Mexican border shifted. However, Puerto Ricans share a history of migration with other Latina/o groups from the Caribbean and Central and South America, and all Latina/o groups share an ancestral tie of some sort to the Spanish language.

Latina/o literary history suggests that while there are distinct relationships between various Latina/o groups, there are also many points of intersection. Social activism and community building have been part of Latina/o literary history from its earliest moments. As more Latina/o literature from the nineteenth century is recovered and studied, we have a better picture of the diversity of Latinas/os in the United States at the time. Diaries, chronicles, and Spanish language presses attest to the presence of a variety of Latina/o communities since the earliest historical moments. Mexicans and Cubans—like acclaimed poet, philosopher, and political activist José Martí—began the Spanish language presses of the United States. They worked in pan-Latina/o groups to keep the Latina/o community informed and connected across the Americas. In addition, the late-nineteenth century letters and fiction of California-native María Amparo Ruiz de Burton attest to a Latina/o populace critical of U.S. political policy and social hypocrisy.

What many people do not realize is that the journalism, personal writings and correspondences, and fiction written in the nineteenth century and earlier were followed by significant literary contributions in the early twentieth century. At this time of global economic and social upheaval, many urban areas began seeing increased Latina/o population growth. With this growth came more prominent cultural figures from Latina/o backgrounds. Literary scholars have recognized that the great Modernist poet and essayist William Carlos Williams was of Puerto Rican descent, and some have argued that his ethnic identity and experiences provided the foundation for his critical perspective in *Against the American Grain*.[4] Other Latina/o writers and activists were likewise engaged in facilitating cultural literacy as Latina/o communities grew in urban areas. Pura Belpré, for instance, was the "first Afro-Latina librarian in the New York Public Library system" and also a prolific essayist and children's folklorist (Sánchez González 9–11). Belpré began publishing in the 1930s, but her influence on children and educators continues today, as signaled by the Pura Belpré Award that honors outstanding Latina/o fiction for children and young adults.

The connection between literary production, education, and social activism remained an important component of the literature of the Civil Rights era. Latina/o writers began chronicling their experiences growing up Latina/o in the United States, thus creating a literary portrait of midcentury America not previously depicted. Nuyorican writers like Nicholasa Mohr and Piri Thomas wrote novels and memoirs about urban life in New Jersey and NYC. Chicano writer Rudolfo Anaya explored a Mexican American childhood in the rural Southwest. While these authors began publishing in earnest in the 1970s, they were writing about life in the United States in the 1940s and

1950s. These literary contributions reflected the nationalist movements of the 1960s, in which Chicano and Nuyorican activists began demanding equal rights in the workplace, educational institutions, and government. Nationalist ideologies often replicated patriarchal and homophobic systems that became oppressive when it came to issues of gender and sexuality.

Due, in part, to the successes of past generations of writers, the 1980s and 1990s saw a significant growth in Latina/o literary production. While these new voices were still intent on articulating their previously unwritten experiences in the United States, another set of social critiques emerged in this era as Latina/o authors began addressing inequalities found *within* Latina/o communities. U.S. Puerto Rican and Chicana/o texts were still at the forefront of this expansion, but women writers began to receive more attention than ever before. These women were writing fiction that illustrated the social and political inequalities found in nationalist ideologies. The political tensions between gender, sexuality, and ethnic identities often shaped this literature and became a central thematic concern. At the same time, the literature from Cuban Americans, Dominican Americans, and Central Americans from various countries began to enter more prominently into the Latina/o literary field. In 1990, Cuban American author Oscar Hijuelos became the first Latina/o to win the Pulitzer Prize for Fiction for his novel *The Mambo Kings Play Songs of Love.*

Contemporary Latina/o literature continues many of the thematic, political, and aesthetic projects of the past decades, while still enjoying commercial and critical success. Junot Diaz's bestselling novel *The Brief and Wondrous Life of Oscar Wao,* for example, won the 2008 Pulitzer Prize for Fiction. Nevertheless, the popularity of contemporary Latina/o literature has also complicated how Latinas/os are seen in the United States. Critical discussion about post-1960s Latina/o literature often centers on the following debate: on the one side are critics who suggest that Latina/o literature seeks social justice by drawing attention to the specificity of the Latina/o experience and revealing the many ways that mainstream society oppresses Latinas/os; on the other side are critics who argue that Latina/o literature should use its aesthetic and commercial success to strive for universal status or recognition.[5] As the rest of this introduction shows, Latina/o literature simultaneously achieves both of these aims.

While a brief literary history emphasizes the diversity of Latina/o cultural groups, a thematic survey of Latina/o literature reveals the many points of intersection within the various Latina/o groups in the United States. The most important of these themes and approaches to Latina/o literature can be grounded under the following six topics: Magical Realism; language play and bilingualism; the border and immigration; mestizaje, race, and cultural mixing; family and education; and the urban experience. Each of the sections below introduces one of these topics, providing a summary look at the key critical debates around the idea as well as a brief examination of at least one major text associated with each theme or approach. Finally, a discussion of exemplary texts for children concludes each section. This thematic introduction should provide readers and teachers with a series of perspectives on Latina/o literature written for adults and children.

Magical Realism

One of the most common ways to approach U.S. Latina/o Fiction is through the lens of Magical Realism.[6] One cause of this generic association is the popularity of Latin American magical realism which, as Paul Allatson writes,

> [It] is marked by a range of recurring narrative and plot devices: the collapse of time; the normative integration of supernatural events and figures into daily existence; transformative shape changing; miraculous coincidences; false appearances and their unmasking; the conflation of high and low, elite, folk, and popular cultural forms and worldviews; and the hybrid incorporation of indigenous, African and European perspectives and cultural practices. (148)

Critics of U.S. Latina/o literature have remarked upon the association between contemporary Latina/o fiction and the "boom" of Latin American fiction in the 1960s and 1970s best exemplified by Gabriel García Márquez's *Cien años de soledad* (*One Hundred Years of Solitude*). Karen Christian suggests that the popularity of this Latin American genre has influenced the marketing of U.S. Latina/o fiction to the point that "magical realism has come to be viewed as emblematic of Latina/o culture" (22–23). This connection between the highly popular Latin American fiction and U.S. Latina/o fiction is understandable when considering the Chicana/o literature coming out in the early 1970s. Rudolfo Anaya's *Bless Me, Ultima* (1972), for instance, plays with time and integrates "supernatural events and figures into daily existence" (Allatson 148). This is particularly the case with Anaya's representation of women (as *curanderas* / healers and *brujas* / witches) and indigenous characters that pass on folklore to the young protagonist Antonio. This novel is often taught in high school and university curriculums as a representative of U.S. Latina/o fiction. Magical realism, as a mode, thus becomes entrenched in ideas about U.S. Latina/o writing.

Ellen McCracken also asserts that this association of Latin American and U.S. Latina/o fiction has more to do with marketing than with generic or thematic concerns. Latin American literature is not always manipulating magical realism, nor is U.S. Latina/o literature always using Latin America as a literary model. McCracken discusses how this association plays out in Cuban American author Cristina García's case:

> The common thread in several of the reviews is the implicit or explicit comparison of *Dreaming in Cuban* to the work of Gabriel García Márquez and Latin American magical realism, two of the most common reductive modes by which the U.S. cultural mainstream has appropriated Latin American fiction of recent decades as a palatable Third World commodity. (22)

While McCracken recognizes some magical realist elements in García's work, which are, "in principle, more susceptible to mainstream exoticizing and containment," she argues, "the novel deploys these themes in modes that often work against such containment" (26). In other words, read closely, U.S. Latina/o fiction often employs a wide variety of writing strategies, often to combat, parody, or ironize the exoticization of their work and of U.S. Latinas/os at large.

Language Play / Bilingual Text

If magical realism is one of the first things people think about in relation to Latina/o literature, certainly one of the first things people notice when reading these texts is the presence of Spanish. While canonical American authors have played with multilingual texts (T. S. Eliot's modernist *The Wasteland* and Cormac McCarthy's Border Trilogy), Latina/o authors have infused their works with various levels of Spanish language references in order to communicate the relationship between English and Spanish in their everyday lives. Alfred Arteaga asserts that the nature of Chicana/o poetics and language play parallels the experience of dual cultures and in-between spaces of identity construction found in Eliot and Pound (69). Arteaga associates Chicana/o poetics and language play with Bakhtin's notion of heteroglossia, "the context of historical, interlingual, and interdiscursive factors that come into play in, and affect meaning of, any utterance"(72). This concept is useful as a way to understand U.S. Latina/o writing because of the complex history of U.S. Latinas/os, the influence of Spanish and English on texts, and the constant cultural and discursive interplay in these texts.

While it is helpful to recognize the heteroglossic elements of U.S. Latina/o writing, it is also important to note that not all U.S. Latinas/os speak Spanish. There are second-, third-, and fourth-generation U.S. Latinas/os who have not grown up speaking the language at home and whose only Spanish was gleaned in high school or college course work. Indeed, authors such as Cherríe Moraga have openly declared their initial discomfort with Spanish and the anxiety language causes when attempting to build solidarity with Latinas who have more "authentic" Spanish skills (43). Nevertheless, Arteaga is right to note the predominance of language play and a heteroglossic understanding of culture and language in most Latina/o fiction because even Moraga uses Spanglish (the insertion of Spanish words into English phrases) and Caló (Chicano slang) in most of her plays in order to develop characters that constantly negotiate their Latina/o identity.

Other writers are more comfortable with their Spanish language skills, but choose not to create bilingual or heteroglossic texts. Cuban American author Achy Obejas, for instance, uses very little code switching (or the use of more than one language in a conversation or text) in her fiction, even though she is a professional translator.[7] Despite this difference in her writing style, Obejas often overtly refers to her character's code switching, (inserting phrases like, "he said, in Spanish") while writing the text only in English. The result is an awareness of the multiplicity or hybridity of linguistic experience without the literal Spanish on the page. Interestingly, this produces a sensibility of true bilingualness, as characters are communicating fluidly and fluently in Spanish for entire conversations that can last pages, despite the reader seeing only English. By refusing to allow her characters to code-switch midsentence, there is less of a Spanglish element to her writing and more of a bilingual aesthetic.

U.S. Latina/o picture books are often bilingual, but the way they demonstrate this trait varies. While some books simply provide direct translations of full passages found on the same page, other picture books aimed at teaching certain vocabularies, like Yuyi Morales's Pura Blepré Award winning *Just a Minute*, which helps children count from one to ten in English and Spanish, integrate the vocabulary words in each language in the same sentence. In addition, some Spanglish texts capture the everyday parlance and language play of youth and street culture. Examples of this code switching can be found in Gary Soto's picture book *Chato's Kitchen*, illustrated by Susan Guevara. While the text is predominantly written in English, occasionally the protagonist Chato (a cat) breaks out in Spanglish or slang phrases like, "*Órale*, neighbors" and "No, *de veras, hombres*. I'm ok" (6)[8]. These signs of multilingualness abound in Soto's series of Chato tales following the adventures of an urban cat in a multicultural neighborhood, stories meant to reflect the everyday linguistic experiences of urban Latinas/os in the Southwest.

These varied linguistic representations are important to a Latina/o readership in that they can reflect a familiar speech pattern. However, not all Latinas/os share a similar relationship to Spanish or to urban slang. The language play found in these texts is testament to the matrixes of identity. The politics of language and community are often fraught because of the diverse linguistic experiences within the Latina/o community explained above and the (growing) number of Latinas/os who are not Spanish speakers or readers. Nevertheless, there is an attempt by some writers to manipulate Spanish to demonstrate the complicated relationship between language and culture, between language and identity.

The Border and (Im)Migration

Much of Mexican American and Chicana/o literature evokes or references the border between the United States and Mexico, if not literally, then metaphorically. Gloria Anzaldúa theorized this geopolitical and metaphoric space in her important work, *Borderlands / La Frontera: The New Mestiza*. In this text, she discusses the history of the border, how it was established in 1848 and how this process divided families that would forever be culturally, linguistically, and physically distinct. Anzaldúa, is not, however, the first Chicana or pre-1960s Mexican American writer to evoke this shift in national identification based on a map change versus immigration. As early as 1885, Maria Amparo Ruiz de Burton used this national shift to discuss the economic and social injustices done to Californios whose land and homes were taken from them by Anglo newcomers in *The Squatter and the Don*. However, because of the discourses that would perpetually label Mexican Americans and other Latina o groups as invaders of the American nation-state[9], this historical presence is a theme often illustrated in Latina/o literature.

Although these historical reminders are an important element of Latina/o literature, this fiction also serves to draw attention to the twenty-first-century drama on the border. The violence and danger on the border faced by immigrants to the United States *and* Latinos who are U.S. citizens is often a topic of this literature. For instance, Ana Castillo's *Guardians* (2007) provides a fictional portrait of people living in El Paso and their precarious existence. She uses current events, the disappearance of people on the U.S.-Mexico border, to demonstrate how both U.S. Latinas/os and Mexicans are violently affected. Castillo illustrates how illegal drug trafficking on both sides of the border affects U.S. women who disappear *and* how the illegal carrying of immigrants across the border also leads to the disappearance of people every day. The murder of thousands of women and men on the border between El Paso and Ciudad Juarez is also the topic of Alicia Gaspar de Alba's fictional account *Desert Blood: The Juarez Murders* (2007). This violence on the border is not often dealt with by media sources except to discuss the issues of illegal immigration, border patrols, and U.S. security issues. These writings offer portraits of individual experiences of the atrocities that affect communities within the United States, in Mexico, and in some cases throughout Central and South America.

Immigration and border crossing is also represented in young adult and children's literature. Often, young people share the anxieties of border crossings and articulate these emotions and personal experiences in poignant ways. A semicomic treatment of this theme can be found in Juan Felipe Herrera's bilingual picture book *Super Cilantro Girl / La Superniña del Cilantro*, illustrated by Honorio Robledo Tapia, which has a little girl becoming a superhero to rescue her mother from detention at the border. The anxious girl becomes proactive as a "magical" moment allows her to overcome her powerlessness in the situation and recover her mother. Gloria Anzaldúa's bilingual picture book *Friends from the Other Side* illustrates for children the importance of friendship in helping the innocent victims of border violence, the children who have accompanied parents seeking work and hope for their families. In this text, a little girl helps shelter a classmate. Anzaldúa's children's literature depicts the harsh realities of immigrant children's lives through the eyes of a bilingual Mexican American girl who learns about justice and moral duty. These fictional explorations of real-life border experiences highlight the physical dangers and the day-to-day dilemmas faced by those living in this geopolitical space.

Life on the border, however, is not all about fear, violence, and disappearance. In fact, much literature illustrates the bicultural experience that inhabitants influenced by two cultures (Mexican or another Latin American culture and U.S. American culture) must negotiate. Sandra Cisneros has famously illustrated these cultural negotiations in her works *House on Mango Street* (1989) and her latest novel *Caramelo* (2002). Each of these texts follows a protagonist who grapples with what it means to grow up Mexican American in Chicago. While this may not seem like a border narrative in the traditional sense, Cisneros's texts illustrate the ways a bicultural experience presents a metaphoric border experience. Her protagonists move back and forth between their Latina/o home cultures and the world outside. In the case of *Caramelo*, the protagonist also literally travels back and forth from Chicago to Mexico and demonstrates how both of those cultures work to mold the young female protagonist in the text. In this case, the border is magnified as a symbolic crossing the protagonist must negotiate in order to come to terms with who she is. This cultural mixing is often celebrated in Latina/o literature as a unique and vital aspect of everyday life. In this sense, the cultural borderlands present a space of creativity and personal comfort with being in-between cultural identifications.

Mestizaje, "Race," and Cultural Mixing

Race is one of the important issues in Latina/o culture, how it is perceived both in the United States and throughout the Americas. Rafael Pérez-Torres theorizes this central concern: "In discussions of Latin American and Chicana/o identity and culture, the notion of racial mixture plays a dominant role. At heart, a recognition of multiple racial and cultural influences—African, Native American, European, Asian—composes the rich and troubled story of mestizaje in the Americas. Consequently, mestizaje has become both the metaphor and the precondition for cultural production in the 'New' World. Critical, visual, musical, and written arts deploy mestizaje as a thematic and formal marker of identity" (xi). This process or racial mixture, or mestizaje, is analogous to the notion of creolization and hybridity. Border theorists and those interested in the historical formation of this group of people use mestizaje to describe the racial formation and ethnic background of Latinos.

But, as Pérez-Torres suggests, mestizaje is also about cultural mixture and highlights the experiences of Latinos in the United States. Mestizos can simultaneously experience themselves as "American" and stay connected to their home culture. Gloria Anzaldúa describes the ability to live with multiplicity in a "black and white" world as "mestiza consiousness" in *Borderlands / La Frontera*. Latino fiction dealing with mestizaje often focuses on young people growing up in families where there is a real generational difference in regards to the relationship to cultural mixture. In fact, most first-generation protagonists have to grapple with what it means to be an "American" who often has a very different relationship to her parents' and grandparents' country of origin. Cristina García's novel *Dreaming in Cuban* presents this as Pilar, the youngest of the protagonists, experiences a different perspective on Cuba than her anti-Castro mother. In Julia Alvarez's *How the García Girls Lost Their Accents*, the girls anguish over their Dominicanness when arriving in New York. The desire to become American results in a coming together of different cultures.

Sometimes, the coming together of cultures has to do with discovering one's "ethnic" identity. Michele M. Serros has written several works of fiction that deal with suburban angst complicated by ethnic identity. In her work, *Chicana Falsa and Other Stories of Death, Identity, and Oxnard*, Serros challenges assumptions about what it means to be Mexican American and Chicana in California. In her poem "La Letty," she notes the transition between childhood and adolescence that marks a shift in the narrator's relationship to her "sister, bestfriend," (2) who,

> had once been "Leticia,"
> "Tish" for short,

> but now
> only two weeks into junior high,
> She is "La Letty"
> *y que*
> *no mas.* (1)

The narrator of this poem watches the transformation of "La Letty," highlighting the way her sister *learns* how to be Chicana, and subsequently tries to teach her lessons in authenticity. The narrator is labeled a "Chicana falsa" by her sister Leticia because she does not dress or speak the same as her "sister, bestfriend" anymore. Serros highlights the complexity of identity again in another poem, "JohnwannabeChicano," which begins, "John Michael Smith, III is / a Chicano" (33). In this poem, the title character desires to belong to the Chicano youth culture and performs the "look" and the language. This cultural blurring demonstrates the interconnected cultures that influence each other: a "white" American youth wants to be Chicano, a Chicana youth is not Chicana enough, and "Tish" can become "La Letty" by virtue of a wardrobe, some makeup, and an attitude. In her adolescent fiction *Honey Blonde Chica* series, Serros continues her look at cultural fusion by following an upper-class, privileged, non-Spanish-speaking, Latina, Evie Gomez, through a variety of teenage dilemmas and identity crises. Through these characters, Serros helps dispel stereotypic expectations about how Mexican American and Chicana youth are "supposed" to look and sound and from which socioeconomic status they are "supposed" to come. Her characters instead share the fact that they are working through their cultural and racial mestizaje.

Such identity crises regularly appear in Latina/o literature and are linked to the difficulty in sorting an identity between multiple cultural backgrounds. Protagonists may or may not identify as Latina/o or as American in these texts; instead there is a negotiation of identity, or more commonly, an articulation of cultural mestizaje—the seamless incorporation of multiple cultural influences in everyday life. Abraham Rodriguez's novels brilliantly describe the everyday lives of young Nuyoricans negotiating culture and identity. In *The Buddha Book,* a group of high school students scoff at the Puerto Rican pride embraced by their public school because it does nothing to abate their bleak everyday existence filled with violence, drugs, and little hope. Instead these students hold large parties and produce underground graphic journalism to disclose the falsehoods they are fed at school. Rodriguez's latest novel, *South by South Bronx* revises this disillusionment with the New York art scene by highlighting the travails of two men in their thirties, a Nuyorican writer and painter, who get caught up in a mystery. The discussions about art and culture in this text illustrate the way multiculturalism in the 1990s operated simultaneously to celebrate and limit art by people of color. Rodriguez thus presents dilemmas of identity as they manifest in institutions of learning and culture that control the discourses about the individual, discourses that have very little to do with reality.

The "racial" and cultural mixing, or mestizaje, illustrated in Latina/o literature appears differently in various eras of literary production. Up until the 1990s most of the literature dealing with these issues focused on the conflicts between cultures. Serros and Rodriguez represent a new generation of writers influenced by popular youth cultures who are comfortable with the postmodern notion of the performative nature of identity. While these texts may not seem overtly political on the surface, they mock the notion that Latinas/os can be identified or defined by one particular cultural, racial, or linguistic marker.

Family and Education

Family plays an important role in illustrating generational shifts and cultural negotiations in Latina/o literature. The stereotypic representation of the strong father, loving mother, nurturing grandmother and the loving children under their care has been the topic of many works of fiction, including Rudolfo Anaya's *Bless Me, Ultima*. These idealized notions of family can operate, however, to reproduce the patriarchal ordering of family that limits the role of women to these stereotypes. Rosa Linda Fregoso argues that representations of idyllic Mexican American families in literature and film "respond in many ways to the family values rhetoric of the nineties by reviving the myth of a singular, ideal familia. . . . traditional images of la familia ignore the diversity of actual familia life in most Chicano/a households" (72). Contemporary U.S. Latina/o literature has dealt with these romantic idealizations of the family that, according to Fregoso and others, stemmed from the various nationalist movements in the 1960s. The politics of Civil Rights required a strong family image to fortify the calls for justice of that era. Writers like Cherríe Moraga have challenged these idealized notions through contemplations of dysfunctional families in her play *Shadow of a Man* and nontraditional configurations of families in her memoir *Waiting in the Wings: Portrait of a Queer Motherhood*.

Despite these alternative views, the family continues to represent the site for Chicano and Latino cultural connections. Lyn Di Iorio Sandín begins her work with this claim: "The protagonists of contemporary U.S. Latino/a fiction are caught in a bind. On the one hand, they face the pressures of assimilation into mainstream American culture. On the other, they are profoundly enmeshed in families closely tied to their communities of origin" (1). Sandín here articulates the tensions between closely knit families championing cultural mores that may be at odds with dominant or mainstream America. Thus, while these alternative views may seem at odds with the stereotypical Latina/o family that is lifted up as an example of family values to mainstream culture, they represent a clearer picture of the tensions found between parent and child in Latina/o literature. While not every parent child relationship is conflicted, it is true that to be a Latina/o family does not necessitate the perfect heteronormative, nuclear family structure.

In Latina/o fiction for children and adolescents, these family images are often nontraditional but they are, for the most part, very positive representations. Extended family members offer insight and support when parents are at odds with children. Grandparents, aunts, and even neighbors present positive role models for the children. In these stories, children are mentored through difficulties in their lives. For instance, Julia Alvarez's novel for young readers, *How Tía Lola Came to Visit Stay*, presents a great aunt from the Dominican Republic coming to Vermont to help a young boy, Miguel, cope with his parents' divorce. Alvarez depicts Tía Lola as Miguel sees her: a bright, cheerful, loving, and somewhat "tropical" character at odds with the community in Vermont. Alvarez thus shows how Miguel reproduces some of the immigrant stereotypes for Dominicans through his embarrassment of Tía Lola's dress and her English language ability. As the story progresses, however, Miguel's perceptions of his aunt change as everyone accepts her and as she helps him adjust to the new challenges in his life. This representation of generational and national difference is telling in that we see how Miguel has internalized the ways non-Latinas/os see Latinas/os (particularly immigrants) in a negative light. In many ways, it takes outside acceptance for Miguel to accept his family and his Dominican roots. This story highlights the ways outside prejudices affect Latina/o families and how children must negotiate the family and the world outside. These kinds of stories can help motivate the development of cultural pride in a young generation of Latinas/os, especially because of the ever-growing numbers living in traditionally non-Latina/o communities. These stories can also help non-Latinas/os (particularly if they are educators) realize the impact their perceptions can have on Latina/o young people and their families.

The cultural pride developed through texts about the family is often connected to the education system. There are many examples, such as Cisneros's famous short story collection, *The House on Mango Street,* that depict the nightmares endured at the hands of nuns or teachers and in the schoolyard. The family can, in these instances, provide a source of encouragement. At other times, like in Juan Felipe Herrera's bilingual picture book *The Upside Down Boy*, illustrated by Elizabeth Gómez, the education system supports and encourages Latina/o students and their families. Herrera's text shows the protagonist's transition from migrant laborer to elementary school student and writer. The journey from anxiety to excitement and success presents how important the education setting is in developing confidence to learn and in encouraging young Latina/o writers.

The importance of family and education in Latina/o fiction is not necessarily an obvious point in that each supplies tensions and joys for the protagonists. U.S. Latina/o literature presents a complex relationship between protagonists and these institutions meant to foster care and growth. However, paying attention to these tensions creates a better understanding of the challenges faced by young Latinas/os attempting to succeed in the U.S. and the families who are simultaneously fostering this success and encouraging cultural pride. The institutional failure to understand these challenges is often the topic of fiction dealing with the urban experience.

Urban Experience

Whether discussing east coast "ghetto fiction" or west coast "barrio" production, Latina/o literature about the urban experience is often an exercise in contradictions. On the one hand, life in the ghetto or barrio is difficult. Economic strains and violence affect the protagonists of this fiction, as does the depressed environment. Schools are not havens from these challenges. Neither do family dynamics offer assistance to overcome the many challenges of barrio life. Nevertheless, there is something communal and familial communicated in urban fiction. Raúl Homero Villa has written of the urban landscape, noting, "many of the cultural practices produced and exercised in the barrios have tended toward positive articulations of community consciousness, which contribute to a psychologically and materially sustaining sense of 'home' location" (5). Latina/o fiction relating to the urban therefore presents an insider's view of "home" or of neighborhood that complicates the stereotypical image of the "ghetto" or "barrio" experience.

From its earliest publications, Latina/o fiction has dealt with the urban space and inhabitants as an articulation of the Latina/o experience. As mentioned before, Nicholasa Mohr and Piri Thomas engaged in the production of this fiction in order to voice the experiences of urban youth in the 1950s. *Down These Mean Streets*, a creative retelling of Thomas's struggles as a black Puerto Rican involved in gangs on the streets of New York, is one of the most often taught texts by a Nuyorican author. Since the

1990s, Abraham Rodriguez has taken up the writing of ghetto fiction, with the aim of critically drawing attention to the plights of young people in the Bronx. As mentioned before, *The Buddha Book* offers a particularly bleak portrait of youth violence and disillusionment. The young people in Rodriguez's novels have very little hope that their Puerto Rican identity will provide them with any advantage in life. Rodriguez uses his characters to perform social critiques of education, the legal system, state government, the economy, the entertainment industry, and gender and racial inequality. The novel is a portrait of the disenfranchised youth within a disenfranchised Latina/o community in the Bronx. Nevertheless, there is always a sense in Rodriguez that the characters have control over the streets and over their collective dilemmas. These authors are simultaneously shedding light on misrepresented and/or misunderstood populations of urban youth in order to dispel nonurban ideas about their culture and to comment on dominant culture.

Other authors write novels about the urban experience to bring to light the experiences of young women. As Villa suggests, this literature depicts the barrio as a complex space that functions as home and a site of danger. This is perhaps best illustrated in Lorna Dee Cervantes's poetry. In her collection *Bird Ave* from the recently published *Drive: The First Quartet*, Cervantes chronicles the lives of nine young girls in a gang on the streets of San Jose, California, in the 1960s. These poems suggest the dangers these girls face on the streets, dangers from sexual predators, from authorities, and from other girls. But a less obvious image is that of the way these girls form a powerful bond that allows them agency and freedom that they do not find in their homes. A somewhat less empowering, but nevertheless nuanced, view of gang life for young women is seen in Yxta Maya Murray's more contemporary novel *Locas,* which chronicles the lives of two teenage girls who end up with two very different relationships to the street. These fictional depictions of urban life provide a historical record of girls' involvements in urban street culture that demonstrates how young women have been fighting off attacks on their bodies, spirits, and minds for a long time. More importantly, these narratives portray intelligent, strong young women who *can* counter the effects of patriarchy on their lives through their communal efforts.

These east and west coast depictions of the fraught ghetto and barrio communities are exemplary of the Latina/o urban fiction produced since the 1970s. These are stories that ask readers to lay aside stereotypes of street life and urban teens and see a more nuanced experience. "Barrio" or "ghetto" fiction is not full of "bad" kids; instead it illustrates the systemic (economic, social, educational, patriarchal, etc.) problems that keep smart, capable individuals in harm's way. Nevertheless, it is important to note that not all Latina/o urban fiction deals solely with gang life. Many novels not only share this theme, but also depict other characters in much different urban situations. Junot Diaz is an example of someone who writes about urban situations from the perspective of young men operating outside of gang culture. These narratives have led to larger perspectives of this literature as communicating just as much about gender and race as about violence and freedom.

Conclusion

Latina/o literature in the United States has grown in volume and in diversity in recent years. In the contemporary moment, it is Latina/o children's literature that has come to represent an exciting new addition to this field of study. Interestingly, these children's authors have continued the thematic concerns found in Latina/o literature more broadly. This is why it is important to have at least an idea of the literary history and the themes Latina/o authors have engaged. This context illustrates that these stories are part of a larger tradition of writing in the United States.

As this literature continues to grow, we can expect to see children's literature engaged with issues of transnationalism and global perspectives, themes that are beginning to emerge in Latina/o literature like Cristina García's *Monkey Hunting,* which chronicles a Chinese family with members in China, Cuba, and the United States, or *A Handbook to Luck* which has three protagonists from different parts of the globe: Cuba, San Salvador, and Tehran. García's texts show that as Latina/o literature develops further, so will the scope of its social justice concerns and its popular appeal. Latinas/os will thus continue to produce great literature with important messages for the Americas and beyond.

Notes

1. Arlene Dávila explains, "Since the 2000 census showed Latinos to be the United States' largest minority, there has been a growing debate about their values, political attitudes, and impact on U.S. national identity" (*Latino Spin* 1). In an earlier study, she comments on the development of the term "Latino" and its current use: "First generalized by federal agencies in the 1970s, a common identity for the diversity of "Latino" populations has since been nourished through census categories, state policies, and the media, prompting questions about the political implications of this development and the ways in which people reject or embrace the identification of "Latino" or "Hispanic" in everyday life" (*Latinos, Inc.* 2).

2. The term "Nuyorican" refers specifically to the Puerto Rican community in New York. The founders of the Nuyorican Poetry Café, a performance and cultural space since the 1970s, coined the term. Nuyoricans are often born and raised in New York City (NYC). The original writers articulated the experiences of the streets and of biculturalism. Nuyorican artists continue this process; but as Rodriguez's work shows, they challenge not only mainstream cultural and social injustices, but those perpetuated within the Latina/o community too.

3. Lisa Sánchez González writes of this move to citizenship: "Throughout the twentieth century, most Puerto Ricans who moved to the mainland United States were the working poor, economic exiles of a colony devoted exclusively to serving the interests of U.S. corporations and military . . . Thus scholars often refer to this Puerto Rican colonial dispersion as a *diasporan*—as opposed to immigrant—experience" (1–2). I will discuss the various Latin communities in another section, but here I also want to note that part of a dispersal of peoples connects with movement and migration.

4. Lisa Sánchez González makes this claim about William Carlos Williams in a foundational literary history of Puerto Ricans in the United States, *Boricua Literature: A Literary History of the Puerto Rican Diaspora* (2001). The information on Arturo Shomburg and Pura Blepré also come from this literary history.

5. I use the "Civil Rights era politics" as a marker of this literature specifically because of the debate laid out by Raphael Dalleo and Elena Machado Sáez in *The Latino/a Canon and the Emergence of Post-Sixties Literature*. Here Dalleo and Machado Sáez critique the claims made by what they call "multiculturalist" and "anticolonial" critics suggesting that contemporary Latina/o literature is no longer political. The multiculturalists suggest Latina/o literature has now assimilated to the U.S. mainstream, whereas anticolonial critics suggest recent literature has lost political potency (5–6). The authors suggest that "rather than turning away from politics, contemporary Latino/a writers are renewing that political tradition by engaging with the triumphs and defeats of the past, formulating political projects that will mark our future horizons in substantial and creative ways. Seeing this renewal requires developing new lenses that acknowledge the ways in which the relationship between literature and the public sphere is being redefined in light of post-sixties realities—the market's centrality in the creation, dissemination, and reception of virtually all contemporary cultural texts" (Dalleo and Machado Sáez 7).

6. Paul Allatson defines Magical Realism in the following way: "Magical realism is a literary genre that attempts to account for realities characterized by the pluralization of worlds and signifying traditions, the intersections between rational and prerational epistemes, and the hybridization of modern and traditional cultural practices. While the concept of the 'magical real' had earlier proponents in Europe in the 1920s, the genre came to international attention with the so-called literary boom in Latin American writing of the 1960s and 1970s, and has since been identified by critics in many national literatures." (147–48).

7. Obejas's latest translation is Junot Diaz's Pulitzer Prize winning novel, *The Brief Wondrous Life of Oscar Wao* (2007).

8. "Yo, neighbors" and "No, for reals, guys. I'm ok." (Translation mine.)

9. In his work *Brown Tide Rising*, Otto Santa Ana suggests, "[C]ontemporary public discourse reveals a dismal portrayal of Latinos in today's society. Latinos are not integrated into their nation. . . . Latinos are never the arms or heart of the United States; they are the burdens or disease of the body politic. Likewise Latinos are characterized as foreigners invading their own national house" (10). U.S. Latina/o Literature counters this discourse of otherness by offering full portraits of the Latina/o experience in the United States.

Works Cited

Allatson, Paul. *Key Terms in Latino/a Cultural and Literary Studies*. Malden: Blackwell Publishing, 2007.

Alvarez, Julia. *How the García Girls Lost Their Accents*. New York: Plume Contemporary Fiction, 1992.

———. *How Tía Lola Came to Visit Stay*. New York: Yearling, 2001.

Anaya, Rudolfo. *Bless Me, Ultima*. New York: Warner Books, 1994.

Anzaldúa, Gloria. *Borderlands / La Frontera: The New Mestiza*. San Francisco: Aunt Lute Books, 1987.

———. *Friends from the Other Side*. San Francisco: Children's Book Press, 1997.

Arteaga, Alfred. *Chicano Poetics: Heterotexts and Hybridities*. Cambridge: Cambridge UP, 1997.

Castillo, Ana. *The Guardians*. New York: Random House, 2007

Cervantes, Lorna Dee. *Drive: The First Quartet*. San Antonio: Wings Press, 2006.

Christian, Karen. *Show and Tell: Identity as Performance in U.S. Latina/o Fiction*. Albuquerque: U of New Mexico P, 1997.

"Cinco de Mayo." *Building Chicana/o Latina/o Communities Through Networking*. University of California. 18 January 2009. http://clnet.ucla.edu/cinco.html.

Cisneros, Sandra. *Caramelo*. New York: Alfred A. Knopf, 2002.

———. *The House on Mango Street*. New York: Vintage Books, 1984.

Dalleo, Rafael, and Elena Machado Sáez. *The Latino/a Canon and the Emergence of Post-Sixties Literature*. New York: Palgrave Macmillan, 2007.

Dávila, Arlene. *Latino Spin: Public Image and the Whitewashing of Race*. New York: New York UP, 2008.

———. *Latinos Inc.: The Marketing and Making of a People*. Berkeley: U of California P, 2001.

Díaz, Junot. *The Brief Wondrous Life of Oscar Wao*. New York: Riverhead Books, 2007.

Fregoso, Rosa Linda. *Mexicana Encounters: The Making of Social Identities on the Borderlands*. Berkeley: U of California P, 2003.

García, Cristina. *Dreaming in Cuban*. New York: Ballantine Books, 1992.

———. *Monkey Hunting: A Novel*. New York: Alfred A Knopf: 2003.

———. *A Handbook to Luck*. New York: Alfred A Knopf: 2007.

Gaspar de Alba, Alicia. *Desert Blood: The Juarez Murders*. Houston: Arte Público Press, 2007.

Herrera, Juan Felipe. *Super Cilantro Girl / La Superniña del Cilantro*. Illustrations by Honorio Robledo Tapia. San Francisco: Children's Book Press, 2003.

———. *The Upside Down Boy / El niño de cabeza*. Illustrations by Elizabeth Gómez. San Francisco: Children's Book Press, 2000.

Hijuelos, Oscar. *The Mambo Kings Play Songs of Love*. New York: Farrar Straus Giroux, 1989.

McCracken, Ellen. *New Latina Narrative: The Feminine Space of Postmodern Ethnicity*. Tucson: U of Arizona P, 1999.

Moraga, Cherríe L. *Shadow of a Man. Heroes and Saints & Other Plays*. Albuquerque: West End Press, 2000.

———. *Waiting in the Wings: Portrait of a Queer Motherhood*. Ithaca: Firebrand Books, 1997.

Morales, Yuyi. *Just a Minute: A Trickster Tale and Counting Book*. San Francisco: Chronicle Books, 2003.

Murray, Yxta Maya. *Locas: A Novel*. New York: Grove Press, 1997.

Pérez-Torres, Rafael. *Mestizaje: Critical Uses of Race in Chicano Culture*. Minneapolis: U of Minnesota P, 2006.

Rodriguez, Abraham. *The Buddha Book*. New York: Picador, 2001.

———. *South by South Bronx*. New York: Akashic Books, 2008.

Ruiz de Burton, María Amparo. *The Squatter and the Don*. New York: The Modern Library, 2004.

Sánchez González, Lisa. *Boricua Literature: A Literary History of the Puerto Rican Diaspora*. New York: New York UP, 2001.

Sandín, Lyn Di Iorio. *Killing Spanish: Literary Essays on Ambivalent U.S. Latino/a Identity*. New York: Palgrave Macmillan, 2004.

Santa Ana, Otto. *Brown Tide Rising: Metaphors of Latinos in Contemporary American Public Discourse*. 1st ed. Austin: U of Texas P, 2002.

Serros, Michele M. *Chicana Falsa and Other Stories of Death, Identity, and Oxnard*. Valencia: Lalo Press, 1994.

———*Honey Blonde Chica*. New York: Simon Pulse, 2007.

Soto, Gary. *Chato's Kitchen*. Illustrated by Susan Guevara. New York: The Putnam and Grosset Group, 1997.

Thomas, Piri. *Down These Mean Streets*. New York: Vintage Books Press, 1997.

Villa, Raúl Homero. *Barrio-Logos: Space and Place in Urban Chicano Literature and Culture*. Austin: U of Texas P, 2000.

CHAPTER 16

Conflicting Inclinations: Luis J. Rodríguez's Picture Books for Children

Phillip Serrato

Today's world of the child demands a new literature, for the literature of the past does not meet their needs.

Gerald A. Reséndez, "Chicano Children's Literature" (109)

Today's students of children's literature are living in an interesting era of book publishing for children. They may analyze new books of contemporary realistic fiction and contemplate the different directions that authors can choose to pursue.

Donna E. Norton, *Through the Eyes of a Child* (369)

The failure of books for children to reflect and address the experiences of Chicana/o children prompted Chicana/o authors in the 1960s and 1970s to start writing their own books for young people. As Gerald Reséndez points out, prior to the emergence of these books, the texts that could be found in American schools and libraries—for example, Leo Politi's *Juanita* (1946) and Maurine Gee's *Chicano, Amigo* (1972)—did nothing more than "[perpetuate] stereotypes, . . . [enable] a negative self-image of [Chicana/o] children, [and foster] a serious misunderstanding of the Chicano and [Chicana] culture" (108). Frustrated with the racism and various distortions that inhered in American children's literature, Nephtalí de León, Ernesto Galarza, Alonso Perales, Alurista, and others began penning picture books, short stories, and poetry collections—oftentimes exclusively in Spanish—that embodied the values of educational advancement and cultural validation. As Reséndez stresses, these authors' overarching objective was "to express the unique experience of the Chicano child, to deal with reality rather than with the exotic, romantic, and unreal, and to capture the flavor and soul of what it is to be Chicano" (109). Notably, in several cases an investment in "deal[ing] with reality" compelled authors to depict the racism, poverty, and other hardships that they could see devastating too many Chicana/o children's lives.

By the 1990s—a decade during which a widespread interest in multiculturalism among teachers, librarians, and other concerned adults undergirded a marked increase in the publication of books for children by Chicana/o authors (Brady 219; Fernandez E3)—authors began to portray more ambitiously the realities that ail Chicana/o communities and that impact the lives of children in these communities. Going far beyond cultural validation, novelists such as Francisco Jiménez and Gloria Velásquez and picture book authors such as Gloria Anzaldúa and Juan Felipe Herrera engaged, in a comparatively more forthright manner, subjects such as immigration, racial discrimination, gang violence, and homosexuality. Of course, anytime writers for children confront their readers with weighty social concerns or complicated themes, anxiety arises about young audiences' readiness for such material. Thus, unsurprisingly, while works such as Velásquez's *Tommy Stands Alone* (1995) and Anzaldúa's *Friends from the Other Side* (1997) have received praise for boldly addressing some of the salient issues that young people today encounter, they have also been the targets of complaints precisely because of their boldness.

The picture books of Luis J. Rodríguez illustrate the conflicting inclinations that contemporary Chicana/o authors struggle to resolve as they continue to develop stories for children around challenging issues. With striking depictions of poverty and violence, Rodríguez modulates the ambitious spirit of new realism into the picture book genre, thus breaking new ground within the genre. Through their appeal to new realism, *América Is Her Name* (1998) and *It Doesn't Have to Be This Way* (1999) can be read as attempts to speak to the fact that many Chicana/o childhoods are distinguished by experiences with different forms of hardship. Curiously, however, each book concludes with a tidy and uplifting resolution that seems to be at odds with the aggressive commitment to depicting unpleasant realities that otherwise distinguishes each text. While, on one level, such a discrepancy bespeaks a hesitancy in the world of children's publishing to put on the market texts that are overly harsh or "depressing," it also emblematizes ambivalence on the part of contemporary Chicana/o authors about how they can best help contemporary youth negotiate the facts of their lives.

Telling It Like It Is

Given his background as a gangbanger-turned-author who has chronicled in his "adult" writings how mean life on the streets of urban America can be, it is not surprising that Luis Rodríguez's picture books for children are as intense as they are. Rodríguez first gained literary notoriety for his autobiography, *Always Running: La Vida Loca, Gang Days in East L. A.* (1993). According to Rodríguez, the book's unflinching recapitulation of his descent as a teenager into a life of violence, crime, and drugs was meant to discourage his son, Ramiro, from following in his father's gangbanger footsteps (Rodríguez, "Behind *la vida loca*" 103). Today, Rodríguez devotes his energies to steering "at-risk" young people across the country away from gangs, drugs, crime, and dropping out of school. Committed to opening young people's eyes to alternative prospects in life, he is constantly touring, delivering public lectures, and running workshops at sites ranging from public schools to youth detention facilities. The two picture books for children that he has written so far result from his ambition to prompt critical thinking in young people about their destinies and to help them come to terms with the issues that affect them. To maximize the impact of his works on especially urban Latina/o youth, he incorporates into his books elements of realism not ordinarily found in picture books for children. Through this realism, ideally, his works can assume a special relevance (and thus utility) for contemporary youth.

In *América Is Her Name*, his first picture book for children, Rodríguez reveals his interest in producing an innovative, more relevant type of literature for children by presenting a narrative about a young immigrant girl trying to live with (and through) a number of personal and familial challenges. In this manner, Rodríguez offers a different type of protagonist as well as a storyline not ordinarily found in picture books for children. Introducing this new type of protagonist and some of her struggles, the opening page relates:

A Mixteca Indian girl walks through the Pilsen barrio in Chicago. She has honey-brown skin and elongated eyes that are large and dark; her thick hair is in braids. She was born in the mountains of Oaxaca. She still remembers the goats, pigs, and thatch-roofed house they once called home. Now she is in a strange place she can't even pronounce. She dreams of Oaxaca in Spanish.

América is her name. América Soliz. She is nine years old and has two brothers and a sister. Her mother's name is Nayeli, a Mixteco name which means "Flower of the Fields." América's father Oscar works the factories of southwest Chicago. He sleeps all day and works all night. She rarely sees him. Her uncle, Tío Filemón, lives with them. He also works. And he drinks. América dreams that he doesn't drink.

Endowed with a distinctly racialized physiognomy, América physically resembles girls who may not be accustomed to seeing themselves in books or in other realms of popular culture, thus creating an opportunity for a hitherto overlooked sector of girl readers to identify finally with a protagonist. The admiration that charges Rodríguez's description of América is especially important because it counters the abjuration of the Indian body that historically has decimated the esteem of many dark-skinned Latina girls and women. By suturing readers into an appreciation of América vis-à-vis her appearance, Rodríguez works to interrupt the disparagement of girls who look like her as well as undo (if not preempt) any shame felt by girl readers who may have such a body.

Most compelling about the first page of the story is its inventory of the multiple tiers of distress that complicate América's experience. Besides geographical and cultural dislocation, América must contend with an absent father and an alcoholic uncle. A few pages later, readers see that the specter of violence randomly tinges her life when, while on her way to school, she witnesses a boy fire a gun at a group of boys who are taunting him. Once she is in school, América suffers through an intimidating English as a Second Language class with a teacher who later, and with obvious hostility, refers to América as "an illegal." Literally, with every turn of the first few pages, América comes in contact with a new source of grief. Structurally, this mapping of the girl's circumstances provides a setting for this narrative, creating an opportunity for readers to meet the protagonist and become acquainted with some of the distinguishing details of her life. As readers thereby realize some of the challenges that América faces, they can wonder what will become of this girl and how she will deal with the various difficulties she faces.

As the story proceeds, yet more causes for despair accumulate. América's father gets laid off from his job, América's mother comes home upset because someone at the grocery store has called her a "wetback," and Tío Filemón continues to drink. Midway through the book, América hits her emotional low point when her father finds her indulging a new-found interest in writing poetry. When America's father catches her writing a poem at the kitchen table, she reveals to him that poetry has become a meaningful, personal outlet for herself. "I'm writing a poem for me," she explains to her father. With complete insensitivity, however, América's father scolds her, "Don't waste your time. Where are you going to go with writing? Learn to clean house, to take care of your brothers and sisters. Writing for yourself won't pay the bills." Devastated by her father's words, América looks outside of her family's apartment window. The narrative then explains,

América is sad. "Will this be my life?" she wonders. "Not to write. To clean houses, get married, have children. To wait for the factory to feed us." She sees in her mind all of the sullen faces that look out of third-floor windows when she walks to school and the desperate men without jobs standing on street corners. They all seem trapped, like flowers in a vase, full of song and color, yet stuck in a gray world where they can't find a way out. "Will this be my life?"

The depiction of the exchange between América and her father and the girl's subsequent despair is a bold move on the part of Rodríguez on several levels. First of all, he confronts young readers with the somber realization that they may not necessarily be able to count on their family to be a source of encouragement. Family, he shows, can sometimes be unsupportive, insensitive, and inhospitable. Moreover, Rodríguez invites a critical reconsideration (and thus a reorganization) of the machinations of gender within some Latino families by showing the narrow perspective of América's father. To the dismay of his daughter, the father imposes on her oppressive expectations and suppresses her pursuit of the one fulfilling activity she has. In effect, the text destabilizes presumptions about the primacy of family bonds in Latino families as well as the primacy of the patriarch in Latino households.

While some readers might bemoan that América faces an overkill of difficulties—which is perhaps part of the reason a *Publishers Weekly* review dubs the book "ponderous" and "heavy-handed" ("Forecasts" 75)—it seems more appropriate to understand the inclusion of so many harsh realities into this one story as a reflection of the fact that immigrant children in the United States must indeed contend with a panoply of socioemotional conflicts. Numerous sociological studies have documented immigrant children's struggles to navigate an overkill of personal challenges.[1] One study particularly useful for interpreting América as an emblem for immigrant children found that "[Mexican immigrant] families experiencing multiple risk factors (e.g., financial hardship, low maternal education, maternal depression) or numerous negative life events (e.g., serious injury or illness, job loss) tend to have children with more adjustment problems than families experiencing a single risk factor" (Dumka, Roosa, and Jackson 310). Suggesting as much, *América Is Her Name* presents an immigrant child on the verge of being overwhelmed by multiple stressors ("risk factors" and "negative life events") that precipitate "adjustment problems" that in her case take the form of painful isolation, alienation, and introversion.

Bearing in mind the sociologically realistic underpinnings of the crafting of América, the case can be made that Rodríguez is not merely falling prey to overambition and trying to do too much in his first book for children. Rather, he can be seen trying to produce the kind of book that, as he mentions in an interview, he believes contemporary readers need: one that finally tells the untold stories of immigrant children and acknowledges the realities of their lives (Merina 7). The significance of this kind of book lies in its potential to facilitate the resilience of children living in similar situations by providing an articulation of some of the experiences and anxieties that accrue to cause stress in immigrant children. As long as painful experiences and anxieties remain repressed for children, they are susceptible to the anxiety that accompanies psychological and emotional disorganization and thus remain unable to resolve or at least accommodate their conflicted feelings (De Rios 162). As Rodríguez maps out the situations that certain children face, however, he enables children's cognitive mastery (or understanding) of their circumstances. This mastery, in turn, can contribute to the development of a general coping with (or acceptance of) life circumstances in those readers who identify with América. Concomitantly, the text offers to facilitate the accommodation of the feelings that these situations provoke and thereby alleviate some of the stress that haunts immigrant children.

In *It Doesn't Have to Be This Way*, Rodríguez tells another story that, again in an effort to speak to contemporary childhood realities and concerns, features, at least for most of the book, a particularly aggressive narrative strategy. Waxing autobiographical in his "Introduction" to the text, Rodríguez shares with readers his motivation for writing this book about a boy who considers joining a gang:

> I was involved in gangs from the time I was eleven until I was eighteen. It was a very hard way to grow up. Many of my friends from those years are dead, and I'm very lucky just to be alive. Today I spend a lot of time counseling young people in gangs. I want to show kids growing up that they don't have to go through what my friends and I did. That's why I've written this book.

With this introduction, Rodríguez makes clear his desire to offer a cautionary tale about the pitfalls and perils of *la vida loca*,[2] or life in a street gang. Traumatized by the ordeals through which he lived and feeling fortunate just to be alive, Rodríguez hopes to spare young people the necessity of learning from firsthand experience the truth about gangs. Such a commitment holds special urgency given the warning delivered in a 1998 report that appeared in the journal *Psychology in the Schools* that "Well into the 1990s, America has more youth gangs, more gang member drug involvement, and more gang violence than ever before" (Larson and Busse 373).

As in *América Is Her Name*, *It Doesn't Have to Be This Way* features some gritty elements that are not commonly found in picture books for children but that nonetheless reflect the realities with which many contemporary youth are all too familiar. The story revolves around Monchi, a young Chicano who lives in an unspecified barrio where, he says, "I live with my mom. Inside the houses, through open doors, I [can] see brightly painted walls with lots of pictures. From inside [come] music and the smells of dinners cooking." After introducing Monchi, Rodríguez portrays some of the conflicts that Monchi has to navigate. A few pages into the book, Clever, the leader of the Encanto Locos Pee Wees, a local street gang, approaches and propositions Monchi. In a portrayal of the sort of "direct confrontation" that more than a few barrio youth encounter as early as the elementary school years (Vigil 53–56), Monchi explains,

> On my way home [from Tío Rogelio's house], there is a big tree where I like to sit and read and write poetry. I stopped there for a while, leaning against the tree in the shade.
>
> Suddenly, Clever was standing over me. I stared at a scar on his lower lip. "*Quiuvo?* What's up?" I asked. I tried to sound cool, but I was scared.
>
> "It's about time you joined the Pee Wees," he said. I nodded. It seemed like the only thing I could do. I was glad he wanted to be friends and wasn't going to hurt me. But I knew the Pee Wees did things that got them into trouble.

In Monchi's response, Rodríguez models the multiple levels of pressure and confusion that a youth may feel in this situation. At once, the boy is stunned by his lack of preparedness for this situation as well as leery of giving a "wrong" answer that may upset Clever and potentially lead to Clever's harming him. Afraid of harm and unaware of alternative ways of responding to his predicament, which is how young people may really feel in such a situation, Monchi says that agreeing with Clever "seemed like the only thing I could do".

Interestingly, after laying out a situation with which many readers may identify, Rodríguez starts developing a Brechtian detachment between the reader and the text. As articulated by Brecht, the alienation effect is a crucial means by which theatre can enable in a spectator a careful, detached contemplation of the drama that is being played out in a stage performance. The possibility of a detached contemplation depends, Brecht stresses, upon the capacity of a performance to reveal itself as a performance and not seduce spectators into being swept into a suspension of disbelief. In *It Doesn't Have to Be This Way*, Rodríguez encourages a comparable detached contemplation through what some might consider the shallow handling of certain features of the narrative. In particular, Monchi's assumption that Clever "want[s] to be friends" with him positions readers to think critically about the decision that Monchi faces. Clearly, Monchi misunderstands Clever's intentions. As readers see through the shallow reference to friendship, they can complicate any notion that an invitation to join a gang is tantamount to an invitation to be someone's friend. Hence, I would argue, Rodríguez's narrative transcends critiques of new realist texts as simplistically contrived and "peopled with characters who are more mouthpieces of a particular point of view than fully developed protagonists" (Forman 470). In the case of *It Doesn't Have to Be This Way*, Rodríguz is attempting to speak to the real experiences of contemporary children and efficiently capture the dynamics that they must negotiate in a manner that, paradoxically, creates a critical distance between readers and the situation being depicted. Ideally, readers will, in turn, be able to think twice about the decisions they must make in their own lives.

Once Monchi assents—on an obviously faulty premise—to join the Pee Wees, he participates in activities that position readers to consider what gang membership actually entails. With support from illustrator Daniel Galvez, Rodríguez offers readers insight into some of the dangers of *la vida loca*. Among other things, Rodríguez narrates and Galvez illustrates Monchi's slide into petty crime, his newfound willingness to sneak out of his home at night, and his witnessing of the brutal initiation (or "jumping-in") of a new member into the Pee Wees. As documented by sociologists such as James Diego Vigil, the initiation of a new member into a gang often involves a ritual in which the prospective member is encircled by current members and then beaten for a period of time that may range from 30 seconds to several minutes. Through such a specialized rite of passage, the gang tests the mettle and commitment of the prospective member. On both the narrative and visual levels, the jumping-in that Monchi witnesses in *It Doesn't Have to Be This Way* is meant to be particularly painful for a reader to bear. Alongside Galvez's illustration of a heap of a body on the ground surrounded by a group of boys, one of whom has his foot raised in the midst of stomping the victim, the text states, "Five guys beat on Payaso for sixty seconds—one whole minute! I wanted to close my eyes because it hurt just to watch." Of course, part of the pain for Monchi—which Galvez captures in the boy's twisted expression as he turns away from the savage spectacle—lies in his realization that if he decides to become a full member of the gang, he can expect to be the next heap on the ground. For readers, this moment shows the violent underside of gang life. By revealing a harsh fact of gang life such as this one in this picture book, Rodríguez's aim is obviously to dissuade, if not scare, young people away from gang membership.

The culminating moment of *It Doesn't Have to Be This Way*—both in terms of its narrative structure and its unusual ambition—occurs with a drive-by shooting. On the night that Monchi meets up with the Encanto Locos so that they can jump him into the gang, Monchi's cousin, Dreamer, arrives at the scene. Up to this point in the story, Dreamer has served as a cautionary voice of reason, urging Monchi to stay away from Clever and the Locos. Earlier, for instance, when she spies Monchi fiddling with a knife he recently obtained, Dreamer urges Monchi, "Monchi, I used to hang around with Clever and them guys. I don't like some of the things they do." When she appears on the scene just before Monchi's scheduled initiation, she makes one last effort to tell Monchi, "Don't do this." At the same moment, however, trouble strikes, "We didn't notice a car pull up in the dark with its lights out. Someone in the car yelled, 'Soledad Night Owls!' They are the main enemies of the Locos. Just as we turned, they shot at us. Boom! I dropped to the ground and heard the car speed off." In the aftermath, Monchi finds everyone unscathed except for Dreamer, whom he discovers "moaning in the dirt" in a pool of blood. With fear creeping over him, Monchi notes that "Her face looked strange, pale. There was so much blood." Complementing Rodríguez's narrative efforts, Galvez shows an eerily pale Dreamer lying on the ground with a crimson pool collecting beneath her.

Certainly, petty crimes, gang initiations, drive-by shootings, and bleeding-to-death cousins are not the usual fare that one encounters (or expects to encounter) in picture books for younger children.[3] However, the inclusion of such elements into *It Doesn't Have to Be This Way* constitutes a means by which Rodríguez actually offers to fulfill David Russell's call for a children's literature that can "touch the lives . . . of young [urban] readers with matters that concern them" (Russell 32). As Russell notes, urban youth in particular have historically been stranded by a paucity of literature that captures their experiences. Granted, the matters that urban youth encounter today may not be pretty, and the inclusion of these matters in a picture book may collide with popular sensibilities about appropriate content for picture books for children, but the alternative—the suppression of such material—only denies young readers an opportunity to acknowledge, understand, come to terms with, and negotiate the issues that really affect them.

Happy Endings for Everyone

Interestingly, by the end of *América Is Her Name* and *It Doesn't Have to Be This Way*, both texts lose their new realist momentum. Shortly after we see América on the verge of an emotional collapse in *América Is Her Name*, her life suddenly and dramatically takes a turn for the better. "A few days later," Rodríguez narrates,

> América burst into the kitchen. "Mamá, mamá, tengo un cien!" she says. "I got a hundred on my writing assignment. Even Miss Gable liked it." Her mother beams proudly. "I knew you could do it! You are a poet." Her dad looks up from the television and says, "Well, what do you know. Maybe I've got a poet for a daughter." He stands up. América thinks he is going to yell at her. Instead, he hugs her real tight. "M'ija," he says. "Don't worry. I'll find a job again. I'll work hard, every day, every night if I have to. It's good you're writing poetry."

Although it is heartening, the problem with this conclusion is that it seems too easy. All of a sudden, the different adversarial forces that taxed América are neutralized. Her teacher, who was previously portrayed as intractably racist and hostile, is now a source of encouragement. Her father, who had scathingly rebuked her interest in poetry and who had exhibited entrenched macho attitudes, now encourages his daughter to write. Moreover, her father vows to get a job and even work night and day if necessary, which sounds inspired but which actually does not make complete sense. Her father is unemployed not because of laziness or an unwillingness to work; he is unemployed because he got laid off, which means he is unemployed because of economic realities outside of his control. Thus, a simple avowal to find a job will not be enough to resolve the family's financial woes.

Meanwhile, at the end of *It Doesn't Have to Be This Way*, amidst two pages of hand wringing over whether Dreamer will survive the shooting, Monchi comments, "I never knew anything like this would happen." Such a remark reflects how Monchi serves as a potential surrogate for the reader who, before reading the book, might not have thought too much about the consequences of being in a gang. Notably, all anxiety is relieved, when, finally, "The doctor came out and told us that Dreamer was going to live." The survival of Dreamer here is a key swerve away from the new realist trajectory that the text initially follows, however, for it takes readers out of tough truths and into idealistic, more comfortable endings. At the risk of sounding cruel and insensitive, the survival of Dreamer could be seen as undermining the effort of the book to boldly present to young readers the realities of gangs. With its happier ending, the text stops short of fully showing youth what can indeed happen when one associates with gangs.[4]

Compounding the notably nonrealist, and therefore less than fully effective, style of the ending of *It Doesn't Have to Be This Way* is the handling of Monchi's ultimate decision not to join the gang. At the hospital, Monchi's uncle, Tío Rogelio, advises Monchi, "It doesn't have to be this way, *m'ijo*. I know you want to be a man, but you have to decide what kind of a man you want to be." Remembering these words shortly thereafter, when Clever informs Monchi of the Locos' retaliatory plans, Monchi simply tells Clever, "It doesn't have to be this way." With not another word on Clever's response or the subsequent relationship between Clever and Monchi, the text leaves readers with the implication that Monchi will be able to enjoy trouble free days ahead. This suggestion is terribly problematic, of course, because barrio youth "invited" to join a gang frequently find themselves coerced into joining with the threat of physical violence hanging over any unwillingness they may have. Individuals who decide to decline the invitation often end up living in danger and certainly not happily or even easily ever after.

In all likelihood, cautious publishers can be cited as part of the reason for the rather idealistic endings of *América Is Her Name* and *It Doesn't Have to Be This Way*. Discussing representations in books for children of immigrant experiences, for example, Nelly Hecker and Bob Jerrolds observe that publishers have been hesitant to publish "books that portray the harsh experiences and sadness of immigrants" (128). At the same time, the happy, all too easily resolved endings may reflect Rodríguez's (and other authors') divided sensibilities about strategies for writing for children. Rodríguez himself has professed a desire to give young people hope in their lives as part of his motivation as a writer. As if to offer hope to urban youth mired in the predicaments depicted in *América Is Her Name* and *It Doesn't Have to Be This Way*, Rodríguez models the possibility of the transcendence of apparently dead ends. América appears en route to a more fulfilling future, and Monchi seems safe from the "urban nihilism" that Vincent Pérez identifies as an element of life in a gang (134–35). In this respect, Rodríguez's two texts embody Maria Nikolajeva's inspiring idea that "fiction is not a direct *reflection* of reality but an artistic *transformation* of it" (190).

Even with this in mind, though, one can question how fair it is for Rodríguez to gesture toward such ideal possibilities when their basis in reality (and therefore their relevance to contemporary youth) remains questionable. Indeed, these endings seem acutely ironic because whereas the new realist features of his books nurture resilience, their conclusions seem at odds with the development of resilience. With no fully satisfactory way out of this predicament, it seems that Rodríguez and other similarly ambitious writers for youth are left to continue to wrestle with and work out their conflicting inclinations. Motivating them, of course, will be well-intentioned desires to offer contemporary youth a helpful, relevant, and effective literature to get through life. Carlos Vélez-Ibáñez's discussion of Chicano literature in *Border Visions* is useful for putting the divergent directions of children's authors in perspective. With the premise that "At present, poetry, novels, 'pieces,' and expository narratives by the hundreds dot the Mexican[-American] literary landscape in the search for and expression of place and space—internal and external" (213), Vélez-Ibáñez figures Mexican-American literature as "multiply gifted" and "multifaceted" (213). He then concludes,

> the common thread that unites them in much of the literature is the basic existential search for place, space, and connection, and just as important cultural creation and invention. Whether it is . . . women simultaneously expressing ancient and generating new and innovative modes of writing or . . . men struggling to deconstruct their own inventions, much of [contemporary Mexican-American literature] defies easy classification, pigeonholing, or categorization because it is born of struggle and creation within a region of struggle and creation. This is not a world of easy categories. (213)

Likewise, Chicana/o children's literature is a literature in a productive flux. Alongside Juan Felipe Herrera's pointed *Super Cilantro Girl* we have Pat Mora's measured *Rainbow Tulip*. Also in the mix and not to be overlooked we can find Rigoberto González's innovative *Antonio's Card* as well as Gloria Anzaldúa's brilliantly intertextual *Prietita and the Ghost Woman*. Of course, while each text is critically necessary in its own right, it is also always somehow imperfect. In the final analysis, no author will ever get the balance of critical thinking, age-appropriate content, *and* entertainment value "right," but that is what makes Chicana/o children's literature a powerfully dynamic and rich genre. It is a genre that resists stasis and remains unafraid to search out new ways to be relevant and useful in speaking to contemporary needs.

Notes

1. See, for instance, Grace Kao, "Psychological Well-Being and Educational Achievement Among Immigrant Youth."
2. Translated literally, "*la vida loca*" means "the crazy life." Within urban Chicana/o cultural formations, the phrase has a lengthy history of being used to refer to life in a street gang.
3. Interestingly, amazon.com lists the book's reading level as "Ages 4–8" while the publisher's website lists it as intended for "Ages 6 and up."
4. Admittedly, if Dreamer were to have been killed off in this barrio tale, the text would simply fall into the problematic and stereotypical trap of portraying a female who has to be sacrificed for the sake of a male protagonist's salvation. Indeed, even as it stands, the text can be seen as recycling this stereotype of the

sacrificing female with Dreamer "just" taking a bullet and having a close call with death. The suffering that she endures is for the redemption of Monchi.

Works Cited

Anzaldúa, Gloria. *Friends from the Other Side*. San Francisco: Children's Book Press, 1993.

———. *Prietita and the Ghost Woman*. San Francisco: Children's Book Press, 1995.

Brady, Jeanne. "Multiculturalism and the American Dream." *Kinder-Culture: The Corporate Construction of Childhood*. Eds. Shirley R. Steinberg and Joe L. Kincheloe. Boulder: Westview, 1997. 219–26.

Brecht, Bertolt. "Short Description of a New Technique of Acting which Produces an Alienation Effect." *Brecht on Theatre: The Development of an Aesthetic*. Ed. and trans. John Willett. New York: Hill and Wang, 1964. 136–47.

De Rios, Marlene D. "Magical Realism: A Cultural Intervention for Traumatized Hispanic Children." *Cultural Diversity and Mental Health* 3.3 (1997): 159–70.

Dumka, Larry E., Mark W. Roosa, and Kristina M. Jackson. "Risk, Conflict, Mother's Parenting, and Children's Adjustment in Low-Income, Mexican Immigrant and Mexican American Families." *Journal of Marriage & Family* 59.2 (1997): 309–23.

Fernandez, Maria Elena. "A New Chapter on Cultural Pride." *Los Angeles Times*, 24 September 2000. E1+.

"Forecasts: Children's Books." *Publishers Weekly*, 13 April 1998. 75.

Forman, Jack. "Young Adult Books: Politics—The Last Taboo." *The Horn Book* 61 (July/August 1985): 469–71.

Gee, Maurine. *Chicano, Amigo*. New York: Morrow, 1972.

González, Rigoberto. *Antonio's Card/La Tarjeta de Antonio*. San Francisco: Children's Book P, 2005.

Heale, Jay. "What Publishers Are Publishing and What Children Want to Read." *Bookbird* 36.1 (1998): 36–38.

Hecker, Nelly, and Bob W. Jerrolds. "Cultural Values as Depicted in Hispanic Contemporary Fiction Books Written for Children." *Linking Literacy: Past, Present, and Future*. Ed. Kay Campbell, Bernard L. Hayes, and Richard Telfer. Logan: Logan State U, 1995. 115–24.

Herrera, Juan Felipe. *Super Cilantro Girl*. San Francisco: Children's Book P, 2003.

Kao, Grace. "Psychological Well-Being and Educational Advancement among Immigrant Youth." *Children of Immigrants: Health, Adjustment, and Public Assistance*. Ed. Donald J. Hernandez. Washington, D.C.: National Academy P, 1999. 410–77.

Lamme, Linda Leonard, Danling Fu, and Ruth McKoy Lowery. "Immigrants as Portrayed in Children's Picture Books." *Social Studies* 95.3 (2004): 123–29.

Larson, Jim, and R. T. Busse. "Specialist-Level Preparation in School Violence and Youth Gang Intervention." *Psychology in the Schools* 35.4 (1998): 373–79.

Merina, Anita. "Meet: Luis Rodríguez—Peacemaker." *NEA Today*, 14.6 (Feb 1996): 7.

Nikolajeva, Maria. *Children's Literature Comes of Age: Toward a New Aesthetic.* New York: Garland, 1996.

Norton, Donna E. *Through the Eyes of a Child: An Introduction to Children's Literature.* 7th ed. Upper Saddle River: Prentice Hall, 2006.

Perez, Vincent. "'Running' and Resistance: Nihilism and Cultural Memory in Chicano Urban Narratives." *MELUS* 25.2 (2000): 133–46.

Politi, Leo. *Juanita.* New York: Scribner, 1948.

Reséndez, Gerald A. "Chicano Children's Literature." *Chicano Literature: A Reference Guide.* Eds. Julio A. Marínez and Francisco A. Lomelí. Westport, CT: Greenwood P, 1985. 107–21.

Rodríguez, Luis J. *Always Running: Mi Vida Loca, Gang Days in L.A.* New York: Simon & Schuster, 1994.

———. *América Is Her Name.* Willimantic, CT: Curbstone P, 1998.

———. "Behind *la vida loca.*" *Latina* (Jan 1999): 102–03.

———. *It Doesn't Have to Be This Way.* San Francisco: Children's Book P, 1999.

Russell, David L. "'The City Spreads Its Wings': The Urban Experience in Poetry for Children." *Children's Literature in Education* 29.1 (1998): 31–42.

Velásquez, Glora. *Tommy Stands Alone.* Houston: Piñata Books, 1995.

Vélez-Ibáñez, Carlos G. *Border Visions: Mexican Cultures of the Southwest United States.* Tucson: U of Arizona P, 1996.

Vigil, James Diego. *Barrio Gangs: Street Life and Identity in Southern California.* Austin: U of Texas P, 1988.

CHAPTER 17

Reading Trauma and Violence in U.S. Latina/o Children's Literature

Tiffany Ana López

My writing about children's literature here is part of my larger work in trauma theory and Latina/o literary and cultural studies. In this essay, I explore the ways four writers, Luis Rodríguez, Julia Alvarez, Gloria Anzaldúa, and Roberto Gonzalez, extend their engagements with matters of violence and trauma from their writing for adult audiences into their children's literature. Reading the movement of their writing across genres illustrates the distinct ways authors dealing with matters of trauma and violence repeatedly return to certain scenes of memory and event not so much for finding resolution as for making meaning and instigating change.

Latina/o children's literature is critically instructive because it challenges and expands thinking about trauma. Notably, the kind of writing under discussion in this essay is driven by a keen sense of responsibility by which authors construct themselves as intimately bound to both their audience and story. I offer the term *critical witnessing* to describe the process of being so moved or struck by the experience of encountering a text as to embrace a specific course of action avowedly intended to forge a path toward change. I look at the many forms (writing, teaching, and engaged reading, be it of a written text or a performed life) that critical witnessing takes, beginning with how writers signal the personal as a highly productive springboard for critical engagement. I explore the various ways these Latina/o children's authors position themselves as critical witnesses, sharing stories of survival and healing, explicitly inviting their young readers into a shared circle of critical witnessing and insistently offering their writing as a vehicle toward personal and social change.

To be a critical witness entails more than just telling or repeating a story or event. Rather, critical witnessing works from a story's impact as much as its intention as a means to spotlight the conditions that brought the story into being. It is experienced as a profound level of response, a palpable necessity to create as a means to generate social change. Critical witnessing is more than a focused act of looking or bearing witness. It actively insists that an event is pivotal and in need of expanded context and critical address. Critical is an operative word here, for it is what characterizes this form of witnessing as engaged in a pedagogy of social justice whereby the story instructs in order to reconstruct.

While we live in a society saturated by violence, there is no public critical discourse about violence, especially not one that is made accessible to children. The processes of both coming into and surviving violence too often get buried within predictable melodramatic narratives of evil perpetrators and forsaken victims. While such stories represent very real feelings, these essentialist narratives evade the complexity necessary to produce critical discourse and social change. People come into violence for complicated reasons, and they survive violence in complicated ways. The ability of Latina/o children to navigate an openly hostile and debilitating world depends on their being taught active modes of engagement such as those offered through literatures of critical witnessing.

I am interested in reading Latina/o children's literature as a profound engagement with trauma theory that articulates and documents the ways Latina/o children are burdened by violence and haunted by cultural trauma, from the colonization of lands and bodies to the subjugation of minds and spirits, and the ways its authors map survival strategies. In her book, *An Archive of Feelings*, Ann Cvetkovich writes, "the project of investigating racial histories needs to be a part of interdisciplinary trauma studies" (6). To date, trauma theory has yet to explore the lives of Latinas/os as either individual survivors of violence or as members of a group with a shared history of trauma. I situate my investigation of Latina/o children's literature as a means to necessarily enrich and expand trauma studies. Drawing from Rudolfo Anaya's fruitful observations in his foreword to *Growing Up Chicana/o*, Latina/o literature is "a creative history, told in the form of stories. . . . It is fair to say that as long as our literature was not available to white America, this country did not really know the life of the [Latina/o] community" (Lopez 7). If our stories of violence remain untold, they remain unheard, a defining part of our lives unknown; and without documentation, stories of violence cannot be analyzed or a counterdiscourse theorized. Latina/o children's literature of critical witnessing provides a window into the world of Latina/o children and the various and complex ways they are forced to grapple with situations and histories of violence.

Within a cultural moment in which affirmative action, bilingual education, and head start programs have been effectively dismantled and issues of immigration and migrant labor continue to get positioned as sources of political scapegoating, even criminality, Latina/o children's literature offers a critically urgent space. Many Latina/o youth lack a consistent sense of economic, social, and emotional stability. Narratives produced by the dominant culture portray the individual as responsible and, if only properly motivated, fully capable of remedying problems. Lack of access to economic resources (employment, education, health care) is seldom portrayed as tethered to the workings of the larger social fabric. Absent is a critical discourse that forcefully spotlights institutionalized oppression and demands a larger public accountability. As Cvetkovich observes,

> Because trauma can be unspeakable and unrepresentable and because it is marked by forgetting and disassociation, it often seems to leave behind no records at all. . . . Trauma puts pressure on conventional forms of documentation, representation, and commemorations, giving rise to new genres of expression . . . that call into being collective witnessing and publics. . . . It thus demands an unusual archive. (7)

The Latina/o children's literature I explore in this essay provides what Cvetkovich describes as an "unusual archive." All of the writers I have chosen for discussion have published a collection of personal essays or a memoir and clearly translate their thinking about the ways violence has shaped their identity into their writing for children which, I posit, reads as a form of mentoring on the page. They work from their experience with personal, cultural, and/or historical crisis points to show readers a path toward a horizon of healing. Each thus works to create a form of storytelling that will help to usher young readers through various forms of violence and to fortify them as survivors of trauma, readers of culture, and agents of change.

Luis Rodríguez and the Practice of Complete Literacy

I begin with a discussion of Luis Rodríguez because his work so aptly represents what it means for a writer to position himself as a critical witness. He explicitly constructs himself as a mentor on the page through such phrasings as "The more we know, the more we owe" (Rodríguez, *Always* 11) and "It is not enough to prepare our children for the world; we must also prepare the world for our children" (*América*), and he focuses on forms of violence that most readers readily understand as clearly harmful to Latina/o youth: gang warfare, racism, poverty. In the preface to his groundbreaking memoir targeted toward juvenile audiences, *Always Running—La Vida Loca: Gang Days in L.A.*, Rodríguez dedicates the work to his son Ramiro, whom he fears is following in the footsteps of his own personal history of struggle against the pull of gang life. Seeing his same battles with violence and gangs repeated by his son, compounded by a growing lack of school, community, and job programs, propels Rodríguez to write his memoir as a book of outreach and guidance for others in a similar state of crisis. He clarifies, "My hope in producing this work is that perhaps there's a thread to be found, a pattern or connection, a seed of apprehension herein, which can be of some use, no matter how slight, in helping to end the rising casualty count for the Ramiros of this world, as more and more communities come under the death grip of what we called 'The Crazy Life'" (Rodríguez, *Always* 11). In outlining the program he sees necessary for fully empowering youth in facing a world delimited by the scope of violence that informs gang culture, Rodríguez offers the term *complete literacy* to describe "the ability to participate competently and confidently in any level of society one chooses" (9). This term carries much critical import as it signals the paramount importance of stability (self-awareness, forethought, emotional introspection, critical engagement) in healing from violence. Rodríguez's memoir offers what Cvetkovich terms an "unusual archive" by documenting forms of violence that, because they occur in marginalized communities, appear invisible to the dominant culture.

By showing young readers how to navigate through the most challenging of situations and events—those charged by histories of trauma and violence—Rodríguez works to offer a fortifying inoculation against systemic forms of violence. He documents this history and emphasizes it as one of collectively experienced violence to counter the ways it has been naturalized and, as such, accepted as part of the construction of identity and culture; furthermore, he provides a critical language to help others recognize these forms of violence as culturally traumatic, such as when he describes the work "an indictment against the use of deadly force which has been the principal means this society uses against those it cannot accommodate" (Rodríguez, *Always* 10). Notably, Rodríguez defines "deadly force" as not just physical violence, but also inclusive of entrenched, ongoing, and systemic forms of emotional, social, and economic oppression that route youth into gang life. He writes, "'The Crazy Life' in my youth, although devastating, was only the beginning stages of what I believe is now a consistent and growing genocidal level of destruction predicated on the premise there are marginalized youth with no jobs or future, and therefore expendable" (6).

Here, he defines poverty and racism as forms of violence that give rise to the formation of gangs as "sophisticated survival structures" (8).

For Rodríguez, physical violence and stereotypes operate in tandem within this structuring language. If the formative years of Latina/o children are structured by violence, and it is perceived as carrying tremendous cultural currency, as they struggle to express themselves and find a way in the world, violence will most likely be the language they employ. His detailing of his gang years illustrates how dominating structures of violence only fester and give rise to reactive substructures. Rodríguez writes about why he felt drawn to join a gang: "I had certain yearnings at the time, which a lot of us had, to acquire authority in our own lives in the face of police, joblessness and powerlessness. Las Lomas was our path to that, but I was frustrated because I felt the violence was eating us alive" (Rodríguez, *Always* 113). Stereotypes enact a particularly potent form of violence on Latina/o youth in their power to destroy confidence and limit competence. In his early collection of poetry, *Poems across the Pavement,* Rodríguez' poem, "Piece by Piece" offers a key image he returns to in *Always Running,* a "jacket made of lies/—tailor made in steel," an image that spotlights the ways stereotypes from the dominant culture enact a form of violence because of the ways they restrict how Latina/o youth envision who they can be and what they can do. He writes,

> If you came from the Hills, you were labeled from the start. . . . Already a thug. It was harder to defy this expectation than just accept it and fall into the trappings. It was a jacket I could try to take off, but they kept putting it back on. The first hint of trouble and the preconceptualizations proved true. So why not be proud? Why not be an outlaw? Why not make it our own? (Rodríguez, *Always* 84)

When youth are disempowered economically and socially (i.e., through stereotypes), they search for new languages in their quest to feel empowered. Rodríguez exposes the structuring force of stereotypes to clarify for readers that to participate in gangs is to participate in the perpetuation of stereotypes and pass on the wounds of violence they seek to ameliorate. Rodríguez returns to the metaphor of the jacket and affirms to his son: "You have a worth . . . outside [the stereotypes] that [have been] imposed on you since birth. Stop running" (251). To stop is to carve a space for contemplation and redirection, both of which are necessary for combating violence.

In *Always Running* Rodríguez also offers the hope that young readers, particularly young males, will see their lives reflected in his own story. This is what defines him as a critical witness. In reading about his carving a path toward changing his life, they might then see their own possibilities for change reflected within the narrative. Often what we are unable to recognize in ourselves, we more readily recognize in others. Throughout the memoir, Rodríguez spotlights his struggles during his formative years with extreme poverty, lack of educational opportunity, institutionalized racism, and burdensome definitions of masculinity. Notably, he positions all as mutually informative and as existing on a continuum of violence, a spectrum that spans from verbal assault to physical attack and includes both individual and institutional violations. He offers readers a frank and graphic accounting of his involvement with gang violence and emphasizes while there are many things he did of which he is not proud, he must remember so that he does not forget; the violent person he was in the past informs the critical voice of personal and social change he represents today. Notably, he provides a context for what led to his involvement in gangs and what eventually empowered him to leave. All hinged on his discovery of new languages. He writes, "I felt disjointed, out of balance, tired of just acting and reacting. I wanted to flirt with depth of mind, to learn more about my world. My society. About what to do. I became drawn to the people who came to work at the community centers; they were learned" (113). He ultimately observes, "We needed to obtain victories in language, built on an infrastructure of self-worth" (219).

In this register, mentors play a paramount role in fostering personal and social change and ushering the disenfranchised and wounded into a position of critical witnessing as part of the healing process. A pivotal scene in *Always Running* concerns Luis' mentor, Chente, who spins a globe and asks him to find Las Lomas, the neighborhood territory that has been the source of his devoted involvement in gang warfare. Rodríguez cannot. This lesson sparks his thinking about the ways individual acts on a small scale have the power to resonate into a global context and instigate change. He muses, "I thought about the globe. Chente was right. A bigger world awaited me" (Rodríguez, *Always* 236). Chente's probing insights motivate Rodríguez to begin taking small steps toward demonstrating leadership from within the gang, believing others might make similar observations about the world if only he could find a way to make Chente's brand of pedagogy accessible to his fellow gang members. At a party he experiments with influencing others by speaking a new language, one of questioning the presumed social norms: he refuses to smoke a joint being passed around. It is a small but significant act: "As soon as somebody took a stand and turned it down, the others did the same" (Rodríguez, *Always* 235). Luis finds himself filled with a newfound sense of confidence to take further steps toward making changes in his life by speaking with a greater sense of authority and occupying a position of leadership: "I figured I could help the homeboys become warriors of a war worth fighting for. . . . if they had something more meaningful in their lives; if only" (237).

The scene reads as a microcosm of the memoir, which offers itself as a kind of social atlas, helping young readers find and navigate their place in the world. It exemplifies how personal experience provides a highly generative springboard for critical engagement and how creating change depends on being able to reflect back on one's experiences and place them in a larger comparative framework; to do this, one needs critical witnesses to show the way. Rodríguez only comes to see himself as a role model through his mentor Chente's profound observations about his life: "You have to make a choice now. Either the craziness and violence—or here, learning and preparing for a world in which none of this is necessary. . . . There are a lot of people involved in your life now. When you win, we win; but when you go down, you go down alone" (159). Most significantly, through these mentoring conversations Chente gives Luis the precise language he needs to carve a path for not only changing his life but also reaching out to others.

Notably, Rodríguez's account of his experiences with his mentor illustrates the new ways he comes to see language and, in the process, himself. Rodríguez explains why he was able to even allow himself to learn from Chente: "I looked up to him. . . . He was someone who would influence me without judging me morally or telling me what to do. He was just there. He listened, and when he knew you were wrong, before he would say anything, he would get you to think" (Rodríguez, *Always* 114). Chente teaches him to see that language is power and requires responsibility: "There are choices you have to make not just once but every time they come up" (132). His conversations with his mentor are what facilitate Rodríguez's emotional transition away from gang life by empowering him with the skills to observe critically the limited communication of gang violence. He analyzes a gang key phrase, "*de volada*" ("just do it, right now and without thought or hesitation" [n.p.]), as evidence of how gangs train one *not* to think for oneself (79) and stifle independent thinking so as to promote a collective voice that speaks through the language of violence: "[O]nce you are asked to do a hit, you can't refuse, can't question or even offer an excuse" (118). In the end, Rodríguez' memoir dramatizes the tension between the life that is expected of a young man and the life he chooses to live for himself.

Literature of critical witnessing boldly investigates the complex spectrum of subjectivities defined through violence and trauma. People commit acts of violence for complicated reasons, and people survive violence in complicated ways. Throughout his work, Rodríguez emphasizes that while one might engage in violent acts, this does not make one evil, nor is engaging in the language of violence necessarily a permanent thing. The language of violence can be replaced by other performative languages, such as poetry and teaching. Violence is emphatically portrayed as a language of poverty and desperation, conditions that can be mitigated.

Rodríguez's two illustrated children's books, *It Doesn't Have to Be This Way* and *América Is Her Name*, build on his memoir in their portrait of the ways violence impacts the lives of Latina/o youth and in the books' emphasis on the role of mentors in ushering youth through struggle by providing a language for navigating toward the future. Mentors show the child protagonists how to fully articulate their feelings, assert their observations, critically assess a situation, and find a sense of choice about possible actions in scenarios that appear to offer an incredibly delimited range of possibilities.

Mentors hold a particular significance in the lives of Latina/o youth growing up in the inner city. If a child's home life and/or community life is unstable, then teachers and school provide an incredibly vital space. As *Always Running* illustrates, children turn toward gangs to fill a void when their needs for emotional stability are not being fully met. In his introduction to *It Doesn't Have to Be This Way*, Rodríguez speaks frankly to his young readers about the autobiographical connections between himself and Monchi, the book's protagonist: "I know why young people join gangs: to belong, to be cared for, and to be embraced. I hope we can create a community that fulfills these longings, so young people won't have to sacrifice their lives to be loved and valued in this world" (Rodríguez 3). This brief introduction is accompanied by images of young Luis striking a tough pose contrasted with images of an adult Rodríguez today counseling youth, autographing books, and sitting with his family. The book thus begins by emphasizing the possibilities for transformation beyond one's circumstances which are made visually measurable through the photos that document Rodríguez' journey from young gang member to a professional writer and community activist.

Like *Always Running*, *It Doesn't Have to Be This Way* shows the pernicious process by which youth get routed into the violence of gang life, beginning with the initial allure of gang life and the emotional needs gangs fulfill. Significantly, Monchi is never invited to join a gang. Rather, his joining is presumed as a rite of passage into adulthood. The local gang approaches him and declares, "It's about time you joined the Pee Wees." After Monchi is brought into the gang by being called to witness another member get "jumped in" (beat up for 60 seconds by the entire gang acting as a unit), he dons the uniform (baggy pants, flannel shift, a bandanna) and immediately finds people treat him differently, "At school, I got respect. Girls talked to me, and older gang members gave me the handshake."

As Rodríguez recounts in *Always Running*, mentors provide alternative role models who are pivotal to combating violence and instilling new survival strategies. Monchi has two key role models readily available to him: Clever, the local gang leader, and Tío Rogelio, his uncle. The former offers to teach him the language of intimidation and criminality; the latter, the language of caring and commitment. Throughout his work Rodríguez emphasizes the need for youth to have adults who value what they have to say. In *It Doesn't Have to Be This Way*, Tío Rogelio occupies the role played by Chente in the memoir. Monchi's time spent with his uncle under the protective hood of a car compares to Rodríguez's descriptions of his time spent with Chente at the youth center: both locations provide an intimate and protected arena for storytelling and the imparting of life lessons. Like Chente, Tío Rogelio speaks to Monchi from a place of genuine caring. He invites him into a space of personal exchange, "Tell me one of your stories." In contrast, Clever tells Monchi what to do and he only interacts with him in the larger public space of gang territory.

In Rodríguez's work, mentors emphasize that violence is not a natural part of the environment by calling attention to the systems that sustain it. In *It Doesn't Have to Be This Way*, as a mentor on the page, Rodríguez reveals an economy of violence, from the man who commissions Monchi and other kids to steal bikes, to Clever who brings kids into the gang and calls the shots (something literalized in the shooting of Monchi's cousin, Dreamer). This difficult social terrain underscores the need for children to have mentors in their lives to combat the potent and systemic force of gangs. Most significantly, Rodríguez shows the need for kids to have adults who compassionately listen to their stories and simultaneously encourage their critical engagement with the world. A successful mentor is an active listener. Like Chente, Tío Rogelio does not judge Monchi; rather, he offers difficult questions and observations intended to empower and direct Monchi to make his own decisions about how to respond to a situation of life crisis. Tío Rogelio offers, "I know you want to be a man, but you have to decide what kind of man you want to be." His counsel sparks Monchi's thinking about his connections to others. He thereafter understands himself as responsible for the welfare of his cousin Dreamer, "It was because of me that she got shot." And like the young Rodríguez concludes through his conversations with Chente, through his conversations with his uncle, Monchi begins to realize his potential for being, rather than following, a leader.

When Clever commands Monchi to join a retaliation drive-by shooting to avenge Dreamer's getting shot ("It's tonight! You got to come"), Monchi confidently reiterates Tío Rogelio's words, "It doesn't have to be this way." This scene illustrates the incredibly important role of mentors on the well being of families (Monchi's and Dreamer's) and communities (Monchi's school and neighborhood) because of their transformative impact on Latina/o youth. At the end of the book, Monchi returns to his special time with Tío Rogelio fixing cars and sharing stories. He speaks about meeting Clever and making the decision not to join a gang, to which his uncle responds, "That was a brave thing. . . . I have a lot of respect for you." Monchi shares with the reader, "Nobody ever said that to me before. It made me feel real good." This scene shows Monchi's transformation after receiving from his uncle the love and support Rodríguez reports Latina/o youth too often seek and receive from gangs. The closing lines of the book indicate the potential of mentors to change the direction of a young person's life by redirecting thought about collective force and group action. Tío Rogelio shares, "We can make good things happen, mijo, if we all work together" to which Mochi responds, "I liked the sound of that."

Rodríguez's second children's book, *América Is Her Name,* further illustrates the paramount role mentoring plays in the cultivation of complete literacy as a strategy of combating and healing from trauma. In the background of *América* loom poverty and the threat of violence. The illustrations in the book contrast the world of struggle against the violence of poverty with the universe of poetry and the imagination. América's father has lost his job and lashes out in anger at family members, such as when he demeans her attempts to write poetry. Her mother struggles with experiences of overt racism, and her uncle drinks out of sadness and homesickness. América's teacher appears equally burdened, always yelling at the school children, frustrated with their linguistic and social struggles.

Mr. Aponte, a visiting poet to her school, inspires América to use poetry as a means to remember her homeland in Oaxaca and narrate her feelings and observations about immigrant life in Chicago. Mr. Aponte affirms, "When you use words to share feelings with somebody else, you are a poet, and poets belong to the whole world. Never forget this." With these words, he invites América into a circle of critical witnessing. Mr. Aponte's visit is brief, but the lessons he imparts are shown to have incredible force, resonating with América and guiding her through the crisis points at home. When América's father first sees her writing poetry, he responds, "Don't waste your time. Where are you going to go with writing. . . . Writing for yourself won't pay the bills." To escape scrutiny and ridicule, América writes her stories and poems secretly "because there's no one to read them to." This passage emphasizes that América does this not because no one is physically present, but because no one in her family values her creative expression of self. In the face of economic hardship, it is difficult for many families to envision and support the long-term benefits of a humanities-based education when the immediate reality is one of economic survival. Mr. Aponte helps to fortify América with skills of introspection and communication to get her through times of conflict. She finds comfort in finding a sense of community in the writing and sharing of poetry and in time she confidently asserts to her father that she writes for herself ("I'm writing a poem for me"). Reading and writing thus provide América with an alternate vision that allows her to define herself outside the boundaries of the poverty, racism, and violence that encircle her life. Notably, América's mother begins to join her at the kitchen table where they spend time writing and exchanging poetry. This scene highlights América's leadership skills within her own family and the potential of children to pass on to adults what they learn from their mentors.

In this way, Rodríguez portrays the long reach of mentoring, notably how a child can pass on the acquisition of new languages in ways that impact the family unit and, by extension, perhaps the entire community, a potential signaled by Rodríguez naming his protagonist América. When América comes home with a perfect test score, her mother proudly declares, "I knew you could do it! You are a poet." Her dad takes time to stop watching television to marvel, "Well, what do you know. Maybe I've got a poet for a daughter.'" Inspired by her accomplishments during a time of shared family struggle, he avows, "Don't worry. I'll find a job again. I'll work hard, every day, every night if I have to. It's good you're writing poetry." The book concludes with América proudly musing, "That sounds good to the Mixteca girl, who some people say doesn't belong here. A poet, América knows, belongs everywhere." As he does in his memoir and previous children's book, Rodríguez portrays the power of mentoring to urge complete literacy into action. It allows América to work through a period of family crisis, and furthermore it inspires members of her family to affirm their own sense of strength. Notably, in his endnotes for both *It Doesn't Have to be This Way* and *América is Her Name*, Rodríguez shares that the writing was inspired by stories shared with him by children during his work as a visiting writer in classrooms across the United States.

In her essay, "Not Outside the Range: One Feminist Perspective on Psychic Trauma," Laura Brown provides an important set of distinctions regarding the ways the dominant culture reads and defines trauma and survivors:

> Our definitions of trauma have been narrow and constructed within the experiences and realities of dominant groups in cultures. The dominant, after all, writes the diagnostic manuals and informs the public discourse, on which we have built our images of "real" trauma. "Real" trauma is often that form of trauma in which the dominant group can participate as a victim rather than as the perpetrator or etiologist of the trauma. (102)

Brown also offers an important contrasting term from the work of feminist therapist Maria Root, "insidious trauma," defined as "the traumatogenic effects of oppression that are not necessarily overtly violent or threatening to bodily well-being at the given moment but that do violence to the soul and spirit" (107). In the second half of this essay, I am interested in the ways Latina/o children's authors engage with what Brown terms "insidious trauma" and how their work illustrates various stages in the practice of critical witnessing.

The New Mestiza as Critical Witness in the Work of Gloria Anzaldúa

Gloria Anzaludúa's notion of *mestiza consciousness* is important to the reading of trauma and violence in Latina/o children's literature because, like Rodríguez's concept of complete literacy, it works to provide a discourse that enables its practitioners to navigate the world with a sense of confidence and competence. In her landmark cross-genre feminist text, *Borderlands / La Frontera*, Anzaldúa defines the critical practice of the new mestiza:

> The new mestiza copes by developing a tolerance for contradictions, a tolerance for ambiguity. She learns to be an Indian in Mexican culture, to be Mexican from an Anglo point of view. She learns to juggle cultures. She has a plural personality, she operates in a pluralistic mode—nothing is thrust out, the good, the bad and the ugly, nothing rejected, nothing abandoned. Not only does she sustain contradictions, she turns the ambivalence into something else. (79)

The new mestiza is a type of critical witness. She actively positions herself as driven to pass on her skills of survival born from struggle and values the complexities of her resulting subjectivity. Anzaldúa translates this practice into her children's book, *Friends from the Other Side*, imbuing her protagonist Prietita with the characteristics of the new mestiza as critical witness. While sitting on the branch of a tree in her backyard, Prietita meets an impoverished boy named Joaquín when he comes to her home selling firewood. She observes, "his Spanish was different from hers" and notices his small bony arms covered with boils. Prietita's cousin and friend call him names, such as "wetback" and "mojado." In speaking with him, Prietita learns Joaquín is from Mexico, which the children refer to as "the other side." He and his mother live in a shack and are plagued with worry that their family will be split apart by the Border Patrol should they be caught and deported.

Notably, Prietita works under the mentorship of an herb woman to become a healer. Her apprenticeship requires that she learn to recognize variations in the landscape and discern the difference between things that are toxic and things that are healing. With each observation about Joaquín and how he is treated within her community and culture as well as within larger society, Prietita is challenged to take some sort of action that speaks to her level of commitment to healing wounds, both literal and symbolic. Throughout the book, Prietita is tested: will she stand up to her cousin's ignorant and hurtful epithets, will she rebuke a lifelong friend for his violent gestures? Is she ready to learn how to concoct healing remedies, such as those needed to cure the boils on Joaquín's arms? Can she become a discerning reader of the social as well as the natural landscape?

In *Borderlands / La Frontera*, Anzaldúa refers to the border as a *herida abierto*, a "1,950 mile-long open wound/dividing a *pueblo*, a culture" (3). As Phillip Serrato and I observe in our essay "A New Mestiza Primer: Borderlands Philosophy in the Children's Books of Gloria Anzaldúa," the boils that cover Joaquín's arms are strongly visually representative. These physical wounds "signify the larger ruptures that exist within the Chicano/ Mexican social body, the intracultural divisions between Chicano/ Mexicano, legal citizen/illegal alien, boy/girl" (López and Serrato 208). Joaquín's boils externalize the ways he has been made to absorb emotionally the violence of poverty and racism. To further underscore this point, Anzaldúa provides an introduction that draws on her own experiences growing up in South Texas, close to the border. She describes as a young girl having witnessed women and children crossing the border in search of work because none existed in their homeland, and she then exposes the term "wetback" as an ignorant and hurtful construction: "Many of them got wet while crossing the river, so some people on this side who didn't like them called them 'wetbacks' or 'mojados.'" Anzaldúa's story shows how these words are emotionally and physically potent with a very real power to maim and wound, to fuel racism and lead to violence, illustrated in her describing one of the boys attempting to punctuate his calling Joaquín a wetback by throwing a rock at him. Additionally, she describes the Border Patrol van as ominously prowling the neighborhood in search of Joaquín and his mother.

The violence of history that informs such language and events is spotlighted in the book when a Border Agent inquires, "Does anyone know of any illegals living in this area?" To which a neighborhood woman responds, "Yes, I saw some over there," as she points to "the gringo side of town." Anzaldúa's writing of this comment signals a traumatic event in Chicano history, the United States' taking of lands through the Treaty of Guadalupe Hidalgo (something she discusses at length in *Borderlands*), which is also referenced within the Chicano political vernacular in the darkly humorous phrase, "we didn't cross the border; the border crossed us."

The "other side" in the title of this book refers not only to the other side of the border, but also to a new location of thought, a narrative space driven by empathy and understanding, rather than presumptions born from stereotypes, fear, or ignorance. Anzaldúa portrays Prietita's process of becoming a critical witness for Joaquín. She befriends him and takes the time to learn about his family and their struggle. She saves part of her lunch each day to share with Joaquín, and when the Border Patrol conducts their neighborhood sweep, she provides him and his mother with a safe place to hide, taking them to the herb woman because "she'll know what to do." When Prietita's cousin and her friends taunt Joaquín with "Hey man, why don't you go back to where you belong? We don't want any more mojados here" and threaten to hurl a rock to punctuate their words, Prietita speaks out: "What's the matter with you guys? How brave you are, a bunch of machos against one small boy. You should be ashamed of yourselves!" The closing lines of the book are spoken by the herb woman, who acknowledges Prietita's coming into a position of critical witnessing with the capacity to help usher others through their trauma: "Prietita, I'm going to show you how to prepare these herbs in a paste you can use to heal Joaquín's arms. It's time for you to learn. You are ready now." From her mentorship Prietita has learned to be a critically engaged observer. She understands how to intervene in violent situations and how to draw on multiple resources. Additionally, her confidence and competence make her a leader among her peers and allow her to pass on her lessons to others, such as her cousin and his friends, and by extension, the readers of this book. These narrative moments illustrate the position of the new mestiza as a critical witness, someone inspired by her mentor to serve in a position of guidance and leadership for others.

Critical Witnessing and Self-Empowerment in Rigoberto Gonzalez's Children's Books

In his focus on Chicana/o children grappling with the violence of poverty and the debilitating force of representation, Rigoberto Gonzalez's children's books extend many of the critical engagements that characterize the works of Luis Rodríguez and Gloria Anzaldúa. His first illustrated children's book, *Soledad Sigh-Sighs / Soledad Suspiros*, portrays a day in the life of eight-year-old Soledad whose entire family works long shifts that require her to come home from school by herself and sit each day in an empty home well into the evening. While neighbors check in on Soledad, she is responsible for finishing her homework, heating her own dinner, preparing herself for bed before her family's return, and assuring everyone that she is safe. The title of the book refers to her habitual physical response to the stress of her life:

> By the time everyone comes home, Soledad is asleep on the living room couch. Her math book lies at her side with a worksheet sandwiched between the pages like a slice of Swiss cheese. When Mami wakes her up it is already morning and time to wash-dry-dress to go to school. Papi and Titi wave at her from behind their cups of coffee. . . . Soledad Sighs again. If only she didn't have to be alone after school.

Soledad's routine is unexpectedly disrupted and her spirits lifted when she meets two neighborhood girls who insist on visiting her at home. The girls play together in the small apartment and point things out to Soledad that, in her growing daily boredom, she missed seeing as resources for play and creativity. It is a "the grass is always greener on the other side" kind of story: "'You know what, Soledad?' Nedelsy asks, 'I think you're pretty lucky, having fun with your friends sometimes and being on your own at others." Soledad does not view her situation in this light; however, her friend's envy prompts her to see her life through a new lens. Her friends provide a mirror into which she sees her life from a new perspective: "'Oh, look, Jahniza,' Nedelsy says. 'A treasure box!' Soledad places her finger on her chin. Why didn't she see that crate there before?" Significantly, the book ends not with a change in the family's circumstances, but rather with a change in Soledad's response to those circumstances. When Soledad's mother arrives home early and discovers Soledad's newfound friends, Soledad sighs "but in a happy way," content to know she has access to friends when she needs them.

Gonzalez's insights and observations in this book are translated in part from his two adults works, his memoir, *Butterfly Boy*, and a collection of autobiographical fiction, *Crossing Vines*. The latter draws on his experiences growing up as the son of migrant farmworkers and delivers a series of interwoven short stories, many of which are focused on how children forced to join their families working in the fields effectively have their childhood suspended. The debilitating impact of such hard labor and the burden of imposed responsibilities set them apart from their peers. In his memoir, Gonzalez details the aftershock of such experiences: his early adulthood is driven by an intense conflict between wanting to live alone and fearing solitude, wanting to feel a part of a community and always feeling out of sync with his peers, tensions that clearly inform his involvement in a series of emotionally and physically abusive relationships. As an adult, he finds himself unconsciously searching for the sense of nurturing and play excised from his childhood due to his family's struggle against the tide of poverty that required his conscription into migrant farm labor while still only a child. Gonzalez's children's books are born from his understanding that this erasure of childhood is a form of violence even though it is not typically discussed as such. His children's books very much read as stories delivered to counter the combined debilitating forces of emotional and economic violence. In part, it is their invisibility that defines them as violence. Soledad sighs because she is supposed to keep any sense of suffering silent. In being expected to contribute to her family's economic survival, she is asked to have a level of understanding beyond her years; her childhood is a secondary concern to the family's struggle against poverty.

Gonzalez's second children's book, *Antonio's Card / La Tarjeta de Antonio*, also looks at an invisible yet debilitating force of violence: compulsory heterosexuality and homophobia, especially as they impact children. In her essay, "Learning from the Death of Gwen Araujo?—Transphobic Racial Subordination and Queer Latina Survival in the Twenty-First Century," Linda Heidenreich writes of the case of Gwen Araujo, a transgender Latina youth murdered by young men from her own neighborhood. While Araujo's family and friends supported her throughout her struggles to openly express her identity, her larger structuring world of school and neighborhood did not. Heidenreich clarifies, "In fact it is outside her family that she was most unsafe. Her mother asked that bathroom accommodations be made for her at school. The school refused. Students began to harass her; eventually she gave up and dropped out" (51). Heidenreich echoes Brown's and Cvetkovich's insistence that such violence demands being read as a shared public trauma: "Her death sent a message to all of us who are queer, but especially to those of us who are queer and Latina, queer and raced, queer and mixed race—we are not safe—even when loved and embraced by our own families, as was Gwen Araujo" (52).

Antonio's Card / La Tarjeta de Antonio portrays the pressures of compulsory heterosexuality on a young boy forced to grapple with whether or not to publicly display in his classroom the Mother's Day card he has made for Leslie, his mother's partner and his second mother. While Antonio is a masterful speller and loves words, he lacks the language to articulate his conflicting feelings to either Leslie or his mother but especially not to anyone at school. While he loves Leslie, he fears other children in the class will laugh at his card—and, by extension, at him and his family—for the image of Leslie privileged over that of his biological mother will make it clear that his family does not represent the norm Antonio sees defined by his peers on their Mother's Day cards; his definition of mothering is complex and defies singular representation. In Gonzalez' portrait of Antonio's struggle to articulate his fears, he illustrates how though they may lack the critical language, Latina/o youth with queer *familia* are well aware of the powerful social structuring of compulsory heterosexuality and homophobia as its by-product.

As someone drawn to spelling, Antonio is also incredibly well aware of the power of language to wound: "Words are more than letters. Words hurt feelings. He doesn't want to hear the kids laughing at his card. He doesn't want to see the kids pointing at Leslie." The book details Antonio's observations about how people react to those who are different, specifically those outside heteronormativity, and the difficult internalized thought process he must engage in order to come to his final decision about whether or not to display his card for Leslie. The turning point in the story occurs when Leslie picks him up from school and takes him to her studio to unveil her own Mother's Day present for Antonio's mom, a beautiful canvas portrait. Gonzalez spotlights Antonio's emotional response to seeing this work:

> Antonio feels a lump in his throat. He can hardly speak. Antonio imagines what his afternoons would be like without Leslie, while his mother is at work. In his mind, he sees a solitary tree, and beneath the leaves he sees a solitary boy. No one to read with, no one to play spelling games with or curl up next to. He doesn't want ever, ever to have to write the word L-O-N-E-L-Y.

Leslie's confident display of her love for Antonio's mother inspires him to emulate it and confidently display his own artistic declaration of love for Leslie whom he clearly considers to be a mother: "Suddenly Antonio feels so lucky that Leslie is part of his family. And that is nothing to be ashamed of." The book concludes with Antonio proudly taking Leslie back to school to share his own artwork with her, his Mother's Day card.

That Antonio makes a card evidences that this is a story about the burdens of representation, specifically the impact of representations of compulsory heterosexuality, writ large in the dominant culture through such holidays as Mother's Day, on youth living in queer family structures. In *Borderlands*, Anzaldúa writes of her response to learning that one of her students thought homophobia meant a fear of going home, "I thought, how apt. Fear of going home. And of not being taken in. We're afraid of being abandoned . . . for being unacceptable, faulty, damaged. Most of us unconsciously believe that if we reveal this unacceptable aspect of the self our mother/culture/race will totally reject us" (20). As Heidenreich's essay makes clear, there is great significance to Gonzalez's focus on school as a site of emotional conflict. Teachers very much provide a form of public mothering. What is the impact for queer youth to believe that their public parents will reject them? Heidenreich's essay confirms Antonio's fear is legitimate as it is grounded in a history of violence, no matter that it is one only recently formally documented.

Notably, Gonzalez's children's books evidence a philosophy that widely characterizes Latina/o literature: children must be given the tools to act with awareness and vision, what Rodríguez terms confidence and confidence. As with many of the children's books that have been discussed thus far, in *Antonio's Card* it is not the circumstances that change, but the child's thinking about his circumstances and, even more importantly, his ability to make productive sense of his own struggle. As with Anzaldua's *Friends from the Other Side*, Antonio must learn to proudly defend and embrace difference. While Antonio reaches a point of resolution, Gonzalez's book shows the difficulty of his doing so on his own without the guidance of a mentor or fellow critical witnesses to help usher him through his struggle.

The Alchemy of Violence in Julia Alvarez's *Secret Footprints*

I conclude this essay with a discussion of Julia Alvarez's *The Secret Footprints* because it powerfully illustrates the ultimate goal of healing from trauma and violence: for survivors to see themselves defined as bigger than the events of trauma alone and to be able to read through their own stories of violence toward stories of hope, play, and joy, to fully celebrate life in all its complexities and contradictions.

Notably, Alvarez's children's book stands in dialogue with her other engagements with the history, culture, and people of the Dominican Republic, most especially its history of political violence and how it impacts the definition of self and community. For example, her juvenile novel, *finding miracles*, is a story about a girl adopted into a Jewish family in

Vermont who discovers that she is an adoptee from "a country recovering from a brutal history of dictatorship and political corruption." This purposefully vague book jacket description leaves the country unnamed, thus directing readers to emphasize the enduring resonance of violent events rather than to isolate them in a particular place or time. This is underscored by the book's mention of historical figures, such as the Mirabal Sisters, who also figure prominently elsewhere in Alvarez' adult fiction (*In the Time of Butterflies*). These moments of translation illustrate the pivotal role the history of violence in the Dominican Republic has for Alvarez as a writer and her sense of responsibility to honor the survivors of that history, evidenced by her repeatedly casting a spotlight on the lasting scars of trauma and violence so that they may be fully articulated and critically analyzed, shame and secrecy adamantly refused. Indeed, *The Secret Footprints* is about making secrets visible, a continuance of Alvarez's ongoing portraits of survivors' shared struggle to unburden themselves of secrets of what trauma theorists term *the unspeakable*.

Based on a mythological story Alvarez heard throughout her growing up years in the Dominican Republic, *The Secret Footprints* unfolds the tale of the ciguapas, a beautiful people whose feet are on backward ("so their toes face where they have come from") and who live in underground ocean caves; they occasionally come on to land to investigate their human counterparts and, sometimes, even lure them to their caves. Alvarez's version of the story portrays a young ciguapa who puts herself in danger by coming too close to humans. The elder ciguapa warns the younger to be most careful not to get caught: "Doctors will want to put us in a cage and study us." In part, the ciguapa story is about the power of difference as something simultaneously desired and feared. The ciguapas are extraordinarily beautiful, but their feet *are* on backwards, making it hard to read their footprints and track them down. In this way, *The Secret Footprints* is also a story about the power of language, both spoken and performed. The backward nature of the ciguapa feet requires learning how to read their tracks, something the humans in the story simply cannot learn to do. The image of feet on backwards also provides a potent metaphor for what it means to live with the residues of trauma; the ciguapa's footprints physically leave an imprint that simultaneously points to the past while moving forward into the future. Their footprints also symbolize trauma survivors' need to approach things from a different perspective.

In her closing author's notes to *The Secret Footprints*, Alvarez provides details about the ciguapa myth and its specific cultural context within the literature and history of the Dominican Republic as well as her own family. She shares,

Sometimes my mother and aunts would try to scare me at night by saying that if I didn't go to sleep quickly or if I turned on my light after lights-out, the ciguapas would come and take me away. They thought I would be scared, but I was secretly excited by the thought of seeing a ciguapa. I never did. Still, I haven't given up. Sometimes I leave my wash out on the line overnight and stick a piece of candy or an apple in the pocket of my pants or jacket, just in case. I know it's a long way from the Dominican Republic to Vermont, especially if your feet are on backward. But I have to tell you, sometimes that piece of candy or apple is gone from that pocket in the morning. My husband says it could be squirrels or maybe even a raccoon.

I know better.

Alvarez's writing here, like her telling of the ciguapas myth, reflects a wonderfully directed sense of Rodríguez's concept of complete literacy. She speaks with confidence (about wanting to see a ciguapa) and competence (about ciguapa mythology). She refuses to accept her mother's warning that the ciguapas are dangerous or her husband's claim that they don't exist in Vermont, and she refuses to stop believing in the promise of a ciguapa visit, though, admittedly, she is geographically quite far from her—and their—homeland. Refusing to deny them, she embraces and acknowledges their centrality in her life as they share in the history of the Dominican Republic and, consequently, in the history of its violence which demands documentation and the bearing of witness.

Significantly, Alvarez also simultaneously embraces the power and possibility of play and magic, casting herself a role within the story as the human who will always leave treats for the ciguapas. For children who grow up in a world structured through violence, elements of imagination and play are typically put under erasure; adult survivors must actively recover them. Susan Brison, a feminist philosopher and survivor of rape, writes of her struggle to heal from violence and asserts that while she understands the powerful pull of trauma that will always structure her life, she also recognizes and celebrates the signs of healing and recovery evident in her embrace of beauty and joy:

[R]ight now, as I look out at the freshly mown field behind our house in Vermont, all I see and hear is new life—shoots of grass, lupines, pine trees, fireflies, crickets, frogs, small things singing. And I'm surrounded by the warmth and sweetness of friends and family and music. We may call such things reasons to live, but reason has little to do with it. They are the embodiments of our wishes and passions, the hopes and desires that draw us into the future. (xii–xiii)

Alvarez's illustrated children's book is likewise a magnificent celebration of the imagination and a passionate assertion of creative vision and voice. She makes clear for readers that her storytelling comes from a deeply personal place that should be honored and celebrated, a gesture with the potential to inspire other readers to be both witnesses and writers, the possibilities of which she is well aware. In *Something to Declare*, she shares that as a child reading, she often found "kinship with the girl on the cover of my storybook" (*Something to Declare* 135). In *finding miracles*, an English teacher affirms to her students, "Stories are how we put the pieces of our lives together" (3). As illustrated in the books under discussion in this essay, reading provides children with a portal to other imaginative worlds and, as such, offers the possibilities of new languages that might be applied in the working through of personal and cultural traumas. *The Secret Footprints* represents a profound alchemy of violence, a refusal to see a boogeyman where a ciguapa might exist, an insistence on the possibilities of its visit by actively and enthusiastically baiting the pocket.

Latina/o children's literature is essential to understanding trauma narratives because it powerfully reminds us that violence impacts the lives of children as well as adults. It insists that children are critically engaged thinkers with powerful emotional intelligence. The goal of this literature of critical witnessing is to equip children with strong emotional shock absorbers so that they may possess the levels of confidence and competence required to make personal and social change. It is critically generative in large part because it poses questions and it seeks to be pedagogical, to leave a child with a lesson of some sort to apply to the future building of self and community. It shows children a situation and offers various scenarios designed to fortify them with a sense of knowledge about how they themselves might navigate through situations charged by violence. For children who grow up in worlds defined through trauma and violence, books can provide an important source of stability in their lives, the experience of reading providing a window to a world in which violence is not the norm and where there are avenues toward empowerment. The story confirms it doesn't have to be this way: stories of violence can be read as stories of hope.

Special acknowledgment goes to Helen Lovejoy and Joelle Guzman for their ongoing conversations with me about the work of this project and to Sonia Valencia for her outstanding research assistance.

Works Cited

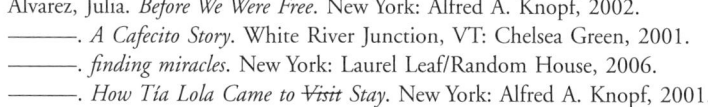

Alvarez, Julia. *Before We Were Free*. New York: Alfred A. Knopf, 2002.
———. *A Cafecito Story*. White River Junction, VT: Chelsea Green, 2001.
———. *finding miracles*. New York: Laurel Leaf/Random House, 2006.
———. *How Tía Lola Came to Visit Stay*. New York: Alfred A. Knopf, 2001.

———. *The Secret Footprints*. New York: Alfred A. Knopf, 2000.

———. *Something to Declare*. Chapel Hill: Algonquin Books, 1998.

Anzaldúa, Gloria. *Borderlands / La Frontera: The New Mestiza*. San Francisco: Spinsters/Aunt Lute, 1987.

———. *Friends from the Other Side / Amigos Del Otro Lado*. San Francisco: Children's Book Press, 1993.

———. *Prietita and the Ghost Woman / Prietita Y La Llorona*. San Francisco: Children's Book Press, 1995.

Brison, Susan J. *Aftermath: Violence and the Remaking of a Self*. Princeton: Princeton UPress, 2002.

Brown, Laura. "Not Outside the Range: One Feminist Perspective on Psychic Trauma." *Trauma: Explorations in Memory*. Ed. Cathy Caruth. Baltimore: Johns Hopkins University P, 1995. 100–112.

Cvetkovich, Ann. *An Archive of Feelings: Trauma, Sexuality, and Lesbian Public Cultures*. Durham: Duke UP, 2003.

González, Rigoberto. *Antonio's Card / La Tarjeta de Antonio*. San Francisco: Children's Book Press, 2005.

———. *Butterfly Boy: Memories of a Chicano Mariposa*. Madison: University of Wisconsin P, 2006.

———. *Crossing Vines: A Novel*. Norman: University of Oklahoma Press, 2003.

———. *Soledad Sighs-Sigh / Soledad Suspiros*. San Francisco: Children's Book Press, 2003.

Heidenreich, Linda. "Learning from the Death of Gwen Araujo?—Transphobic Racial Subordination and Queer Latina Survival in the Twenty-First Century." *Chicana/Latina Studies* 6.1 (2006): 50–86.

López, Tiffany Ana, ed. *Growing Up Chicana/o*. New York: William Morrow and Company, 1993.

López, Tiffany Ana, and Phillip Serrato. "A New *Mestiza* Primer: Borderlands Philosophy in the Children's Books of Gloria Anzaldú." *Such News of the Land: U.S. Women Nature Writers*. Eds. Thomas S. Edwards and Elizabeth A. De Wolfe. Hanover: UP of New England, 2000. 204–16.

Rivera, Tomás. *Y no se lo tragó la tierra/ . . . And the Earth Did Not Devour Him*. Trans. Evangelina Vigil-Piñon. Houston: Arte Publico Press, 1992.

Rodríguez, Luis J. *Always Running: La Vida Loca: Gang Days in L.A.* New York: Simon & Schuster, 1994.

———. *América Is Her Name*. Willimantic, CT: Curbstone Press, 1998.

———. *The Concrete River*. Willimantic, CT: Curbstone Press, 1991.

———. *Hearts and Hands: Creating Community in Violent Times*. New York: Seven Stories Press, 2001.

———. *It Doesn't Have to Be This Way: A Barrio Story / No Tiene Que Ser Así: Una Historia del Barrio*. San Francisco: Children's Book Press, 1999

———. *Poems across the Pavement*. Chicago: Tia Chucha Press, 1989.

Sources for Further Study

This list does not include items that are listed in the chapters' Works Cited.

Ethnic American Literature Resources/ Cross Culture

Baker, Houston A., Jr. *Three American Literatures: Essays in Chicano, Native American, and Asian-American Literature for Teachers of American Literature.* New York: MLA, 1982.

Bishop, Rudine Sims. "Children's Books in a Multicultural World: A View from the USA." *Reading against Racism* Ed. E. Evans. Buckingham: Open UP, 1992. 19–38.

Day, Frances Ann. *Multicultural Voices in Contemporary Literature: A Resource for Teachers.* Portsmouth, NH: Heinemann, 1994.

Hade, Daniel D. "Reading Children's Literature Multiculturally." *Reflections of Change: Children's Literature Since 1945.* Ed. Sandra L. Beckett. Westport, CT: Greenwood Press, 1997. 115–21.

Lee, A. Robert. *Multicultural American Literature: Comparative Black, Native, Latino/ a and Asian American Fictions.* Jackson: UP of Mississippi, 2003.

Maitino, John R., and David R. Peck, eds. *Teaching American Ethnic Literatures.* Albuquerque: U of New Mexico P, 1996.

Rochman, Hazel. *Against Borders: Promoting Books for a Multicultural World.* Chicago: ALA Books, 1993.

Rogers, Theresa and Anna O. Soter, eds. *Reading across Cultures*: *Teaching Literature in a Diverse Society.* New York: Teachers College Press, 1997.

Rothenberg, Paula. "Beyond the Food Court: Goals and Strategies for Teaching Multiculturalism." *Feminist Teacher* 13.1 (2000): 61–73.

African American

Awkward, Michael. "Introduction." *Inspiriting Influences: Tradition, Revision, and Afro-American Women's Novels* New York: Columbia UP, 1989. 1–14.

Baker, Houston A. Jr. *Blues, Ideology, and Afro-American Literature: A Vernacular Theory.* Chicago and London: U of Chicago P, 1984.

Bell, Bernard. *The Contemporary African American Novel: Its Folk Roots and Modern Literary Branches.* Amherst: U of Massachusetts P, 2005.

Carby, Hazel. *Reconstructing Womanhood: The Emergence of the Afro-American Woman Novelist.* New York: Oxford UP, 1987.

Collins, Patricia Hill. *Black Feminist Thought: Knowledge, Consciousness, and the Politics of Empowerment.* 2nd ed. New York: Routledge, 2000.

Ellis, Trey. "The New Black Aesthetic." *New Bones: Contemporary Black Writers in America.* Eds. Kevin Everod Quashie, Joyce Lausch, and Keith D. Miller. Upper Saddle River: Prentice Hall, 2001. 261–72.

Gates, Henry Louis, Jr. "African American Criticism." *Redrawing the Boundaries: The Transformation of English and American Literary Studies.* Ed. Stephen Greenblatt and Giles Gunn. New York: Modern Language Association, 1992. 303-320.

———. *Black Literature and Literary Theory.* New York: Methuen, 1984.

Graham, Maryemma, Sharon Pineault-Burke, and Marianna White Davis. *Teaching African American Literature.* Oxford: Routledge, 1998.

Hale, Dorothy. "Bakhtin in African American Literary Theory." *ELH* 61 (1994): 445–71.

Harris, Violet J. "Multicultural Curriculum: African American Children." *Young Children* 46 (1991): 37–44.

Hooks, Bell. *Ain't I a Woman: Black Women and Feminism.* Boston: South End Press, 1980.

Johnson-Feeling, Dianne. *Telling Tales: The Pedagogy and Promise of African American Literature for Youth.* New York: Greenwood Press, 1990.

Kutenplon, Deborah, and Ellen Olmstead. *Young Adult Fiction by African American Writers, 1968–1993: A Critical and Annotated Guide.* New York: Garland, 1996.

Leadbeater, Bonnie J. Ross, and Niobe Way, eds. *Urban Girls: Resisting Stereotypes, Creating Identities.* New York: New York UP, 1996.

Leitch, Vincent B. "Black Aesthetics." *American Literary Criticism from the 30s to the 80s.* New York: Columbia UP, 1988. 332–65.

Lester, Julius. *On Writing for Children and Other People.* New York: Penguin, 2004.

Mitchell, Angelyn, ed. *Within the Circle: An Anthology of African American Literary Criticism from the Harlem Renaissance to the Present.* Durham: Duke UP, 1994.

Napier, Winston, ed. *African American Literary Theory: A Reader.* New York: New York UP, 2000.

Olaniyan, Tejumola. "African American Critical Discourses and the Invention of Cultural Identities." *African American Review* 26 (1992): 533–45.

Peterson, Dale. "Response and Call: the African American Dialogue with Bakhtin and What It Signifies." *Bakhtin in Contexts: Across the Disciplines.* Ed. Amy Mandelker. Evanston: Northwestern UP, 1995. 89–98.

Russell, Kathy, Midge Wilson, and Ronald Hall. *The Color Complex: The Politics of Skin Color among African Americans.* New York: Harcourt, Brace and Jovanovich, 1992.

Sims [Bishop], Rudine. *Shadow and Substance: Afro-American Experience in Contemporary Children's Fiction.* Urbana: NCTE, 1982.

Stepto, Robert. *From Beyond the Veil: A Study of Afro-American Narrative*. Urbana: U of Illinois P, 1979.

Smith, Katharine Capshaw. *Children's Literature of the Harlem Renaissance*. Bloomington: U of Indiana P, 2006.

Smith, Karen Patricia, ed. *African-American Voices in Young Adult Literature: Tradition, Transition, Transformation*. Lanham: Scarecrow Press, 1994.

Smith, Valerie. *Self-Discovery and Authority in Afro-American Narrative*. Cambridge: Harvard UP, 1987.

Smitherman, Geneva. *Talkin & Testifyin: The Language of Black America*. Boston: Houghton Mifflin, 1977.

———. *Talking That Talk: Language, Culture and Education in African America*. New York: Routledge, 2000.

Tate, Claudia. "Race and Psychoanalysis." *Psychoanalysis and Black Novels: Desire and Protocols of Race*. New York: Oxford UP, 1998.

Taylor, Gail Singleton. "Pass It On: The Development of African-American Children's Literature." *Negro Educational Review* 50.1–2 (1999): 11–17.

Williams, Mary Thompson, and Helen Bush Caver. "African-Americans in Children's Literature: From Stereotype to Positive Representation." *Journal of African Children's Youth Literature* 3 (1991/92): 11–25.

Asian American

Chae, Youngsuk. *Politicizing Asian American Literature: Towards a Critical Multiculturalism*. New York: Routledge, 2008.

Cheung, King-Kok, ed. *An Interethnic Companion to Asian American Literature*. New York: Cambridge UP, 1997.

Chiu, Monica. *Filthy Fictions: Asian American Literature by Women*. New York: Alta Mira Press, 2004.

Chu, Patricia P. *Assimilating Asians: Gendered Strategies of Authorship in Asian America*. Durham: Duke UP, 2000.

Davis, Rocio G. "Ethnic Autobiography as Children's Literature: Laurence Yep's *The Lost Garden* and Yoshiko Uchida's *The Invisible Thread*." *Children's Literature Association Quarterly* 28.2 (2003): 90–97.

———. "Metanarrative in Ethnic Autobiography for Children: Laurence Yep's *The Lost Garden* and Judith Ortiz Cofer's *Silent Dancing*." *MELUS* 27.2 (2002): 139–56.

Davis, Rocio G., and Sami Ludwig, eds. *Asian American Literature in the International Context: Readings on Fiction, Poetry and Performance*. Munster: Lit, 2002.

De Manuel, Delores, and Rocio G. Davis, eds. "Asian American Children's Literature." Special Issue of *The Lion and the Unicorn* 30.2 (2006).

Ho, Wendy. *In Her Mother's House: The Politics of Asian American Mother-Daughter Writing*. Walnut Creek: Alta Mira Press, 1999.

Kim, Elaine H. *Asian American Literature: An Introduction to the Writings and Their Social Context*. Philadelphia: Temple UP, 1982.

Lawrence, Keith, and Floyd Cheung, eds. *Recovered Legacies: Authority and Identity in Early Asian American Literature.* Philadelphia: Temple UP, 2005.

Lee, Rachel C. *The Americas of Asian American Literature: Gendered Fictions of Nation and Transnation.* Princeton: Princeton UP, 1999.

Lim, Shirley Geok-lin, and Amy Ling. *Reading the Literatures of Asian America.* Philadelphia: Temple UP, 1992.

Ling, Amy. *Between Worlds: Women Writers of Chinese Ancestry.* New York: Pergamon Press, 1990.

Njeri, I. "Sushi and Grits: Ethnic Identity and Conflict in a Newly Multicultural America." *Inventing America: Readings in Identity and Culture.* Eds. G. Gabriella and M. Owell. New York: St. Martin's Press, 1996. 512–28.

Oh, Seung Ah. *Recontextualizing Asian American Domesticity.* New York: Lexington Books, 2008.

Wong, Sau-ling Cynthia. *Reading Asian American Literature: From Necessity to Extravagance.* Princeton: Princeton UP, 1993.

Wong, Sau-ling Cynthia, and Stephen H. Sumida, eds. *Resource Guide to Asian American Literature.* New York: MLA, 2001.

Wu, Jean Yu-wen Shen, and Min Song, eds. *Asian American Studies: A Reader.* New Brunswick: Rutgers UP, 2000.

Xiaojing, Zhou, and Samina Najmi, eds. *Form and Transformation in Asian American Literature.* Seattle: U of Washington P, 2005.

Yamamoto, Traise. *Masking Selves, Making Subjects: Japanese American Women, Identity, and the Body.* Berkeley: U of California P, 1999.

Latino/a

Acevedo, Luz De Alba, et al. *Telling to Live: Latina Feminist Testimonios.* Durham: Duke UP, 2001.

Ada, Alma Flor. *A Magical Encounter: Latino Children's Literature in the Classroom.* Boston: Allyn and Bacon, 2003.

Anaya, Rudolfo A., and Francisco A. Lomelí. *Aztlán: Essays on the Chicano Homeland.* Albuquerque: El Norte Publications, 1989.

Aranda, Jose, Jr. *When We Arrive: A New Literary History of Mexican America.* Tucson: U of Arizona P, 2003.

Augenbraum, Harold, and Margarite Fernandez Olmos. *U.S. Latino Literature: A Critical Guide for Students and Teachers.* Westport, CT: Greenwood Press, 2000.

Brady, Mary Pat. *Extinct Lands, Temporal Geographies: Chicana Literature and the Urgency of Space.* Durham: Duke UP, 2002.

Castañeda, Antonia Shular, Tomás Ybarra-Frausto and Joseph Sommers, eds. *Chicano Literature: Texts and Context.* Englewood Cliffs: Prentice-Hall, 1972.

Caulfield, Carlota, and Darien J. Davis, eds. *A Companion to US Latino Literatures.* Woodbridge, UK: Boydell & Brewer, 2007.

Dávila, Arlene. *Latino Spin: Public Image and the Whitewashing of Race*. New York: New York UP, 2008.

———. *Sponsored Identities: Cultural Politics in Puerto Rico*. Philadelphia: Temple UP, 1997.

Day, Frances Ann. *Latina and Latino Voices in Literature for Children and Teenagers*. Portsmouth, NH: Heinemann, 1997.

———. *Latina and Latino Voices in Literature: Lives and Works*. Westport, CT: Greenwood Press, 2003.

Figueras, Consuelo. "Puerto Rican Children's Literature: On Establishing an Identity." *Bookbird* 38.2 (2000): 23–27.

Freiband, Susan, and Consuelo Figueras. "Understanding Puerto Rican Culture Using Puerto Rican Children's Literature." *MultiCultural Review* 11.2 (2002): 30–34.

Garcia, Laura E., Sandra M. Gutierrez, and Felicitas Nuñez, eds. *Teatro Chicana: A Collective Memoir and Selected Plays*. Austin: U of Texas P, 2008.

Jimnez, Francisco, ed. *The Identification and Analysis of Chicano Literature*. New York: Bilingual Press/Editorial Bilingue, 1979.

Pérez-Torres, Rafael. *Mestizaje: Critical Uses of Race in Chicano Culture*. Minneapolis: U of Minnesota P, 2006.

———. *Movements in Chicano Poetry: Against Myths, against Margins*. Cambridge: Cambridge UP, 1995.

Poey, Delia. *Latino American Literature in the Classroom: The Politics of Transformation*. Gainesville: UP of Florida, 2002.

Ramos, Henry A. J., ed. *The History of Barrios Unidos: Healing Community of Violence*. Houston, TX: Arte Público Press, 2007.

Saldívar-Hull, Sonia. *Feminism on the Border: Chicana Gender Politics and Literature*. Berkeley: U of California P, 2000.

Shirley, Carl R., and Paula W. Shirley. *Understanding Chicano Literature*. Columbia: U of South Carolina P, 1988.

Sommers, Joseph, and Tomás Ybarra-Frausto, eds. *Modern Chicano Writers: A Collection of Critical Essays*. Englewood Cliffs: Prentice-Hall, 1979.

Torres, Edén E. *Chicana Without Apology: The New Chicana Cultural Studies*. New York: Routledge, 2003.

Trujillo, Carla, ed. *Living Chicana Theory*. Berkeley: Third Woman Press, 1998.

Vasquez, Edith M. "La Gloriosa Travesura de la Musa Que Cruza/The Misbehaving Glory(a) of the Border-Crossing Muse: Transgression in Anzaldúa's Children's Stories." *Entre Mundos/Among Worlds: New Perspectives on Gloria Anzaldúa*. Ed. Ana Lousie Keating. New York: Palgrave Macmillan, 2005. 63–75.

Native American

Allen, Paula Gunn. *Studies in American Indian Literature: Critical Essays and Course Designs*. New York: MLA, 1983.

Ballinger, Franchot. *Living Sideways: Tricksters in American Indian Oral Traditions*. Norman: U of Oklahoma P, 2004.

Bataille, Gretchen M. *Native American Representations: First Encounters, Distorted Images, and Literary Appropriations*. Lincoln: U of Nebraska P, 2001.

Berman, Joan. "Native American Children's Literature in the Classroom: An Annotated Bibliography." *Humboldt State University Library*. 7 December 2008. http://library.humboldt.edu/~berman/naclit.htm.

Brill de Ramirez, Susan Berry. *Contemporary American Indian Literatures and the Oral Tradition*. Tucson: U of Arizona P, 1999.

Caldwell-Wood, Naomi, and Lisa A. Mitten. "Selective Bibliography and Guide for 'I' Is Not for Indian: The Portrayal of Native Americans in Books for Young People" *ALA/OLOS Subcommittee for Library Services to American Indian People/ American Indian Library Association*. Native Culture Links. 1991. 07 December 2008. http://www.nativeculturelinks.com/ailabib.htm.

Davis, Mary B, ed. *Native America in the Twentieth Century: An Encyclopedia*. Assistant eds. Joan Berman, Mary E. Graham, and Lisa A. Mitten. New York: Garland, 1994.

Hirschfelder, Arlene, Paulette Fairbanks Molin, and Yvonne Wakin. *American Indian Stereotypes in the World of Children: A Reader and Bibliography*. Lanham, MD: Scarecrow, 1999.

Hirschfelder, Arlene, and Yvonne Beamer Wakim. *Native Americans Today: Resources and Activities for Educators Grades 4-8*. Westport, CT: Libraries Unlimited, 2000.

Pulitano, Elvira. *Toward a Native American Critical Theory*. Lincoln: U of Nebraska P, 2003.

Reese, Debbie. *American Indians in Children's Literature*. 07 December 2008. http://americanindiansinchildrensliterature.blogspot.com/.

Stott, Jon C. *Native Americans in Children's Literature*. Phoenix: Oryx P, 1995.

Treuer, David. *Native American Fiction*. Saint Paul: Graywolf P, 2006.

Velie, Alan R., ed. *Native American Perspectives on Literature and History*. Norman: U of Oklahoma P, 1994.

Wiget, Andrew, ed. *Handbook of Native American Literature*. New York: Garland, 1996.

Further Reading of Primary Texts

Frosch, Mary, ed. *Coming of Age in America: A Multicultural Anthology*. New York: New Press, 1995.

Gallo, Donald R, ed. *Join In: Multiethnic Short Stories by Outstanding Writers for Young Adults*. New York: Delacorte, 1993.

African American

Curtis, Christopher Paul. *Bud, Not Buddy*. New York: Delacorte, 1999.

———. *The Watsons Go to Birmingham—1963*. New York: Delacorte, 1995.

Grimes, Nikki. *Bronx Masquerade*. New York: Dial, 2002.
———. *Jazmin's Notebook*. New York: Dial, 1998.
Hamilton, Virginia. *Her Stories: African American Folk Tales, Fairy Tales, and True Tales*. New York: Blue Sky, 1995.
———. *The House of Dies Drear*. New York: Macmillan, 1968.
———. *M. C. Higgins, the Great*. New York: Macmillan, 1974.
———. *The People Could Fly: American Black Folktales*. New York: Knopf, 1985.
———. *The Planet of Junior Brown*. New York: Macmillan, 1971.
———. *Sweet Whispers, Brother Rush*. New York: Philomel, 1982.
———. *Zeely*. New York: Simon & Schuster, 1967.
Johnson, Angela. *The Other Side*. Georgetown, ME: Orchard, 1998.
———. *Toning the Sweep*. Georgetown, ME: Orchard, 1993.
Myers, Walter Dean. *Fallen Angels*. New York: Scholastic, 1988.
———. *Hoops*. New York: Delacorte, 1981.
———. *Monster*. New York: HarperCollins, 1999.
———. *Scorpions*. New York: Harper & Row, 1988.
———. *Slam!*. New York: Scholastic, 1996.
Nelson, Marilyn. *Carver: A Life in Poems*. Honesdale, Pennsylvania: Front Street, 2001.
Taylor, Mildred. *The Friendship*. New York: Dial, 1987.
———. *The Land*. New York: Phyllis Fogelman, 2001.
———. *Let the Circle Be Unbroken*. New York: Dial, 1981.
———. *The Road to Memphis*. New York: Dial, 1990.
———. *Roll of Thunder, Hear My Cry*. New York: Dial, 1976.
Woodson, Jacqueline. *I Hadn't Meant to Tell You This*. New York: Delacorte, 1994.
———. *If You Come Softly*. New York: Penguin, 1998.
———. *Locomotion*. New York: Putnam/Penguin, 2003.
———. *Miracle's Boys*. New York: Putnam, 2000.

Asian American

Brainard, Cecilia Manguerra, ed. *Growing Up Filipino: Stories for Young Adults*. Santa Monica, CA: PALH, 2003.
Gilmore, Rachna. *A Group of One*. New York: Henry Holt, 2001.
Ho, Minfong. *Rice without Rain*. New York: Lothrop, Lee & Shepard, 1990.
Hong, Maria, ed. *Growing Up Asian American*. New York: Morrow, 1993.
Houston, Jeanne Wakatsuki, and James D. Houston. *Farewell to Manzanar*. Boston: Houghton Mifflin, 1973.
Kadohata, Cynthia. *Outside Beauty*. New York: Atheneum, 2008.
Lee, Marie G. *F is for Fabuloso*. New York: Avon, 1999.
———. *If It Hadn't Been for Yoon Jun*. Boston: Houghton Mifflin, 1993.
Park, Linda Sue. *A Single Shard*. Paramount, CA: Clarion, 2001.
———. *When My Name Was Keoko: A Novel of Korea in World War II*. Paramount, CA: Clarion, 2002.

Staples, Suzanne Fisher. *Shabanu: Daughter of the Wind*. New York: Laurel Leaf, 2003.
———. *Under the Persimmon Tree*. New York: Farrar, Straus and Giroux, 2005.
Uchida, Yoshiko. *The Best Bad Thing*. New York: Atheneum, 1983.
———. *The Happiest Ending*. New York: Atheneum, 1985.
———. *A Jar of Dreams*. New York: Atheneum, 1981.
———. *Journey to Topaz*. New York: Scribner, 1971.
Wong, Janet S. *Minn and Jake*. New York: Frances Foster Books, 2003.
———. *A Suitcase of Seaweed and Other Poems*. New York: McElderry, 1996.
Yee, Lisa. *Millicent Min, Girl Genius*. New York: Arthur Levine, 2003.
———. *Stanford Wong Flunks Big-Time*. New York: Arthur Levine, 2005.
Yee, Paul. *The Bone Collector's Son*. Tarrytown: Marshall Cavendish, 2004.
Yep, Laurence. *Child of the Owl*. New York: Harper & Row, 1977.
———. *Dragon's Gate*. New York: HarperCollins, 1993.
———. *Dragonwings*. New York: Harper & Row, 1975.

Latino/a

Ada, Alma Flor. *Gathering the Sun: An Alphabet in Spanish and English*. Trans. Rosa Zubizarreta. New York: Lothrop, Lee and Shepard Books, 1997.
———. *Mediopollito / Half-Chicken*. Trans. Rosalma Zubizarreta. New York: Bantam Doubleday Dell, 1995.
———. *My Name Is María Isabel*. New York: Atheneum Books, 1993.
———. *The Lizard and the Sun / La Lagartija y el Sol*. New York: Bantam Doubleday Dell Books for Young Readers, 1997.
———. *Under the Royal Palms: A Childhood in Cuba*. Atheneum, 1998.
———. *Where the Flame Trees Bloom*. New York: Atheneum, 1994.
———. *Yours Truly, Goldilocks*. New York: Aladdin Paperbacks, 1998.
Alarcón, Francisco X. *Angels Ride Bikes and Other Fall Poems / Los Ángeles Andan en Bicicleta y otros poemas de otoño*. San Francisco, CA: Children's Book Press, 1999.
———. *From the Bellybutton of the Moon and Other Summer Poems / Del Ombligo de la Luna y otros poemas de verano*. San Francisco, CA: Children's Book Press, 1998.
———. *Laughing Tomatoes and Other Spring Poems / Jitomates Risueños y otros poemas de primavera*. San Francisco, CA: Children's Book Press, 1997.
Algarin, Miguel, and Bob Holman, eds. *Aloud: Voices from the Nuyorican Poets Café*. New York: Owl Books, 1994.
Alicea, Gil C., and Carmine DeSena. *The Air Down Here: True Tales from a South Bronx Boyhood*. San Francisco, CA: Chronicle Books, 1995.
Alvarez, Julia. *A Cafecito Story*. White River Junction, VT: Chelsea Green, 2001.
Atkin, S. Beth. *Voices from the Fields: Children of Migrant Farmworkers Tell Their Stories*. Boston: Little, Brown, 1993.
———. *Voices from the Streets: Young Former Gang Members Tell Their Stories*. Boston: Little, Brown, 1996.
Balgassi, Haemi. *Tae's Sonata*. Paramount, CA: Clarion, 1997.
Behar, Ruth, ed. *Bridges to Cuba / Puentes A Cuba*. Ann Arbor: U of Michigan P, 1995.

Canales, Viola. *The Tequila Worm*. New York: Wendy Lamb Books, 2005.

Cantú, Norma Elia. *Canícula: Snapshots of a Girlhood en la Frontera*. Albuquerque: U of New Mexico P, 1995.

Carlson, Lori M., ed. *Barrio Streets Carnival Dreams: Three Generations of Latino Artistry*. New York: Henry Holt & Co., 1996.

————, ed. *Cool Salsa: Bilingual Poems on Growing Up Latino in the United States*. Orlando: Holt, 1994.

Castillo, Ana. *My Son, the Eagle, the Dove: An Aztec Chant*. New York: E. P. Dutton, 2000.

Castillo, Ana, ed. *Goddess of the Americas: La Diosa de las Américas*. New York: Riverhead Books, 1996.

Cisneros, Sandra. *The House on Mango Street*. Houston, TX: Arte Público, 1984.

Cofer, Judith Ortiz. *An Island Like You*. Georgetown, ME: Orchard, 1995.

————. *The Meaning of Consuelo*. New York: Farrar, Straus & Giroux, 2003.

————. *Call Me Maria*. New York: Orchard Books, 2004.

————. *Silent Dancing: A Partial Remembrance of a Puerto Rican Childhood*. Houston, TX: Arte Público, 1990.

Corpi, Lucha. *Where Fireflies Dance / Ahí, donde bailan las luciérnagas*. San Francisco: Children's Book Press, 1997.

Cruz Martinez, Alejandro. *The Woman Who Outshone the Sun / La Mujer Que Brillaba Aún Más Que El Sol*. San Francisco: Children's Book Press.

Delacre, Lulu. *Salsa Stories*. New York: Scholastic, 2000.

Flores, Carlos Nicolás. *Our House on Hueco*. Lubbock: Texas Tech U, 2006.

Fontes, Montserrat. *First Confession*. New York: Norton, 1991.

Gallo, Donald R. *Cinnamon Girl: Letters Found inside a Cereal Box*. New York: Joanna Cotler Books, 2005.

————. *Downtown Boy*. New York: Scholastic, 2005.

Garza, Carmen Lomas. *Family Pictures / Cuadros de Familia*. San Francisco: Children's Book Press, 1990.

————. *In My Family / En mi familia*. San Francisco: Children's Book Press, 1996.

————. *Making Magic Windows: Creating Papel Picado/Cut-Paper Art*. San Francisco: Children's Book Press, 1999.

————. *Making Windows / Ventanas Mágicas*. San Francisco: Children's Book Press, 1999.

Gonzalez, Ralfka, and Ana Ruiz. *My First Book of Proverbs / My Primer Libro de Dichos*. San Francisco: Children's Book Press, 1995.

González, Rigoberto, and Rich Heide, eds. *Under the Fifth Sun: Latino Literature from California*. Santa Clara: Santa Clara UP, 2002.

Hernández, Jo Ann Yolanda. *White Bread Competition*. Houston: Piñata Books, 1997.

Hernández-Gutiérrez, Manuel de Jesús, and David William Foster, eds. *Literatura Chicana, 1965–1995: An Anthology in Spanish, English, and Calo*. New York: Garland, 1997.

Herrera, Juan Felipe. *Calling the Doves / Canto a Las Palomas*. San Francisco: Children's Book Press, 1995

———. *Cilantro Girl / La Superniña del Cilantro*. San Francisco: Children's Book Press, 2003.

———. *Crash Boom Love*. Albuquerque: U of New Mexico P, 1999.

———. *Featherless / Desplumado*. San Francisco: Children's Book Press, 2004.

———. *Grandma & Me at the Flea / Los Meros Meros Remateros*. San Francisco: Children's Books Press, 2002.

———. *Laughing Out Loud, I Fly / A Carcajadas Yo Vuelo*. New York: HarperCollins, 1998.

———. *The Upside Down Boy/El Nino de Cabeza*. San Francisco: Children's Book Press, 2000.

Hijuelos, Oscar. *Dark Dude*. New York: Atheneum, 2008.

Jimenez, Francisco. *Breaking Through*. Boston: Houghton Mifflin, 2001.

———. *La Mariposa*. Boston: Houghton Mifflin Company, 1998.

———. *The Circuit: Stories from the Life of a Migrant Child*. Albuquerque: U of New Mexico P, 1997.

Johnston, Tony. *Any Small Goodness: A Novel of the Barrio*. New York: Blue Sky Press, 2001.

López, Josefina. *Real Women Have Curves: A Comedy*. Woodstock, IL: Dramatic Publishing, 1996.

Loya, Olga. *Momentos Magicos: Tales from Latin America Told in English and Spanish*. Atlanta: August House, 1997.

Martinez, Floyd. *Spirits of the High Mesa*. Houston, TX: Arte Público, 1997.

Martinez, Victor. *A Parrot in the Oven*. New York: HarperCollins, 1996.

Mendez-Negrete, Josie. *Las Hijas de Juan: Daughters Betrayed*. Durham: Duke UP, 2006.

Mohr, Nicholasa. *All for the Better: A Story of El Barrio*. New York: Steck-Vaughn, 1993.

———. *El Bronx Remembered: A Novella and Stories*. Harper Keypoint, 1975.

———. *Felita*. New York: Bantam Doubleday Dell, 1979.

———. *Going Home*. New York: Bantam Doubleday Dell, 1986.

———. *Nilda*. Houston, TX: Arte Público Press, 1986.

Mora, Pat. *Confetti: Poems for Children*. New York: Lee & Low Books, 1996.

———. *The Desert is my Mother / El Desierto es mi Madre*. Houston: Piñata Books, 1994.

———. *The Gift of the Poinsettia / El Regalo de la Flor de Nochebuena*. Houston: Piñata Books, 1995.

———. *Marimba!: Animales from A to Z*. New York: Clarion Books, 2006.

———. *My Own True Name: New and Selected Poems for Young Adults*. Houston: Arte Público, 2000.

———. *The Night the Moon Fell: A Maya Myth*. Toronto: Groundwood Books/ Douglas & McIntyre, 2000.

———. *This Big Sky*. New York: Scholastic Press, 1998.

———. *Tomas and the Library Lady*. New York: Alfred A. Knopf, 1997.

Muñoz, Elias Miguel. *Brand New Memory*. Houston: Arte Público, 1998.

Osa, Nancy. *Cuba 15*. New York: Delacorte Press-Random House, 2003.

Ponce, Mary Helen. *Hoyt Street: An Autobiography*. Albuquerque: U of New Mexico P, 1993.

Rodriguez, Abraham, Jr. *The Boy without a Flag: Tales of the South Bronx*. Minneapolis: Milkweed Editions, 1992.

Rodríguez, Joseph. *East Side Stories: Gang Life in East L.A.* New York: Powerhouse Books, 1998.

———. *Juvenile*. New York: Powerhouse Books, 2004.

Rodriguez, Luis. *Trochemoche: Poems*. Willimantic, CT: Curbstone Press, 1998.

Rodriguez, Richard. *Hunger of Memory: The Education of Richard Rodriguez—An Autobiography*. New York: Bantam Books, 1982.

Ryan, Bryan, ed. *Hispanic Writers: A Selection of Sketches from Contemporary Authors*. Detroit: Gale Research, 1991.

Ryan, Pam Muñoz. *Becoming Naomi León*. New York: Scholastic, 2004.

———. *Esperanza Rising*. New York: Scholastic, 2000.

Sáenz, Benjamin Alire. *A Gift from Papá Diego / Un regalo de Papá Diego*. El Paso, TX: Cinco Puntos Press, 1998.

———. *He Forgot to Say Goodbye*. New York: Simon and Schuster, 2008.

———. *Sammy and Juliana in Hollywood*. El Paso: Cinco Puntos Press, 2004.

Saldaña, Ren, Jr. *The Jumping Tree*. New York: Delacorte, 2001.

Salinas-Norman, Bobbi. *The Three Pigs / Los Tres Cerdos: Nacho, Tito, and Miguel*. Oakland: Piñata Publications, 1998.

Serros, Michele. *Chicana Falsa, and Other Stories of Death, Identity, and Oxnard*. New York: Riverhead Books, 1998.

———. *Honey Blond Chica*. New York: Simon Pulse, 2006.

Soto, Gary. *Buried Onions*. San Diego, CA: Harcourt Brace, 1997.

———. *Chato's Kitchen*. New York: Putnam, 1995.

——— *Gary Soto: New and Selected Poems*. San Francisco: Chronicle, 1995.

———. *Local News*. New York: Scholastic Inc., 1993.

———. *Jessie De La Cruz: A Profile of a United Farm Worker*. New York: Persea Books, 2000.

——— *Petty Crimes*. Orlando, Florida: Harcourt Brace, 1998.

———. *Snapshots from the Wedding*. New York: Putnam & Grosset Group, 1997.

———. *Taking Sides*. Orlando, Florida: Harcourt, 1991.

———. *Too Many Tamales*. New York: Putnam, 1993.

Steven, Jan Romero. *Carlos and the Cornfield*. Trans. Patricia Hinton Davison. Flagstaff: Northland Publishing, 1995.

———. *Carlos and the Skunk*. Trans. Patricia Hinton Davison. Flagstaff: Rising Moon, 1997.

———. *Carlos and the Squash Plant / Carlos y La Planta de Calabaza*. New York: Scholastic, 1993.

Tafolla, Carmen. *Baby Coyote and the Old Woman / El Coyotito y la Viejita*. San Antonio: Wings Press, 1993.

Taylor, Sheila Ortiz. *Imaginary Parents*. Albuquerque: U of New Mexico P, 1996.

Testa, Maria. *Nine Candles*. Minneapolis: Carolrhoda Books, 1996.

Trujillo, Carla. *What Night Brings.* Willimantic, CT: Curbstone Press, 2003.

Valdes-Rodriguez, Alisa. *Haters.* New York: Little, Brown, 2006.

Veciana-Suarez, Ana. *Flight to Freedom.* Georgetown, ME: Orchard, 2002.

Viramontes, Helena Maria. *The Moths and Other Stories.* Houston: Arte Público Press, 1985.

Villanueva, Alma Luz. *Luna's California Poppies.* Tempe: Bilingual Press/Editorial Bilinge, 2002.

Villareal, José Antonio. *Pocho.* New York: Bantam Doubleday Dell, 1959.

Native American

Allen, Paula Gunn, and Patricia Clark Smith. *As Long as the Rivers Flow: The Stories Of Nine Native Americans.* New York: Scholastic, 1996.

Bruchac, Joseph. *Code Talker: A Novel about the Navajo Marines of World War II.* New York: Dial, 1995.

———. *Crazy Horses' Vision.* Illus. S. D. Nelson. New York: Lee & Low, 2000.

———. *Eagle Song.* Illus. Dan Andreasen. New York: Dial, 1997.

———. *Pushing Up the Sky: Seven Native American Plays for Children.* Illus. Teresa Flavin. New York: Dial, 2000.

Bruchac, Joseph, and Gayle Ross. *The Story of the Milky Way, a Cherokee Tale.* Paintings by A. Virginia. Stroud. New York: Dial, 1995.

Carlson, Lori Marie, ed. *Moccasin Thunder: American Indian Stories for Today.* New York: HarperCollins, 2005.

Dorris, Michael. *Morning Girl.* New York: Hyperion, 1992.

———. *Sees behind Trees.* New York: Hyperion, 1996.

Erdrich, Louise. *Grandmother's Pigeon.* Illus. Jim La Marche. New York: Hyperion, 1996.

——— *The Porcupine Year.* New York: HarperCollins, 2008.

Harjo, Joy. *The Good Luck Cat.* Illus. Paul Lee. Orlando, Florida: Harcourt, 2000.

Lacapa, Kathleen, and Michael Lacapa. *Less Than Half, More Than Whole.* Illus. Michael Lacapa. Flagstaff, AZ: Northland, 1994.

Littlechild, George. *This Land Is My Land.* San Francisco: Children's Book Press, 1993.

O'Harrell, Beatrice. *Longwalker's Journey: A Novel of the Choctaw Trail of Tears.* New York: Dial, 1999.

Ortiz, Simon. *The People Shall Continue.* Illus. Sharol Graves. San Francisco: Children's Book Press, 1998.

Riley, Patricia, ed. *Growing Up Native American.* New York: Morrow, 1993.

Rumbaut, Hendle. *Dove Dream.* Boston, MA: Houghton Mifflin, 1994.

Sanderson, Esther. *Two Pairs of Shoes.* Illus. David Beyer. Bonita, CA.: Pemmican, 1998.

Savageau, Cheryl. *Muskrat Will Be Swimming.* Illus. Robert Hynes. Flagstaff, AZ: Northland, 1996.

Strete, Craig Kee. *The World in Grandfather's Hands.* Paramount, CA: Clarion, 1995.

Tallchief, Maria, and Rosemary Wells. *Tallchief: America's Prima Ballerina.* Illus. Gary Kelly. New York: Viking, 1999.

Tapahonso, Luci. *Songs Of Shiprock Fair.* Illus. Anthony Chee Emerson. Walnut, CA: Kiva, 1999.

Tingle, Tim. *Crossing Bok Chitto: A Choctaw Tale of Friendship and Freedom.* Illus. Bridges. El Paso, TX: Cinco Puntos, 2006.

———. *Walking the Choctaw Road.* El Paso, TX: Cinco Puntos Press, 2003.

Van Camp, Richard. *A Man Called Raven.* Illus. George Littlechild. San Francisco: Children's Book Press, 1997.

Van Camp, Richard. *The Lesser Blessed.* Vancouver: Douglas & McIntyre, 1996.

Waboose, Jan Bourdeau. *Skysisters.* Illus. Brian Deines. Toronto, Canada: Kid's Can Press, 2000.

Notes on Contributors

Yvonne Atkinson is Assistant Professor of English at Mt. San Jacinto College in Menifee, California where she teaches African American literature, American literature, and multiethnic literature and composition. She has published articles on the Mammy figure in *AMERICAN@* and *A Gift of Story and Song: An Encyclopedia on Twentieth Century African American Writers*. She has also published on African American oral traditions in *The Aesthetics of Toni Morrison, Critical Essays on Toni Morrison's Beloved,* and *Studies in the Literary Imagination*.

Joseph Bruchac is the author of more than 120 books for children and adults, including *March toward the Thunder, Hidden Roots, The Winter People*, and *Our Stories Remember*. He received the Lifetime Achievement Award from the Native Writers Circle of America.

Rocío G. Davis is Associate Professor of American Literature and Director of the Institute of Liberal Arts at the University of Navarra (Spain). Some of her publications are *Begin Here: Reading Asian North American Autobiographies of Childhood* and *Transcultural Reinventions: Asian American and Asian Canadian Short Story Cycles*. She has also coedited *Ethnic Life Writing and Histories: Genres, Performance, and Culture*; *Literary Gestures: The Aesthetic in Asian American Writing*; and *Asian American Literature in the International Context: Readings on Fiction, Poetry, and Performance*.

Melinda L. de Jesús is Chair of Diversity Studies and Associate Professor of Diversity Studies and Critical Studies at the California College of the Arts in Oakland, California. She writes and teaches about youth and popular culture, feminist/gender studies, and comparative American ethnic studies. She recently edited *Pinay Power: Peminist Critical Theory*, the first anthology of Filipina/American feminisms. Her writing has appeared in *Challenging Homphobia*; *The Lion and the Unicorn*; *Meridians: Feminism, Race, Transnationalism*; *Radical Teacher*; *MELUS Journal*; *The Children's Literature Association Quarterly*; *The Journal of Asian American Studies*;

LIT: Literature, Interpretation, Theory; Works and Days; and *Delinquents and Debutantes: Twentieth Century American Girls' Culture.*

Elizabeth Gargano is an Associate Professor of English at the University of North Carolina at Charlotte. She is the author of *Reading Victorian Schoolrooms: Childhood and Education in Nineteenth-Century Fiction,* and her articles have appeared in *Children's Literature* and *Children's Literature Association Quarterly.*

Tanya González is Assistant Professor of English at Kansas State University where she teaches American Literature, Cultural Studies, and Latina/o Studies. She has published on the work of Cherríe Moraga and poet Lorna Dee Cervantes and is currently working on a book length project titled *The Good, The Bad, and The Ugly: Latina Subjectivity in Literature and Popular Culture.*

P. Jane Hafen (Taos Pueblo) is a Professor of English at the University of Nevada, Las Vegas. She is author of *Reading Louise Erdrich's Love Medicine* and editor of *Dreams and Thunder: Stories, Poems, and The Sun Dance Opera by Zitkala-Sa.*

Cynthia Kadohata is the author of *CRACKER! The Best Dog in Vietnam,* *Weedflower,* and *Kira-Kira,* a Newbery-award winner. She has also written for adults, including *The Floating World* and *The Glass Mountains.* Her most recent novel, *Outside Beauty,* is for adolescents.

Neal A. Lester, Chair and Professor of English, teaches at Arizona State University. His area of specialization is African American literary and cultural studies. The author of four books--*Ntozake Shange: A Critical Study of the Plays* (1995); *Understanding Zora Neale Hurston's Their Eyes Were Watching God: A Student Casebook to Issues, Sources, and Historical Documents* (1999); *Once upon a Time in a Different World: Ideas and Issues in African American Children's Literature* (2006); and *Racialized Politics of Desire in Personal Ads* (2007). He is currently completing a coedited collection on the works of poet and performance artist Sapphire and looking at revisions of the children's 1899 story *Little Black Sambo.*

Tiffany Ana López is Associate Professor of English at the University of California, Riverside. Her research and teaching focuses on issues of violence and trauma in American literature across genres, from autobiography, fiction, drama and performance, to prison narratives and children's books. She is editor of the journal *Chicana/Latina Studies: The Journal of Mujeres Activas en Letras y Cambio Social* and an educational writer and teaching artist for the Mark Taper Forum's P.L.A.Y.—Performing for Los Angeles

Youth. Her publications include *Growing Up Chicana/o* and the forthcoming *The Alchemy of Blood: Violence as Critical Discourse in U.S. Latina/o Writing*.

Phillip Serrato is Assistant Professor of English and Comparative Literature at San Diego State University, where he is on the faculty of the National Center for the Study of Children's Literature. A specialist in Chicana/o literary and cultural studies, he has previously published essays on subjects such as the history of Chicana/o children's literature, the portrayal of Latina/o identity and difference in the children's television program *Dragon Tales*, and the racist debasement of Latinos within the ranks of professional wrestling.

Katharine Capshaw Smith is an Associate Professor of English at the University of Connecticut, where she teaches courses in African American literature and children's and young adult literature. She has published essays on childhood, gender, and race, and her monograph, *Children's Literature of the Harlem Renaissance*, won the 2006 award for best scholarly book from the Children's Literature Association.

Michelle Pagni Stewart is an Associate Professor of English at Mt. San Jacinto College in Menifee, California, where she teaches children's and adolescent literature, Native American and multiethnic literature, and composition. She has published articles on Native American children's literature in *Children's Literature Quarterly*, *MELUS*, and *Studies in American Indian Literatures* and has an article on Louise Erdrich's children's novels forthcoming in *Oxford Handbook of Children's Literatures*.

Traise Yamamoto is the author of *Masking Selves, Making Subjects: Japanese American Women, Identity, and the Body*. She is Associate Professor of English at the University of California, Riverside.

Index